HISTORY'S
LOST
TREASURES

HISTORY'S
LOST
TREASURES

AND THE SECRETS BEHIND THEM

Eric Chaline

METRO BOOKS
NEW YORK

METRO BOOKS
New York

An Imprint of Sterling Publishing
387 Park Avenue South
New York, NY 10016

METRO BOOKS and the distinctive Metro Books logo
are trademarks of Sterling Publishing Co., Inc.

© 2013 by Quid Publishing

This 2013 edition published by Metro Books, by arrangement with Quid Publishing.

Conceived, designed, and produced by
Quid Publishing
Level 4 Sheridan House
114 Western Road
Hove BN3 1DD
England

www.quidpublishing.com

ISBN: 978-1-4351-4672-3

For information about custom editions, special sales, and premium and corporate purchases,
please contact Sterling Special Sales at 800-805-5489 or specialsales@sterlingpublishing.com.

Manufactured in Singapore

1 3 5 7 9 10 8 6 4 2

www.sterlingpublishing.com

For Brennan Sharp, Joe Kojdic, and Jose Gallego, three "lost treasures."

CONTENTS

INTRODUCTION

The English word "treasure" comes from the French *trésor* and the Spanish and Italian *tesoro*, which might suggest a link to the words for "gold" in those languages, *or* and *oro*. But this very logical conclusion is, in fact, completely wrong. The word originates from the Latin *thesaurus* and the Greek *thesauros*, meaning a "treasury" or "treasure house," which has no connection with precious metals but is derived from the verbs *thesaurizare* and *tithenai*, "to put" or "to place" (which also gives us a "thesaurus"—a treasury of words). Therefore, from the very first, treasure has been used to define much more than objects made of precious metals and gemstones.

Aficionados of lost treasure "hoards," however—from the Germanic and Old Norse *hord*, *hort*, or *hudz*, meaning "hidden treasure"—will not be disappointed: This book contains history's most fabulous "treasure troves" (from the French *trésors trouvés*, "found treasures"), whose original owners buried them to save them from some terrible near-and-present danger but did not survive to recover them. These include the Bronze Age "Villena treasure" (pp. 40–43) and late Roman "Neptune dish" (pp. 104–107). But things that were hidden for safekeeping were not all material treasures: Spiritual treasures such as the Jewish "Dead Sea Scrolls" (pp. 87–92), the Jain "Chausa treasure" (pp. 100–103), and the Buddhist "Mogao Library Cave" manuscripts (pp. 129–135) were hidden to save them from desecration and destruction.

Many of the treasures that feature in this book were unearthed by archaeologists, such as the extraordinary burial goods excavated from the tombs of ancient civilizations, starting with "The Ram in a Thicket" (pp. 10–14) found in the royal graves of Ur in Mesopotamia (now southern Iraq), "Tutankhamun's death mask" (pp. 30–35), and two other death masks made half a world and two millennia apart: from the Anglo-Saxon tomb-mound in Sutton Hoo (pp. 108–113), England, and from the tomb of the Pakal, the Maya king of Palenque, Mexico (pp. 118–123).

Since the earliest times, shipwrecks have yielded finds of great archaeological, artistic, and scientific, as well as financial, value. One of the most intriguing objects ever found was the mysterious first-century BCE "Antikythera mechanism" (pp. 72–78), which turned out to be an early Greek analog computer. But a more typical example of "sunken treasure" is the wreck of the Spanish New World treasure galleon, "*Nuestra Señora de Atocha*" (pp. 179–182), which carried gold, silver, and emeralds among its fabulous cargo. Among the artworks recovered from the sea are the ancient Greek "Riace warriors" (pp. 51–55), rare examples of Greek bronze statuary that were not melted down to make tools or weapons.

Of course, many of the treasures listed here, such as two of the world's most famous religious artifacts, "the Ark of the Covenant" (pp. 44–50) and "the Holy Grail" (pp. 79–86), known to have existed from written accounts, were lost, and have become the subject of the greatest treasure hunts of all time—both historic and fictional. Others were deliberately destroyed, such as the giant Bamiyan Buddhas (pp. 240–243), Afghanistan, which were dynamited by the fanatical Taliban, or forgotten, such as the treasures of the "Sacred Cenote of Chichen Itza" (pp. 171–174).

Great artworks have been the subject of thefts, such as the Russian "Amber Room" (pp. 223–226), looted by the Germans, and several paintings by Vincent van Gogh (pp. 244–247), taken from a Dutch museum in 2002. Other stolen treasures rumored to exist, such as the bullion thought to have been seized by the Nazis (pp. 213–217) and the Japanese (pp. 218–222) during the Second World War, have yet to be recovered. Finally, our collection features priceless jewels, such as the fabulous Fabergé eggs (pp. 204–208) made for Russia's czars, and the diamond "Patiala necklace" (pp. 227–231) lost from an Indian Rajah's treasury.

In addition to listing the extraordinary circumstances of their loss and, if applicable, recovery, the entries also explain the historical significance of these objects, which often far outweighs their material value. When possible, a dollar value is listed on the opening page of the entry. However, in several cases, the treasure's uniqueness makes it impossible to even estimate a financial value; for these, I have resorted to giving a less tangible but no less significant "historical value."

Apart from being objects of great value, these treasures give readers a sidewise glance at the great events of human history and reveal changing attitudes to the uses of high-status objects. Eleven entries on grave goods indicate that, from the Bronze Age to the Early Middle Ages, treasures were interred with their elite owners, in theory in perpetuity, although in practice most were recycled into the economy by looters. A dozen entries are "cultural" or "sacred" artifacts, whose value is retrospective because of their rarity or because they were associated with a person, idea, or event considered significant by later generations. Twenty-two entries deal with the spoils of war and conquest: vast accumulations of wealth transferred between cultures and continents, often with consequences just as disastrous for the original owners as for the despoilers.

Once reserved for the use of the rich and powerful, the majority of treasures are now owned democratically by institutions, which display them for the edification, education, and enjoyment of the public. We are shocked and dismayed when we learn that a great masterpiece has disappeared from public view, either stolen on the orders of a rogue collector, or bought by a billionaire. Treasures and artworks that were once tangible representations of power, wealth, privilege, and prestige for the few are now held in common by the many, as testament to the diversity and beauty of the natural world and to the skill and creativity of humanity.

TREASURE

Burial goods

Hoards

Shipwrecks

Religious objects or places

Artworks

Gemstones

ABRAHAM'S OFFERING: RAM IN A THICKET

ca. 2600 BCE

Circumstance of loss: Royal burial in the Sumerian city of Ur

Rediscovery: Excavation of the Great Death Pit by Sir Leonard Woolley

Historical significance: Rediscovery of one of the major cities of ancient Sumeria, the biblical Ur of the Chaldees, putative home of Abraham

Value: Confirmation of biblical authority

And Abraham lifted up his eyes, and looked, and behold behind him a ram caught in a thicket by his horns: and Abraham went and took the ram, and offered him up for a burnt offering in the stead of his son.

Genesis 22:13 (King James Version)

According to the Tanakh, the Hebrew Bible, the Old Testament Book of Genesis, and the Islamic Quran, the patriarch Abraham, to whom all three faiths look as their common founder, was a native of the city of Ur of the Chaldees. In antiquity and the Middle Ages, there was no general agreement as to where the city had been, apart from its general location in the Near East. The Islamic candidate was the city of Urfa (ancient Edessa, and modern-day Sanliurfa in southeastern Turkey), but in the mid-nineteenth century, investigations by British archaeologists identified a new possible site. It was a city of much greater antiquity, and one of the earliest and most important urban centers of Sumeria (now southern Iraq), whose name, once the area's cuneiform script had been deciphered by the English linguist and diplomat Sir Henry Rawlinson (1810–95), was the monosyllabic "Ur." British scholars immediately claimed to have identified the biblical "Ur of the Chaldees," and interest in the region intensified. For the next half century, many of its "tells," or ruin mounds, yielded unexpected secrets to their European excavators.

The site of Ur was occupied for over five and a half millennia (compare to London's two millennia and New York's youthful four centuries). The cities of Sumeria were once believed to be the original "cradle" of urban civilization, but historians now know that cities developed independently in many parts of the world. The Western bias for the Near Eastern origins of civilization, however, can be understood if we examine the Christian beliefs of nineteenth-century scholars, who based their research on scripture, and sought to identify the cities of Assyria and Babylonia that were mentioned in the books of the Old Testament. When they were excavated, Ur and the other cities of southern Iraq showed indications of flooding, which many took to be evidence of the Great Flood. However, research has since revealed that the cities of Sumeria regularly experienced flooding. Water, though the lack of it instead of a surplus, led to the abandonment of Ur in 400 BCE, after the course of the Euphrates changed and starved the city of the one resource it could not do without.

Archaeology in the nineteenth century was sometimes little better than tomb-raiding, with researchers from rival countries literally fighting over sites, and stripping them of artifacts, bas-reliefs, and statues that were shipped to fill the new museums of Paris, London, and Berlin. Fortunately, many Near Eastern sites were difficult to access, and if they had no obvious treasures to loot, such as Ur, they were left more or less undisturbed until the twentieth century. After the First World War, the British took over large parts of the Near East from the Ottoman Empire, including Mesopotamia, giving them privileged access to the sites of the Tigris-Euphrates valley. Starting in 1922, the British Museum, in collaboration with Pennsylvania State University, which provided much of the funding for the digs, sent Leonard Woolley (1880–1960) to excavate Ur, where he worked for the next 12 seasons until 1934.

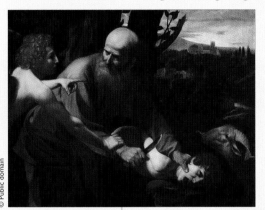

© Public domain

LAST MINUTE
God spared Isaac and sent a substitute.

During his excavation of the site, Woolley made discoveries that rivaled the richest and most famous archaeological find of the period: Tutankhamun's tomb (see pp. 30–35), unearthed in 1922–23. But while Howard Carter (1874–1939) had uncovered a single small tomb belonging to an obscure Egyptian pharaoh, Woolley's dig uncovered an entire civilization, complete with hitherto unseen temples, palaces, libraries, cemeteries, storehouses, and private houses. A great self-publicist who milked his discoveries for every column inch he could get in the British and American press (which he could convert into ready cash to continue his excavations), Woolley not only claimed to have discovered the birthplace of the biblical Abraham but also his house—now, along with the reconstructed ziggurat, the main tourist attraction for the U.S. forces stationed near the ancient city.

According to crime novelist Agatha Christie (1890–1976), who visited the Ur dig in 1928, Woolley brought the otherwise barren, dry-as-dust site to life with his potrayal of the city as it was in the third millennium BCE, although modern scholars have cast doubt on his more colorful descriptions and the claims he made in *Abraham: Recent Discoveries and Hebrew Origins*, which he published in 1936 to expound his biblical theories. Although he was guilty of embroidering to impress the media, visitors such as Christie, and readers of his popular books, Woolley was nevertheless an extremely conscientious archaeologist, whose work at the site established the benchmarks for future archaeological research in the region.

Unlike the previous generation of star archaeologists, such as Heinrich Schliemann (1822–90), who excavated the sites of Troy and Mycenae (see pp. 25–29), and Arthur Evans (1851–1941), who discovered Minoan Knossos, who were not above making the archaeology fit their preconceived notions of what they expected to find, Woolley, his Abrahamic fantasies aside, revealed a civilization quite unlike anything found in the Old Testament. Among the thousands of tombs of the Ur necropolis, Woolley uncovered 16 high-status burials, which he called "royal tombs," although the individuals concerned might not conform to twentieth-century European notions of royalty. His identification was based on the presence of two things: extremely valuable burial goods made of gold, silver, and semi-precious stones—which one would expect to find in the tombs of ancient rulers—and, more shockingly, of the bodies of dozens of male and female attendants sacrificed to accompany their masters and mistresses into the afterlife.

GREAT DEATH PIT

The most extraordinary of Ur's burials, known as "the Great Death Pit," contained the skeletons of 74 male and female attendants interred near the richly attired body of an individual identified from her seal as "Queen" Puabi. Because of the poor preservation of the skulls, which had been crushed by the weight of the soil once the pit had been filled in, Woolley supposed that they died by drinking poison—a relatively peaceful death, even if they had been forced to drink the fateful cup at swordpoint. In 2009, however, a team from the University of Pennsylvania scanned bone fragments from two of the better-preserved skulls and discovered that the victims died when a metal spike had been driven into their heads.

Scattered among the richly dressed skeletons Woolley found objects of great beauty and sophistication, including a pair of standing rams resting their forelegs on a flowering shrub as if they were about to nibble the attached gilded flowers. In keeping with his biblical theories, Woolley described the animals as twin "Rams in a thicket" from the story of the ram sent by god to replace Abraham's son Isaac as a burnt offering (see quote, p. 10). Made of gold, silver, lapis lazuli, and red limestone, shaped over a core of carved wood (which had completely degraded during its long period underground), the statuettes are more likely representations of goats rather than rams, and were either stands for two separate bowls or two legs of a table whose wooden top has not survived. A cylinder seal from Ur bears the image of such a table, so the latter interpretation is most likely to be the correct one.

In Egypt gold was used liberally in royal burials, but in the cities of ancient Sumeria, precious metals were scarce. For the rams, gold and silver were used as thin sheets beaten over the wooden core to which they were glued with bitumen. The lapis lazuli, like the other semi-precious stones adorning the precious objects and jewelry found in the pit, had been imported from Afghanistan, 2,000 miles (3,200 km) away in Central Asia. The rams, now exhibited separately at the University of Pennsylvania Museum of Archaeology and Anthropology, Philadelphia, and the British Museum, London, provide clear evidence of the long-distance trade networks that linked the civilizations of the Bronze Age in the third millennium BCE.

But more than their great artistic merit and their obvious material value (now and at the time they were made), the rams and the other treasures discovered in the royal tombs of Ur are among the few objects the Sumerians made that have survived to tell us about their lives, their beliefs, and their appreciation of the natural world. Lacking stone and timber for construction, the Sumerians built their cities of perishable mud brick, which over the millennia degraded into the huge shapeless mounds that dot the flat alluvial plains of southern Iraq. Unlike the Egyptians and Assyrians, the Sumerians left few statues or carved bas-reliefs. What we know of their culture comes from their libraries of cuneiform texts and a few treasures such as the rams. On p. 10, I have given the historical value of the Ram in a Thicket as "Confirmation of biblical authority," because for many who flocked to the British and Penn State Museums to see them, the rams were proof positive of the truth of the biblical account of Abraham's birth, life, and covenant with God.

TRADE GOODS
The rams are evidence of early global trade networks.

© Magnus Manske | Creative Commons

BOATMAN OF THE SUN: SOLAR BOAT OF KHUFU

2566 BCE

TREASURE

Burial goods

Hoards

Shipwrecks

Religious objects or places

Artworks

Gemstones

Circumstance of loss: Burial of the Pharaoh Khufu

Rediscovery: While clearing debris from around the Great Pyramid of Giza in 1954

Historical significance: The best-preserved ship from antiquity and evidence that the Great Pyramid was built as a tomb

Value: The triumph of archaeology over pseudo-science

The Khufu boat was found in a sealed pit next to the Great Pyramid at Giza. Originally there were five boats buried next to the pyramid, of which all but two had been removed in antiquity. The ship is built primarily of cedar, which must have been imported from Syria-Palestine.

Egyptian Boats and Ships (2008) by Steve Vinson

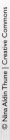

Our second treasure is, like the first, an artifact from the third millennium BCE that is impossible to value because of its extreme antiquity and uniqueness. Unlike the "Ram in a Thicket" (pp. 10–14), the solar boat is not decorated with precious metals or gemstones, but even when it was interred in the shadow of the tomb of its royal owner, it was a high-status object imbued with deep religious significance. Apart from its rarity and holiness, the solar boat is also a treasure in the archaeological sense, as one of the oldest vessels to survive and the best preserved from antiquity, which testifies to the advanced shipbuilding technology of the Egyptian Bronze Age. The solar boat was one of five ritual ships buried with the Pharaoh Khufu (also Kheops or Cheops), whose traditional regnal dates are given as 2589–2566 BCE, and whose greatest claim to fame is the construction of the Great Pyramid of Giza, one of the "Eight Wonders of the World," and the tallest manmade structure on earth until the fourteenth century.

The Great Pyramid is without doubt one of the most studied buildings in the world, as well as one of the most maligned, misunderstood, and misrepresented. The largest of the 138 pyramids so far discovered in Egypt, the Great Pyramid was built like all the others as the tomb of a pharaoh. However, while this function was taken for granted by the ancient Egyptians, it was forgotten by later civilizations that invented much more fanciful origins and functions for the giant structure. One early tradition described the Giza pyramids as the granaries built by the biblical Joseph. More recent authors have sought to recast the Great Pyramid as a repository of all human knowledge—a coded stone archive of human history, past, present, and future; a structure constructed by members of an advanced but now vanished Neolithic civilization, whose original home was on the mythical island of Atlantis; or as physical evidence of contact between humans and alien civilizations whose advanced technology is the only way to explain so awesome a building. These fantastic interpretations usually present the Great Pyramid as a perfect one-off rather than one in a long series of pyramids of different dimensions and designs, starting with the much more modest Stepped Pyramid of Saqqara built a century earlier.

Writers of sensationalist pseudo-history, however, do not bother with inconvenient archaeological evidence that might expose their theories for the crackpot fantasies they are. Although an impressive feat of engineering, the Great Pyramid and its two smaller neighbors in Giza were well within the mathematical, architectural, and technical capabilities of the ancient Egyptians, from measuring and preparing the site, to quarrying, moving, dressing, and polishing the stone, without having recourse to flying saucers or mysterious forces to levitate the stone blocks into position: All that was needed was a great deal of manpower, money, and time—three things that Egypt's early pharaohs had in plentiful supply.

The Great Pyramid is equipped with three burial chambers: one under the structure, which was the traditional location for a royal pyramid burial (though in this case, it was abandoned before it was finished), and two internal chambers dubbed the King and Queen's Chambers and linked to the main entrance by long sloping corridors. The King's Chamber contains a sarcophagus, broken in one corner—evidence that the pyramid was looted in antiquity. In addition to these internal fittings, the pyramid had its own funerary temple complex where rituals were performed to ease the deceased pharaoh's progress through the Underworld; a causeway to the Nile along which the king's body and grave goods would have been brought to the pyramid; several smaller pyramids known as the "Queen's Pyramids"; and the shaft burial of Queen Hetepheres I, Khufu's mother, one of the only early dynastic burials to be discovered intact, apart from the fact that the alabaster sarcophagus meant to contain the queen's mummy was found to be empty.

Finally, confirming the Great Pyramid as the final resting place of a pharaoh was the presence of five solar boats interred in pits around the pyramid. Three of these celestial ships disappeared in antiquity, but two of the pits, hidden by debris that had fallen from the pyramid during an earthquake, were rediscovered in 1954, and were found to have been undisturbed. Opening one pit that had been hermetically sealed for 4,520 years, Egyptian archaeologist Kamal el-Mallakh (1918–87) reported a strong smell of cedar wood.

Ancient Egypt was a river culture that depended for its existence and survival on the Nile, whose annual silt-rich floods fertilized the fields, and whose broad, deep course provided a natural highway from the cataracts

© Roland Unger | Creative Commons

SHIP BURIAL
Five solar barques were buried with Khufu.

"I AM SAILING..."

3-D JIGSAW
The boat was a 1,224-piece cedar-wood puzzle.

deep in the desert all the way to the Mediterranean Sea. It is not surprising that in the myths of this riverine civilization, the sun god Ra sailed across the sky on a boat, while in the traditions of more terrestrial cultures, such as the ancient Greeks, Helios galloped across the sky in a horse-drawn chariot. The ancient Egyptians built their first boats from papyrus, as demonstrated by the intrepid Thor Heyerdahl (1914–2002), who tried to prove that the Egyptians had sailed to the New World by attempting crossings from Africa to South America in the papyrus *Ra* and the totora *Ra II*—the former foundered a few weeks out, while the latter succeeded in reaching Barbados in the West Indies.

Having perfected their papyrus designs, the Egyptians reproduced them in more durable wood for use as trading vessels and as ceremonial barques for their pharaohs. When the Egyptians described their rulers as living gods, they were not speaking metaphorically: The pharaoh in life was a son of the Sun god Amun-Ra, and was represented as the living incarnation of several gods, in particular the falcon-headed Horus; in death, the pharaoh would ascend into the heavens to become an incarnation of Amun-Ra himself crossing the sky in the barque of heaven. The King's Chamber was equipped with two tube-like ducts that led to the outside of the pyramid and were aligned with important stars, which were believed to be the means by which the deceased pharaoh's spirit would ascend from his tomb to the heavens. Compared to Christian imagery that might talk of Jesus or the Virgin Mary's ascension, the Egyptians supplemented the metaphorical imagery with a very physical means: several million tons of stone pyramid complete with burial chamber that was a royal launchpad into space.

The Egyptians believed that the physical body, preserved by the complex process of mummification, was necessary for the survival of the spirit. Hence the dead king needed not only to be preserved as a mummy, but the mummy also needed a home (a pyramid), and everything that the pharaoh would have used in his lifetime: furniture, jewelry, cosmetics, food and drink, and servants (reproduced as scale models rather than sacrificed as in the royal burials of Ur). In keeping with their view of the afterlife, they also provided the pharaoh with the boats that he would need to navigate the vault of heaven when he became one with Amun-Ra.

The treasure that el-Mallakh discovered was a 1,224-piece cedar-wood puzzle, as the boat had been dismantled before it had been sealed into its pit. A flat-bottomed river barge with elegant high sweeping prow and stern post carved in the shape of bundles of papyrus tied with rope, the solar ship is a marvel of the boatbuilder's art. The wood imported from Lebanon was so well preserved that el-Mallakh said the ship might have been interred a year earlier. Its reassembly, however, was a complex puzzle that demanded extensive study of depictions of ancient vessels, as well as of modern-day feluccas still built on the Nile. It took 13 years for the 143-foot (43.6 m) solar barque to be rebuilt, following ancient methods that did not use metal nails but wooden tenons and hemp ropes, and another 15 years before it was exhibited in a museum erected next to the Great Pyramid.

There is no agreement about exactly how the boat was used before it was sealed in its pit. There is evidence that it had been in the water; hence, it had probably sailed on the Nile, though whether this was several times during the pharaoh's lifetime or just the once to transport his mummy from Memphis to the Great Pyramid remains a matter of conjecture. Whichever it was, the vessel, which was moved and steered by six pairs of oars, with its spacious main stateroom at the stern, and two canopied areas on the fore deck, was truly fit for a king, alive or dead. But perhaps more important from the point of view of archaeologists who have had to endure the most absurd theories about the age and function of the Great Pyramid, the boats provide yet more proof that the pyramid was built as a tomb, and not as a giant razor-blade sharpener.

TREASURE

Burial goods

Hoards

Shipwrecks

Religious objects or places

Artworks

Gemstones

DON'T JUDGE A DISK BY ITS COVER: PHAISTOS DISK

1600 BCE

Circumstance of loss: Discovered from sealed depository in the ruins of Phaistos

Rediscovery: Excavation of Phaistos by Luigi Pernier in 1908

Historical significance: The disk may represent the first evidence of movable type

Value: First edition

One clue to the meaning of the object is the context in which it was found. The fact that the Phaistos Disc was unearthed in an underground temple depository has persuaded some researchers of its religious significance, suggesting that the text was possibly a sacred hymn or ritual.

"The Unsolved Puzzle of the Phaistos Disc" in *Hidden History: Lost Civilizations, Secret Knowledge, and Ancient Mysteries* (2007) by Brian Haughton

At first sight the Phaistos disk is not impressive and does not appear to be something that would be of great archaeological significance. About 6 inches (15 cm) in diameter, the light brown fired-clay disk is about the same size as a small side plate or serving dish. Unlike a plate, however, the disk has intricate markings on both sides, arranged in spirals starting from the outside edge to the center. The markings are small incised pictures, some recognizably animal, vegetable, or human, while others are more abstract and open to interpretation but are generally identifiable as tools, weapons, and items of clothing that would have been common during the Aegean Bronze Age. To a layman unfamiliar with ancient ideographic scripts, the disk looks like a kind of children's game; one in which counters move from picture to picture, maybe with the aid of a dice. Had we but found a tablet of rules along with the "game board," we would know what landing on the "Mohican," the "arrow," or the "rosette" would mean, and we might have rediscovered an ancient Minoan version of Snakes and Ladders.

A closer inspection of the markings, however, suggests that the "game board" explanation, which has been put forward several times to explain the disk, is unlikely; while there are 241 separate symbols on the disk, they are made up of an "alphabet" of 45 unique signs, arranged not in individual "squares," as in a game, but in 61 groups within incised lines, varying in length from two to six signs; for example, "rosette-tattooed head-arrow," and "shield-vase-beehive-fish," which suggests that the two spiral sequences represent texts, and that the signs might be "read" as a single letter, as in our alphabet, as a syllable, or as a whole word.

The Bronze Age Minoans and Mycenaean Greeks used two other scripts: the still undeciphered Linear A, and Linear B, composed of 87 syllabic signs and over 100 ideograms, each of which stands for an entire word. In this regard, Linear B is very similar to modern Japanese, which combines *kanji*, Chinese characters, standing for whole words, and two syllabic *kana* scripts, one of which is used to write verb and adjective endings and other parts of speech, and the other to write foreign names and loan words.

Researchers have noted similarities with other ideographic scripts of the region, such as Bronze Age Luwian, which combines syllabic signs with ideograms signifying whole words, commonly animals; for example, a cow or horse's head meaning "cow" or "horse." However, the similarities are conjectural, and translations based on this and other languages are not widely accepted. So far there have been about two dozen linguistic and non-linguistic interpretations of the disk since its discovery a century ago, including translations into Greek, Hittite, and Egyptian, as well as descriptions of it as a calendar, a table of astronomical observations, and, preposterously, as a document from an advanced Atlantean civilization. The author of the latter theory does not explain why the technologically advanced culture that was supposed to exist on Atlantis used an alphabet consisting of such primitive signs, while at the same time, the Minoans and Greeks were already using two abstract syllabic-ideographic scripts.

The association with Atlantis, however, might contain a very small grain of truth. Our earliest source for the Atlantis story, the Athenian Plato (424–348 BCE), placed the mythical island in the Atlantic, "beyond the Pillars of Hercules" (Straits of Gibraltar). However, archaeological discoveries on the nearby Aegean island of Santorini (ancient Thera), north of Crete, revealed the existence of a sophisticated Bronze Age civilization on the island, with trading and cultural links to Crete and mainland Greece, which was destroyed when the island was literally blown apart by a massive volcanic eruption around 1500 BCE. The eruption triggered earthquakes and tsunamis that destroyed or damaged the Minoan settlements on Crete. Hence, the disk might be a relic of Atlantis, as long as we accept that Santorini-Thera and Minoan Crete together were the true inspiration for Plato's island empire that sank into the sea.

BLESS THIS PALACE

No single translation or interpretation of the disk has yet to be widely accepted, the main problem being that this is the only example of the script that has ever been found. The inscriptions on the disk are too short and lack sufficient context to enable the ideographic code to be cracked. To some historians this raises the ugly possibility that the disk is a forgery or a hoax. According to Italian archaeologist Luigi Pernier (1874–1937), who excavated the ruins of the Minoan palace of Phaistos in southern Crete between 1903 and 1905, the disk was in a sealed space underneath the floor of a building that served as the ceremonial gateway of the Phaistos complex. Phaistos is one of several "palaces" found on Crete, which are administrative centers, elite residences, and religious precincts. The most famous Minoan palace is Knossos on the north coast of the island, which is the inspiration of the myth of the monstrous carnivorous half-man, half-bull, who was imprisoned in a labyrinthine palace by his father King Minos.

Interring objects under the floors of important buildings is attested in many cultures of the Near East and Mediterranean. These sometimes bear the name of the builder or restorer of an important building, and outline the circumstances of the (re)construction, or they are placed for ritual reasons as a kind of magical protection for the building. The disk was found mixed with ashes and the bones of cattle, indicating that it may have been placed there as part of a religious ritual involving the burning of sacrificial offerings. Another tablet, bearing an inscription in the mysterious Linear A script, was also found in the same sealed depository, as well as pottery dated to 1700–1600 BCE.

The form of the Phaistos disk inscription, which has several repeated sequences that might be "words," and its context suggested to Pernier that the disk might be a religious text or hymn, though, as with other interpretations, this will not be confirmed until other examples of the script are discovered, allowing for its translation. As long as the disk is genuine, it qualifies as a "treasure" primarily because it is unique—the only known example of an ancient script that could be in Minoan Cretan or could have come from much farther afield.

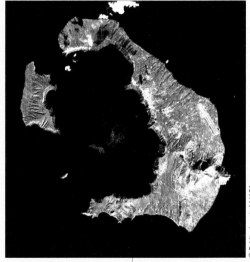

© Public domain | NASA

BLOWN APART
Santorini's destruction is the basis for the Atlantis myth.

There is a second reason why the disk might qualify as a priceless historical artifact, which is the way the disk was inscribed. Other ancient scripts, such as Egyptian hieroglyphs and Mesopotamian cuneiform, were carved in stone, painted on papyrus, or impressed in clay individually. The idea that the same character could be impressed many times over with the same stamp or seal—in other words, what we now call "printing" with standardized "movable type"—is thought to have originated in eleventh-century China over two and a half millennia after the Phaistos disk was sealed in its resting place, and just over three millennia later in the fifteenth century in Europe by Johannes Gutenberg (1395–1468).

The miracle of the Phaistos disk is that the signs were impressed into wet clay with a standardized set of seals—the equivalent of movable type for this 45-character script. We know that this is the case because the "printer" of the disk made corrections to the text, smoothing out the wet clay and stamping over one sign with a different one before the disk was completed and fired. This raises two interesting questions: If the disk was created with some form of movable type devised by a Bronze Age Gutenberg, why have no other examples of the script ever been discovered? Such an invention would make creating impressed clay documents extremely easy—much easier and faster than the process of creating cuneiform tablets with a stylus, of which we have many tens of thousands from sites all over the Near East. A subsidiary question is where are the seal/type forms? No such objects have ever been found in Crete. It is possible that the script on the disk was not native to the island, and that the object was imported from an as yet unidentified culture—an artifact of such rarity and value that it was used in an important foundational ritual when the Phaistos palace was built.

© Aserakov | Creative Commons

ONE-OFF
The disk might be the world's first printed text.

The second question is why, if the disk were indeed inscribed with some kind of printed text, movable type did not take off and spread throughout the civilized world as it would millennia later in East Asia and Europe? One imagines a lone Bronze Age genius—a Minoan or Anatolian Leonardo da Vinci (1452–1519), who single-handedly invented movable type (and maybe the script itself), and then made the disk to demonstrate his invention. According to American author Jared Diamond in *Guns, Germs, and Steel* (1997), the disk is evidence of an invention that appeared long before its time. Diamond's hypothesis, however, seems unconvincing when one considers that highly literate cultures such as Mesopotamia were using writing not just for sacred texts but also for mundane purposes such as accounting, inventories, land deeds, and contracts. Although in certain cultures writing was controlled by ritual specialists and printing might be banned on religious grounds, this was not the case across large parts of the Near East. Unfortunately, we won't be able to answer these questions until we discover other examples of the Phaistos script, which might give further clues to its meaning and origins, or even better, the stamps used to create the disk.

ACCURSED KING: MASK OF AGAMEMNON

1500 BCE

TREASURE

Burial goods

Hoards

Shipwrecks

Religious objects or places

Artworks

Gemstones

Circumstance of loss: Royal burial in pit grave

Rediscovery: Excavation of Mycenae by Heinrich Schliemann

Historical significance: The rediscovery of the ancient culture of Bronze Age Greece

Value: Historical evidence of the Homeric epics

Aegisthus and my wicked wife were the death of me between them. He asked me to his house, feasted me, and then butchered me most miserably as though I were a fat beast in a slaughter house.

Book XI of the *Odyssey* (mid-eighth century BCE) by Homer

King Agamemnon of Mycenae is one of the most famous figures of Greek historical fiction. I say fiction, because his claim to historical existence is based on two rather circumstantial pieces of evidence: The first is a mention in a fourteenth-century BCE Anatolian Hittite document of a "King Akagamunas of the Ahhiyawa," which certain scholars have interpreted as meaning "King Agamemnon of the Achaeans" (an alternative name for the ancient Greeks); and the second is German archaeologist Heinrich Schliemann's (1822–90) claim to have discovered Agamemnon's tomb in Mycenae. Schliemann is much more famous for his identification of the site of Hisarlik in northwestern Turkey as the site of Troy in Homer's *Iliad* (mid-eighth century BCE). He excavated at the site twice: from 1871 to 1873 and from 1878 to 1879.

The tell, or ruin mound, of Hisarlik contains the superimposed remains of nine different cities, numbered Troy I to IX, which range in date from 3000 BCE to 100 BCE. Schliemann identified the early Bronze Age Troy II (dated to 2600–2500 BCE) as the level corresponding to the city besieged and sacked by the Greeks during the Trojan War. He went on to claim that he had found the Trojan King Priam's treasure in the city's ruins. However, both classical and modern scholarship agree that Troy II is at least 1,000 years too early to be the scene of the events recounted in Homer's poem, and that Troy VIIa, which was sacked and burned sometime at the end of the thirteenth century BCE or the beginning of the twelfth century BCE, is the most probable Homeric Troy—if one accepts that the Trojan War was based on a single real event, and is not merely an entirely fictional event or a conflation of several piratical raids by the Mycenaean Greeks on the Asian mainland.

© Public domain

MIXED REVIEWS
Schliemann is both revered as a pioneer and reviled as a fraud.

In the late nineteenth century, at the dawn of scientific archaeology, long before Carbon-14, pollen, and stratigraphic dating techniques had been developed, the study of ancient sites was part science, part treasure-hunting—the balance depending on the character and conscientiousness of the archaeologist concerned. Schliemann was a colorful character— an entrepreneur (some say con artist) and adventurer who came to archaeology in middle age having made his fortune in real estate and import-export. Later archaeologists have criticized his methods and cast doubt on his claims—one going as far as to say that he had managed to do to Troy what the Greeks themselves had failed to do three millennia before; that is, to destroy it completely.

Serious doubts have also been expressed about the authenticity of Priam's treasure, which consists of copper, gold, and electrum jewelry, weapons, and artifacts, because it is unique among finds from the Bronze Age. The treasure—whether genuine, planted but historically more recent, or out-and-out fake—has had a colorful history since its discovery. It was first displayed in Berlin, from where it disappeared at the end of the Second World War in 1945, only to turn up half a century later in a Moscow museum. The ownership of the treasure is still the subject of heated arguments between German and Russian museum authorities.

Despite Schliemann's shortcomings, we must recognize him as one of the great heroes of archaeology, whose discoveries inspired generations of much more conscientious, scientific archaeologists. His interest in the sites linked to the Homeric epics, the *Iliad* and the *Odyssey*, led him to investigate locations other than Troy, including Mycenaean Tiryns, Ithaca, home to the wandering King Ulysses (Odysseus), and Mycenae, home of the leader of the Greek army that sacked Troy, King Agamemnon.

MURDERS MOST FOUL

In Greece's Classical period (sixth to fourth centuries BCE), the Homeric heroes, including Odysseus, Achilles, and Agamemnon, were as familiar and famous among the Greeks as modern-day fictional characters such as James Bond, J. R. Ewing, and Darth Vader are in our own time. They were good, noble, and wise, or evil, ignoble, and devious. Classicists will be horrified by a comparison between modern movie and TV characters and the heroes of ancient Greek classics, but the Homeric epics served much the same functions as our movies and TV shows: as morality tales and as thrilling entertainment.

The legends about Agamemnon's family, the Atreides, named for his father Atreus, read like soap opera, albeit a very bloody one: Imagine *Days of Our Lives* with rape, incest, murder, and cannibalism. The Greeks were big on family curses that were passed from generation to generation, and the Atreides' problems began with Agamemnon's great-grandfather, Tantalus, who killed, cooked, and served up his own son to the gods of Olympus to see if they would realize the deception or go ahead and feast on human flesh. Only one of the gods was fooled, while the others refused to eat the meal. They took their revenge, condemning Tantalus to face eternity standing in a pool of water that he could not drink, and under a tree whose fruit he could not reach. After many other dark family deeds, we come to Agamemnon, whose brother, Menelaus, married Helen, whose affair with Prince Paris of Troy triggered the Trojan War.

The Greek fleet assembled to sail to Troy but was becalmed. When Agamemnon consulted a seer, he instructed him to sacrifice his daughter Iphigenia to appease the goddess Artemis, whom he had offended. He obeyed, lifting Artemis's curse, but earning the undying hatred of his wife Clytemnestra. Ten years later, Agamemnon returned victorious from Troy with a captive Trojan princess whom he had taken as a lover. His wife, who had herself taken a lover during the king's absence, murdered him in his bath, starting a new cycle of killings, retold by the Athenian playwright Aeschylus (524–455 BCE) in the cycle of plays known as the *Oresteia*.

CHEZ LES ATREIDES

The first phase of urban civilization in ancient Greece is known as the Mycenaean period (1600–1100 BCE), named for the Peloponnesian site of Mycenae. Like the Minoan "palaces" of Phaistos (see previous entry) and Knossos on Crete, Mycenaean sites combined elite residential, administrative, religious, and military functions; but unlike Minoan palaces, they were fortified by walls made of huge blocks of stone. While the Minoans appear to have been a relatively peaceful people whose civilization was based on trade, the Mycenaeans were a warrior civilization, as can be seen from their heavily fortified strongholds and the military hardware buried with their kings.

The art and iconography of Mycenaean Greece shows that its culture was deeply influenced by Minoan Crete, though in a more warlike style. For example, while the Minoans delighted in natural scenes of plants and animals, these became Mycenaean hunting scenes. In 1450 BCE, 50 years after the eruption of Santorini-Thera had disrupted and fatally weakened Minoan civilization, the Mycenaeans conquered Crete. Yet they, too, would succumb to invaders when they became victims of the generalized Bronze Age Collapse (1200–1150 BCE) that saw the destruction of all the Mycenaean cities in Greece and the Aegean.

Much as he had done at his other digs in Greece and Turkey, Schliemann arrived at Mycenae convinced that he was going to uncover the ruins of the city described in the Homeric epics—nothing less than the home of Agamemnon and Clytemnestra. The city had been partially explored in the 1840s, but with his fame established by his first dig at Troy, Schliemann had the means to excavate the entire site. He discovered two circles of high-status shaft graves, several of which contained rich burial goods, including weapons, drinking vessels, and five funerary masks made of beaten gold that were placed over the faces of the dead. One of these shows a regal bearded and mustachioed man, whom Schliemann identified as King Agamemnon.

Although several scholars have since accused Schliemann of making and planting the mask to reinforce his Homeric identification of the shaft burial, others accept that the artifact is genuine, though they admit it is unlike the other four masks found in neighboring tombs. But all modern archaeologists agree that the tomb itself cannot belong to a king who fought in the Trojan War, as it dates from around 1550–1500 BCE, some 320 to 370 years before the generally accepted date for the destruction of Troy VIIa. Just as in Hisarlik-Troy, Schliemann claimed that his discoveries in Mycenae had proven the historicity of the *Iliad* and the *Odyssey*.

© DieBuche | Creative Commons

OUT OF TIME
Although identified as Agamemnon, the mask predates the Trojan War.

Schliemann's more cynical critics have suggested that not only did he knowingly make false claims about his discoveries but he also spiced up his digs with planted fakes, such as Priam's treasure and Agamemnon's death mask, to maintain his celebrity status as the world's most successful archaeologist. More charitable commentators have given him the benefit of the doubt and accept that he believed in good faith that he had found Priam's Troy and Agamemnon's tomb in Mycenae, even though that conviction made him overlook facts that did not agree with his beliefs.

"WONDERFUL THINGS": TUTANKHAMUN'S DEATH MASK

1323 BCE

Circumstance of loss: Burial of Tutankhamun

Rediscovery: Excavation by Howard Carter in the Valley of the Kings

Historical significance: The discovery of an almost intact New Kingdom burial

Value: $80 million (contents of Tutankhamun's tomb)

Carnarvon: "Can you see anything?"
Carter: "Yes, wonderful things!"

Exchange between Lord Carnarvon and Howard Carter on opening Tutankhamun's burial chamber

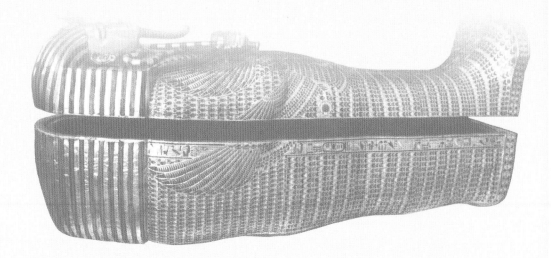

This will be our second visit to Egypt after the entry on Khufu's solar boat (pp. 15–19) dated to the year 2566 BCE. Before we begin, I'd like the reader to appreciate the extraordinary longevity of ancient Egyptian civilization, whose earliest dynasties date back to the end of the fourth millennium BCE. The time span between the beginnings of pharaonic rule in Egypt and Tutankhamun's reign (ca. 1332–ca. 1323 BCE) during the "New Kingdom" (1550–1070 BCE) is two millennia, which is the interval between the present day and the birth of Jesus of Nazareth (ca. 4 BCE–33 CE). Even the gap between the reigns of Khufu (r. 2589–2566 BCE) and Tutankhamun is 1,250 years, the equivalent to taking my readers back from the present to Europe's Dark Ages.

Even when it became a province of the Assyrian, Persian, Macedonian, and Roman empires, Egypt retained its ancient culture, religion, and artistic traditions, which were not completely eradicated until the proscription of paganism by the Christianized Roman Empire in the late fourth century CE. The continuity of religious beliefs, of the institution of divine kingship, and of customs such as the mummification of the dead for over three millennia, is testament to the inner strength and resilience of a culture that cannot only have been imposed from above by the ruling elite but must also have garnered the support of the majority of the population.

Ancient Egypt's long history, however, is not without its episodes of decline. The three "intermediary" periods after the Old, Middle, and New Kingdoms featured societal collapse, civil wars, foreign invasion, and alien domination, but like a kind of self-righting mechanism, Egypt always had the ability to return to its ancestral patterns, altered in many respects, but still recognizably itself. In the temple bas-reliefs showing Alexander the Great (356–323 BCE) and his Macedonian-Greek heirs, the Ptolemaic Dynasty, for example, Egypt's Hellenistic pharaohs are depicted in exactly the same manner, and in the same clothing and postures as the great native pharaohs of the previous millennia.

The Old Kingdom witnessed the birth of pharaonic rule in Egypt and the construction of the pyramids; during the Middle Kingdom Egyptian civilization matured and grew in power but ultimately succumbed to a foreign invader, the Asiatic Hyksos. The New Kingdom represents the apogee of Egypt as a regional power, when her empire encompassed much of the Near East. The most outstanding pharaoh of the period was

Ramesses II (ca. 1303–1213 BCE), whose long rule began two decades after the almost forgotten reign of a young pharaoh, Tutankhamun, whose only real claim to fame is the discovery of his near-intact tomb in the Valley of the Kings in 1922 by British archaeologist Howard Carter (1874–1939).

CHILD OF THE ATEN

Although Tutankhamun himself did very little of note in his nine-year reign, his father was unique in the long annals of ancient Egyptian history as a religious reformer who tried to replace Egypt's sprawling pantheon of gods with a single deity: the solar disk, the Aten. Tutankhamun's father Akhenaten, originally Amenhotep IV (r. ca. 1353–1336 BCE), has been described as the world's first individualist for his attempt to introduce monotheism to polytheistic ancient Egypt. Until his reign, the priesthood of the Temple of Amun-Ra in Karnak (near modern-day Luxor) crowned the pharaoh and assured his religious legitimacy. The priests had naturally grown extremely rich and powerful from royal patronage, as any visitor to the gigantic ruins of Karnak will testify.

© Time & Life Pictures | Getty Images

MAGIC MOMENT
Carter and Carnarvon's first glimpse of the tomb.

For what seems to be genuine religious conviction rather than political expediency to reduce the power of the priesthood, Amenhotep announced that henceforth he would worship only one god, the Aten, in whose honor he built temples in Karnak. He changed his name to Akhenaten, meaning "Strong bull, beloved of Aten." He later built a new capital at Amarna, away from the sanctuaries of Karnak and the influence of the old priesthood. Deprived of royal patronage, the traditional cults of Egypt were weakened but did not disappear. It is unlikely that many outside court circles adopted Atenism, but Amarna was a devotee. Unlike other Egyptian deities, who were human, animal, or human-animal hybrids, the Aten was an abstract solar disk, whose rays tipped with ankhs, the Egyptian cross of life, descended toward the adoring pharaoh and his family.

Although claiming the absolute power and divine status of his forebears, Akhenaten rejected traditional artistic conventions. The bas-reliefs and statues of earlier pharaohs were not realistic portraits but highly stylized, and idealized representations. The visitor to the Egyptian galleries of the British Museum, the Louvre, or the Metropolitan Museum of Art in

New York would be hard pressed to tell one granite pharaoh from another. Akhenaten, on the other hand, was portrayed realistically, a fact made even more shocking because of his ballooning feminine hips and strange elongated face. Several researchers have suggested that he was sexually dysmorphic or even a full hermaphrodite, but as he fathered eight or nine children, he was clearly man enough to procreate. In Amarna, instead of the king at war riding his enemies down in his chariot, Akhenaten is depicted in domestic scenes with his senior wife Nefertiti and his children.

Tutankhaten, "Living image of Aten," was possibly the eighth child of Akhenaten and an unnamed royal consort. He would have been brought up in his father's heretical court in Amarna. As a younger son, Tutankhaten did not succeed when his father died. The exact line of succession is difficult to reconstruct, as Akhenaten's immediate successors were also victims of historical "editing" by the priests of Amun-Ra. Once they had regained power, however, the priests demolished the Aten temples, desecrated Akhenaten's mummy, and tried to erase him and his heretical beliefs from history.

GILDED YOUTH
The idealized death mask marks a return to orthodoxy.

© Aikon | Creative Commons

In around 1332 BCE, they selected the young Tutankhaten to be the next pharaoh, renaming him Tutankhamun ("Living image of Amun") to underline the restoration of Amun-Ra as the supreme deity of the Egyptian pantheon. The choice of a nine-year-old boy as pharaoh suggests that the priests of Amun-Ra and their backers wanted a ruler who they could control and who would not go the way of his father. Studies of Tutankhamun's well-preserved mummy, however, have suggested that the young pharaoh might have died when an injury became infected or that he could have been murdered by his successor, the even more obscure Ay, the last pharaoh of the Eighteenth Dynasty.

Whether his death was accidental or natural, Tutankhamun died well before his time, at about the age of 18. Although the pharaohs had long before stopped building pyramids (as these were an invitation to tomb robbers), during the New Kingdom they excavated elaborate underground tombs in the Valley of the Kings, the largest of which consisted of 120 chambers richly decorated with images of the dead pharaoh, the gods, and ritual texts. Tutankhamun's tomb (KV62) has only four chambers, only one of which, the burial chamber, is decorated. It is likely that the tomb was being prepared for someone else of less elevated status, and that it was quickly co-opted to become the king's final resting place.

There is evidence that the tomb was broken into soon after the king's burial, but the thieves were disturbed and did not reach the king himself. The mummy would be the obvious target of grave robbers because it would be covered in gold amulets and jewelry. The tomb was resealed and Tutankhamun, who had not had much luck in his lifetime, won the jackpot in mummy terms. A later royal tomb was built close to his, and its debris obscured any traces of Tutankhamun's burial completely.

Most of the 63 tombs of the Valley of the Kings were robbed in antiquity, and the most impressive but now empty painted tombs had been opened and explored by nineteenth-century European archaeologists. In 1912, a British researcher wrote: "The Valley of the Kings is now exhausted." Howard Carter and his aristocratic patron Lord Carnarvon (1866–1923) believed they could prove him wrong, but, in the end, it was a very close thing. Disappointed by the lack of discoveries from Carter's years of digging in the valley, Carnarvon told him that 1922 would be his last season.

In early November, however, Carter discovered steps leading down to a hitherto unknown tomb. The stairwell was quickly cleared and he found the stone door at the end of the stairwell intact. Carter made a hole through the top left-hand corner of the doorway and shone a light inside. His brief exchange with Carnarvon is quoted on page 30. Carter had made the find of the century, if not millennium: a nearly intact New Kingdom royal burial. The outer chambers were packed with thousands of artifacts and grave goods—everything that the king might require in the afterlife, including furniture, chariots, food and drink, jewelry and cosmetics. What Carter was desperate to see, however, was the burial chamber; if this, too, were intact, it would be a unique find: the first undisturbed royal mummy.

Breathlessly, Carter broke the seals of the burial chamber and saw that the doors of the elaborate gilt-wood shrine that almost filled the available space in the room were also sealed. Inside was the king's granite sarcophagus, which itself contained smaller coffins, Russian-doll style, which finally revealed the king's mummy. Tutankhamun lay in his coffin just as he had been placed there 3,245 years earlier. His head and upper torso were covered by a funerary mask made with 25 pounds (11 kg) of gold, inlaid with lapis lazuli, carnelian, quartz, obsidian, turquoise—costly semi-precious gems that would have been imported from Central Asia and Africa—as well as with glass and faience. After the Great Pyramid of Khufu, the death mask is probably the most iconic artifact discovered in ancient Egypt.

In addition to the beauty of the funerary goods—the contents of the tomb were conservatively valued at around $80 million—the mask, with its idealized representation of the deceased pharaoh, his expressionless lapis lazuli and faience eyes staring into eternity, his headdress and chin ornamented with the symbols of traditional Egyptian kingship, marks the return of Egypt to religious orthodoxy. Henceforth, until the abolition of paganism in the fourth century, Amun-Ra and the traditional gods would rule unchallenged in Egypt.

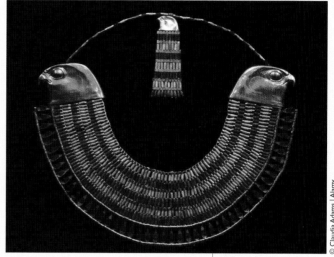

© Claudia Adams | Alamy

GOLDEN PARACHUTE
Pharaohs were buried with vast amounts of gold.

TREASURE

Burial goods

Hoards

Shipwrecks

Religious objects or places

Artworks

Gemstones

TAKING IT WITH HIM: SARCOPHAGUS OF SETI I

1279 BCE

Circumstance of loss: Royal burial of Seti I

Rediscovery: Discovery of the tomb by Giovanni Belzoni in 1817

Historical significance: Although looted of its treasures, Seti's tomb is one of the most impressive in the Valley of the Kings; his alabaster sarcophagus is evidence of how rich the king's burial must have been

Value: £2,000 in 1824

And then, Giovanni came forward between the pillars, holding his candle aloft, he saw something that must have made him catch his breath for its sheer loveliness—something that lay, lambent as a pearl, under the dark blue vault—a great gleaming alabaster sarcophagus.

The Great Belzoni (2006) by Stanley Mayes

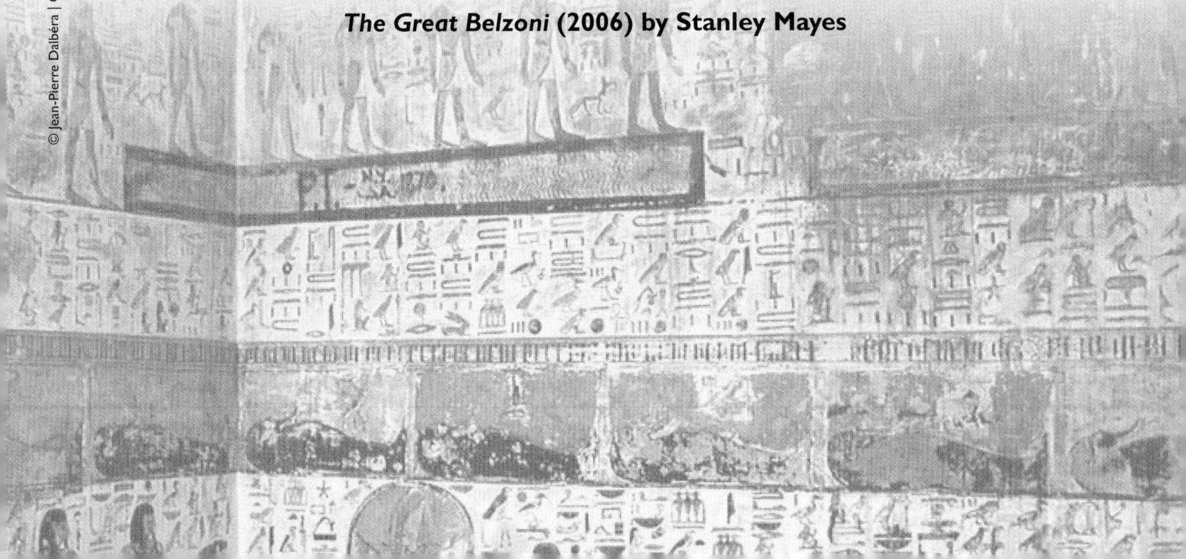

There can be no greater contrast between the owner of the previous lost treasure, the obscure Eighteenth Dynasty Pharaoh Tutankhamun (ca. 1332–ca. 1323 BCE) and Seti I (r. 1290–1279 BCE), the second pharaoh of the Nineteenth Dynasty, and father to one of Egypt's most powerful rulers, Ramesses II (ca. 1303–1213 BCE). Although Tutankhamun's forebears included several of the great warrior pharaohs of the New Kingdom, the end of the dynasty witnessed a period of decline caused in part by the religious reforms of Tutankhamun's father, Akhenaten (r. ca. 1353–1336 BCE).

In certain respects, however, there are parallels between the lives of the two pharaohs. Both had short reigns: Tutankhamun's lasted nine years, and Seti's eleven, and both kings died young of causes unknown. Although there has been speculation that Tutankhamun had been murdered, foul play is not suspected in Seti's death, which has been ascribed to a heart defect, inferred from the unusual placement of his heart in his mummy. The greatest contrast between the two men, however, is their treatment after death.

© Public domain

TOMB RAIDER
Belzoni acquired ancient artifacts for the British Museum.

Tutankhamun was interred in a small tomb, probably built for someone of much less exalted status. It contained only four chambers, only one of which, the burial chamber, was decorated with wall paintings. Perhaps because of the lack of space, or because it had been disturbed by robbers, Tutankhamun's overcrowded tomb looked more like a vault hired for the storage of surplus goods and furniture than a royal mausoleum. The small size of the tomb itself and the obscurity of its owner meant that it remained undisturbed for millennia after its location had been forgotten.

Seti's tomb (KV17) presents a stark contrast. At 450 feet (137 m) long, it is the longest tomb in the Valley of the Kings, and all but two of its eleven chambers are decorated with intricate and brightly colored bas-reliefs and paintings. When the tomb was rediscovered in 1817 by the Italian circus strongman turned archaeologist (though tomb raider might be more appropriate) Giovanni Belzoni (1778–1823), the colors of the paintings and bas-reliefs were so vivid that they looked as if they had only just been painted. Belzoni even found the paints and brushes abandoned by the original artists. Sadly, after 200 years of visitors, vandalism, and the occasional flood because Belzoni failed to protect the tomb from the area's torrential rains, the paintings have suffered serious damage, and KV17 is now rarely opened to the public.

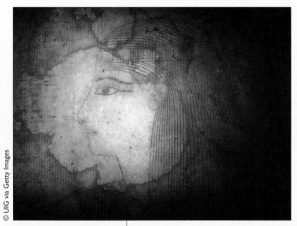

BEDTIME READING
The sarcophagus was covered in images and sacred texts.

Belzoni did not distinguish himself by carefully reconstructing the past with meticulous excavations recording every potsherd, which is the practice of modern scientific archaeology, but by removing large artifacts and shipping them to the British Museum in London. One of the most imposing pieces in the museum's Egyptian sculpture gallery is part of a colossal statue of Ramesses II, pillaged from his mortuary temple in Luxor. Its removal demanded the partial demolition of the temple; therefore, Belzoni was more concerned with pleasing his British employers than preserving the integrity of Egypt's archaeological heritage.

THE BEST MONEY COULD BUY

The pharaohs of ancient Egypt not only believed that they could cheat death by being mummified and magically revived in their tombs, they also believed that they could preserve their wealth, power, and privilege by literally "taking it all with them." The more powerful they were, the grander the tombs and mortuary temples they prepared for their afterlives.

Seti's tomb, apart from the paintings and bas-reliefs that had no commercial value in ancient times (but several of which were removed in the nineteenth century, a few by official vandals and others by looters), had been stripped of anything that could be removed and sold. The eleven chambers were bare, and only their size and magnificence testified to the treasures that they must have contained at the time of the king's burial. If Tutankhamun merited the vast haul of goods, gems, and gold that was found in his small, undistinguished tomb, we can only imagine the wealth that was lavished on a much more important pharaoh, whose successor ensured that his father was given the best royal send-off that money could buy.

While the gilded furniture, the royal chariots, the many guardian statues, the boxes of jewels, the stores of food, wine, incense, and cosmetics, and even the canopic jars containing the king's preserved organs had been looted, there was one artifact too big to move: the stone sarcophagus that would have once protected the king's mummified and bandage-swathed body. The lid had been smashed to get at the king's mummy, which was also missing. Sixty-four years later, Seti's mummy was found and reburied in a much more modest tomb, along with many of the New Kingdom's pharaohs, protected from further desecration but without their treasures. Seti's mummy had been decapitated, no doubt when his death mask — maybe one even more magnificent than Tutankhamun's—had been wrenched off. His rescuers had carefully reassembled him with bandages before his second burial.

Before the discovery of Tutankhamun's tomb, Seti's sarcophagus was one of the few grave goods that testified to the fabulous wealth of New Kingdom burials. Unlike the sarcophagi found in other royal tombs, which were made of dull black or gray granite, Seti's mummiform outer coffin was carved from a massive block of white alabaster, whose intact bottom section measured 9 feet, 4 inches (2.86 m) by 3 feet, 8 inches (1.16 m) by 2 feet, 8 inches (85 cm). The whole was incised with inscriptions, depictions of the gods, and an illustrated version of the sun's nightly journey through the underworld, all picked out in a bright blue metallic paste. The lid, 18 fragments of which have been discovered, and several of which have now been reassembled, depicted a three-dimensional likeness of the king in death.

The sarcophagus arrived London in 1824, one year after its rediscoverer had met his end, dying of a fever while attempting to reach the city of Timbuktu (now in the troubled African state of Mali) on the southern edge of the Sahara Desert. The sarcophagus was initially offered to the British Museum, which refused to pay the astronomical sum of £2,000 for the relic. It remains the centerpiece of the Egyptian collection of the much smaller Sir John Soane's Museum. Unfortunately, 189 years of exposure to the damp British climate and London's polluted atmosphere have turned the alabaster a dull mottled yellow, and the blue paste inlay that once picked out the intricate scenes incised into the sides, lid, and base of the sarcophagus has also disappeared.

CROCK OF GOLD: TREASURE OF VILLENA

ca. 1000 BCE

Circumstance of loss: Hoard buried in a ceramic container during the Bronze Age

Rediscovery: Discovery of two pieces of the hoard in building material led to investigations in the area where the material had been sourced

Historical significance: Showed the metalworking abilities of Spain's Bronze Age smiths; contained pieces made of iron, still rare enough to be considered a precious metal

Value: $500,000 (gold and silver by weight)

The lack of archaeological context means that it is difficult to evaluate the treasure's significance and to date it securely. According to its discoverer, the hoard was hidden by a high-status individual or king, or by a group of individuals in a period of danger.

"José María Soler Museum: The Treasures" from museovillena.com (retrieved February 23, 2013; translated by author)

We finally come to our first "hoard"—a word whose Germanic and Old Norse etymology speaks of both treasure and concealment. Hoards, unlike the caches of burial goods that we have featured so far, are sometimes difficult to date and identify because they usually have little or no archaeological context. By their very nature, they were removed from where they would have normally been kept—a villa, temple, palace, or treasury—and hidden, usually by burying them in some desolate place, to protect them from being looted. Unfortunately, we shall never know the exact circumstances of why a hoard was buried, because someone hiding their money and treasures does not usually take the time to leave a name and address or an explanation.

This creates serious problems for archaeologists and opportunities for anyone who discovers a hoard by chance. In recent years, many hoards have been found by hobbyists with metal detectors. Most detectorists are honest, and not only ask permission of landowners to survey their land, but also report the finds they make to the authorities as "treasure trove." At this point an archaeologist is called in to examine the find. In a few cases, however, a hoard found outside an official archaeological site must present too much of a temptation and may end up on the black market. Of course, the age and style of a hoard may make it very difficult to sell on the open market without attracting the attention of the authorities, and we cannot know how many ancient hoards have been melted down for the still considerable resale value of the precious metal.

The Treasure of Villena, found in the vicinity of the small town of that name, near Alicante in the Valencian Community, southeastern Spain, could have easily disappeared, either melted down or sold illegally. According to the published account of the man who eventually excavated the hoard, local archaeologist José María Soler (1905–96), the initial find was of a solid gold bracelet weighing just over a pound (460 g) in October 1963. The piece consists of five sections, each with a pattern of raised or pierced decorative elements, and was what Soler described as one of the finest pieces of Spanish Bronze Age (1800–700 BCE) goldwork.

A local woman brought the bracelet to the town's jeweler for a valuation. Realizing the antiquity of the piece, he immediately informed Soler and the authorities. The woman said that her husband had found the piece on a building site in the center of town. In November, another woman brought

© Mary Evans | Iberfoto

HEAVY-HANDED
Four solid gold bracelets unearthed near Villena.

IBERIAN ORIGINALS

a similar bracelet to the jeweler to be valued. She claimed that the piece had belonged to her grandmother and had been in the family's possession for many years. Seeing the similarities between the two bracelets, however, the jeweler was not deceived, and he again reported the find.

Both pieces, it seemed, had been found by chance, not in situ where they had been originally buried, but in sand and gravel brought to a building site in the city center. Soler identified where the material had been quarried and in December he made a startling find outside the town: a large incised ceramic pot containing 66 pieces made of gold, silver, iron, and amber, weighing some 22 pounds (10 kg), almost 20 pounds (9 kg) of which was 23.5-carat gold, with a current value for the gold alone of $45,000 — literally a "crock" of gold. When reassembled, the pieces made 49 distinct objects, including bracelets, bowls, bottles, brooches, rings, and buttons, as well as a number of pieces that cannot be identified.

Soler dated the hoard to around 1000 BCE from the incised ceramic container in which it had been buried, the style of the pieces themselves, and because of the presence of iron in the hoard. The division between the Bronze and Iron Ages suggests that there was a sudden shift in technology from one metal to another, but this is now recognized to be an oversimplification. Iron was made in many parts of the world during the Bronze Age. Although iron technology is more complex than that of copper and bronze, it was not beyond the expert smiths of Europe and the Near East. In Spain in the first millennium BCE, however, iron was still a rare and precious metal, which explains its presence alongside gold and silver in the hoard.

The bulk of the objects, however, were made of pure gold, including eleven bowls, made of beaten gold with raised punched decoration creating complex geometric patterns and two gold flasks, with three more bottles made of alloys of gold, silver, and iron. There was also one object—a button—decorated with amber, a semi-precious mineral that would have originated far to the north on the coasts of the Baltic Sea, and would have been traded along a complex trading network to southern Europe and the Near East known as the "Amber Road."

Unlike artifacts found in their archaeological contexts, hoards are difficult to interpret. They may have been made and owned by the people who buried them, or they could be loot hidden after a raid. Hence, the material might be from a completely different time and place. However, in the case of the Villena treasure, the ceramic container in which the hoard had been stored was from the region in which it was found. Soler, who was an expert in the Bronze Age sites of the region, found a smaller hoard about 3 miles (5 km) away, which included what he called a "diadem"—a golden circlet or crown. The proximity and similarity of the two hoards suggested to Soler that a tribal chief or even the king of the local Bronze Age city had buried them during a war or invasion. As is the case with other hoards, the person or persons who buried the Villena Treasure did not live to reclaim it but most likely succumbed to the danger they had anticipated.

While so much about the hoard is conjecture, it has confirmed that the late Bronze Age cultures of southern Spain developed independently from Phoenician and Carthaginian influences. Phoenician traders from the Near East established trading posts in the western Mediterranean in the tenth century BCE. The Villena Treasure predates their arrival by a century, and an analysis of the metal has revealed that it was made from gold mined in northeastern Spain, confirming that the designs of the bowls, flasks, and jewelry are Iberian and not copies of imported Near Eastern models.

TREASURE

Burial goods

Hoards

Shipwrecks

Religious objects or places

Artworks

Gemstones

RADIO TRANSMITTER TO GOD: ARK OF THE COVENANT

587 BCE

Circumstance of loss: During the destruction of Solomon's Temple by the Babylonians

Rediscovery: Not yet found; possible hiding places include Ethiopia, South Africa, Arabia

Historical significance: One of the most sacred relics of the Judeo-Christian tradition; its rediscovery would have deep religious as well as archaeological significance

Value: Salvation

And they shall make an ark of shittim wood: two cubits and a half shall be the length thereof, and a cubit and a half the breadth thereof, and a cubit and a half the height thereof. And thou shalt overlay it with pure gold, within and without shalt thou overlay it, and shalt make upon it a crown of gold round about.

Exodus 25:10–11 (King James Version)

With this entry, we come to a treasure whose value cannot be judged in purely monetary, scientific, or artistic terms. Granted that the Ark of the Covenant, if ever found, would be an object of great antiquity and rarity, on a par with the most priceless of burial goods from ancient Mesopotamia and Egypt, but its real value would be as the central cult object of Judaism, and, by extension, an artifact sacred to the two other "religions of the Book," Christianity and Islam.

From the biblical description quoted overleaf, the Ark of the Covenant was an acacia-wood chest (approximately 52 inches/131 cm long by 31 inches/79 cm wide and deep) gilded inside and out, and topped with a pair of *cherubim* (angels), usually depicted facing one another with their wings outstretched over the chest. The Ark had rings set into its sides so that it could be carried with the aid of two poles without being touched and without touching the ground. The last recorded location of the Ark was the Holy of Holies in the Temple of Solomon (the First Temple) in Jerusalem. Although the Ark was gilt wood, the real treasure was not the ornate wooden chest or the gold leaf that covered it but the "Covenant" that it had been built to contain: the tablets inscribed with the Ten Commandments given by God to Moses on Mount Sinai.

Moses smashed the first tablets after coming down from the mountain to find the people of Israel worshipping an idol in the shape of a golden calf. Having made a second set of commandments, Moses followed divine instructions on how the tablets should be stored and transported. In addition to the Ark itself, God gave Moses a detailed description of the Tabernacle: a tent in which the Ark would be kept during Israel's journey to the Promised Land and the subsequent conquest of Canaan. In the Old Testament, the Ark features as an object of enormous holiness and power and even seeing it could prove fatal to the uninitiated. Only God's anointed, the king and high priest, were permitted to come into direct contact with the Ark, and touching it by accident was fatal.

The Ark's power turned it into a formidable weapon. According to the Old Testament, in around 1400 BCE, the Israelites stormed the city of Jericho. Following the almighty's instructions, the priests carried the Ark around the city and blew rams' horns, which toppled the walls and won the Israelites the city. The historical Jericho is one of the most ancient cities on earth, whose history has included several sieges and sacks.

Detailed archaeological research in the past hundred years, however, has failed to confirm the biblical account of its destruction by the Ark. The only destruction of the city during the Bronze Age dates to the sixteenth century BCE, a century before the supposed biblical event. Even if there were a chronological match, skeptics argue, the most likely explanation for the collapsing walls was probably an earthquake.

The Ark remained in its tented tabernacle, occasionally falling into enemy hands, such as its capture by the Philistines, to whom it brought so much bad luck that they were forced to return it to the Israelites. After King David (ca. 1040–970 BCE) seized Jerusalem from the Jebusites, he vowed to build a temple to house the Ark, but God, speaking through the Prophet Nathan, forbade it. It was David's son Solomon (r. ca. 970–930 BCE) who built the First Temple in around 950 BCE. The Ark finally had a permanent home, where it stood on the Temple's Foundation Stone inside the Holy of Holies, hidden from profane eyes behind a gilded door and a veil of fine linen.

RAIDERS OF MADE-UP HISTORY

In George Lucas's (b. 1944) *Raiders of the Lost Ark*, the hero "Indiana" Jones, played by Harrison Ford (b. 1942), is dispatched to find the Ark of the Covenant before René Belloq (Paul Freeman, b. 1943) can find it for Adolf Hitler (1889–1945). Lucas quite accurately portrayed the Nazis' obsession with occult artifacts and places, which had led them on a fruitless search for Atlantis. In his portrayal of the Ark itself, Lucas's golden reproduction follows the biblical description and many subsequent artistic representations; however, in recreating the history of the Ark after it was removed from the Temple of Solomon, he plots a story that was probably less interesting than the traditions about the fate of the Ark that have come down to us in the intervening three millennia.

In the film, Indy informed the U.S. government agents and the audience that the Ark must be in Egypt, in the city of Tanis, which he claimed had been buried by a giant sandstorm. Although many ancient Egyptian cities were reclaimed by the desert sands once they had been abandoned, this was not the case with the city of Tanis, which stood in the Nile Delta. Quite to the contrary, in the sixth century CE, long after Egypt had become Christian, the city was abandoned because of the risk of flooding from a nearby lake. Indy also named the pharaoh Shoshenq I (943–922 BCE), the biblical Shishaq, as the Egyptian ruler responsible for the removal of the Ark from Solomon's Temple, from whence he would have taken it to Tanis where he had hidden it in the "Well of Souls." The historical Shoshenq did besiege and take Jerusalem in 925 BCE, and the Bible states that he raided the Temple and royal treasury; the Ark, however, was not mentioned as one of the treasures that he took back with him to Egypt.

Although Tanis existed during the reign of Shoshenq, it was not the royal capital, which remained at Memphis. In addition, to the eyes of Egyptians, a gilded chest, however ornate, would not qualify as a "treasure" worth stealing. Such artifacts were fairly commonplace among the possessions of Egyptian pharaohs, as portable shrines or pieces of furniture. Examples of both types were discovered among the burial goods of Tutankhamun (ca. 1332–1323 BCE; pp. 30–35), including a shrine topped with a representation of the wolf-headed patron deity of funerary rites, Anubis, which was briefly taken to be the Ark by an overenthusiastic British media. Another reason to doubt that the Ark fell into Egyptian hands in 925 BCE is that the Temple Mount is honeycombed with tunnels and hidden chambers; therefore, something as sacred and small as the Ark could easily have been hidden from an invader. In addition, the Egyptians had little interest in the gods of conquered peoples, having so many of their own.

A much more likely candidate for the removal of the Ark is the Babylonian King Nebuchadnezzar II (ca. 634–562 BCE), who conquered Jerusalem and sacked the city and the Temple of Solomon in 587 BCE, taking the Jewish king and elite back to Babylon as captives. In the destruction of the city and temple, any hiding place of the Ark might have been revealed. It was also the practice among the Babylonians to take the statues of enemy gods "prisoner," as further evidence of their enemy's complete defeat. Because the Jews never represented God in physical form, the Ark would have been the closest thing to a statue that the Babylonians could take into captivity. Again, however, the Ark is not specifically mentioned as part of Nebuchadnezzar's loot. In fact, it now vanishes from history, and there are no further biblical references to its physical existence.

HIGH JINX
The Ark has inspired many fictional adventures.

© Ivan Montero Martinez | Shutterstock.com

IMPERIAL LOOT
The Romans sacked and
burned the Temple.

There is another good reason why George Lucas could have explored a Babylonian storyline: the German connection. It was a German archaeologist and architect, Robert Koldewey (1855–1925), who excavated the ruins of Babylon, where Nebuchadnezzar, the builder of the fabled "Hanging Gardens," might have deposited the Ark in the Esagila Temple he had built for Babylon's patron god Marduk. Between 1899 and 1917, Koldewey explored the ruins, identifying the city's streets and major architectural complexes. Although he was able to reconstruct the ancient city, outlining its main ceremonial avenue, walls, gates, and principal palaces and temples, he ignored other types of archaeological evidence, discarding potsherds that would have provided a secure means of dating the buildings that he had uncovered.

George Lucas preferred Egypt to Babylon, and he imprisoned Indy with love interest Marion (Karen Allen, b. 1951) in Tanis's "Well of Souls," after the pair unwittingly have handed the Nazis the Ark. Perhaps Lucas thought Egypt was better known and more visually appealing than Babylon. At this point, with the Ark exhumed, the action moves to Nazi bases in the Mediterranean, until, in the closing scenes, Belloq and his Nazi masters open the Ark and are suitably punished, while the virtuous hero survives (one wonders if the God of Abraham would have been so merciful).

STRANGER THAN FICTION

The Well of Souls is a real location, not in Tanis but on Jerusalem's Temple Mount: a small cave directly beneath the Foundation Stone of the Temple. It owes its name to the belief that it is the place where the souls of the dead await the Day of Judgment. Supposedly, no one alive today has ever visited the Well of Souls, giving rise to the story that the Ark may be just a few feet from its original location in the Temple. Even if the Ark had been hidden in a secret chamber beneath the Temple Mount in 925 or 587 BCE, there are good reasons to suggest that it would have been found and removed in the intervening two and a half millennia.

The Jews began rebuilding the Temple in 535 BCE after having been liberated from their Babylonian captivity by their new masters, the Persians. The new building was consecrated in 516 BCE, and expanded and embellished under Herod the Great (74–4 BCE) four and a half centuries later. Although several of the holy artifacts, including the gold menorah (seven-branched candlestick), were returned from Babylon, there is no mention of the Ark of the Covenant or its contents. The Second Temple endured for six centuries, until the year 70 CE, when the Romans destroyed it along with the rest of Jerusalem as a reprisal for a Jewish revolt. The treasures of the Temple, minus the Ark, are shown being looted on the Victory Arch of Titus in Rome. The Romans then rebuilt Jerusalem as Aelia Capitolina, a pagan city dedicated to the father of the gods, Jupiter.

The Temple was never rebuilt, but the Temple Mount has been the scene of intense religious activity ever since. After the Christianization of the Roman Empire, the Byzantines built a church on the site, which was demolished and replaced by the Dome of the Rock and Al-Aqsa Mosque after the Islamic conquest of the city in the seventh century CE. During the Crusader Kingdom of Jerusalem (1099–1192), the mosques were converted into churches and secular buildings, including the headquarters of the Knights Templar (see pp. 79–86). Along with the Egyptians and Babylonians, the Templars are suspected of having found and removed the Ark, taking it to their headquarters in France. When King Philip IV of France (1268–1314) ordered the violent and terminal dissolution of the order in 1307, the Templars are supposed to have hidden the Ark in a secret location in France. But in the past few centuries, several of the more imaginative would-be raiders of the lost Ark have suggested that the holy relic was subsequently transported to North America for safekeeping.

Unless the Ark turns up in a vast U.S. government warehouse (where it was consigned at the end of Lucas's movie), the trail leads not west but south. One tradition has the Ark crossing the desert into Arabia, which was home to thriving Jewish communities that predated the appearance of Islam. The Ark is said to have gone to Yemen and then across the Red Sea to Africa. According to the Lemba, a people native to South Africa and Zimbabwe who claim Jewish descent, the Ark was taken as far south

© Public domain

TRUE VALUE
The Ark held the tablets of the Ten Commandments.

© Public domain

"VOICE OF GOD"
Great Zimbabwe had its
own drum-shaped Ark.

as Great Zimbabwe, a vast city of imposing stone towers and enclosures, which was the capital of the Kingdom of Zimbabwe (1220–1450). The Lemba artifact identified as the Ark was a large wooden drum known as the "Voice of God." It was carried with wooden poles inserted into carved wooden rings, and was said to possess great power like the biblical Ark. The original drum was destroyed, but the replica that was made from its remains is now on display at the Harare Museum.

Ethiopia is the second African country that claims to have the original Ark of the Covenant. The story, written during the Middle Ages, tells of the legendary Ethiopian Emperor Menelik I, son of King Solomon and the Queen of Sheba, who traveled to Jerusalem to meet his father. He obtained the Ark with divine assistance and brought it back with him to his kingdom. According to the Ethiopian Orthodox Church, the Ark, or Tabot, is kept in a church in the ancient city of Axum in northern Ethiopia, where it was used in the coronation rituals of Ethiopia's Christian emperors. Like the biblical Ark before it, the Tabot has only been unveiled for anointed kings and patriarchs of the church.

TWO FOR THE PRICE OF ONE: RIACE BRONZES

ca. 450 BCE

TREASURE

Burial goods

Hoards

Shipwrecks

Religious objects or places

Artworks

Gemstones

Circumstance of loss: Lost at sea, either because of a shipwreck or because of a building falling into the sea

Rediscovery: Found by chance by an amateur diver

Historical significance: Rare examples of Greek bronze originals from the fifth century BCE, which are usually known from Roman copies

Value: Classical ideal

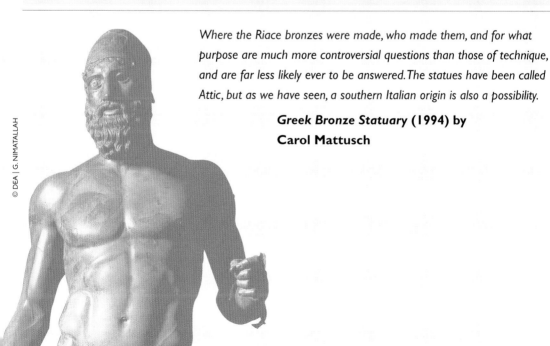

Where the Riace bronzes were made, who made them, and for what purpose are much more controversial questions than those of technique, and are far less likely ever to be answered. The statues have been called Attic, but as we have seen, a southern Italian origin is also a possibility.

Greek Bronze Statuary (1994) by Carol Mattusch

The province of Calabria, the "toe" of Italy's "boot," has two claims to fame that intersected during the discovery of this entry's treasure trove, the "Riace bronzes." In the present, the area is home to the 'Ndrangheta, a Mafioso-style syndicate of criminal families, which is infamous for the sudden and fatal "disappearances" of its enemies; and in antiquity, it was part of Magna Graecia, Greater Greece, an area of southern Italy colonized by the ancient Greeks, which retains a rich heritage of archaeological sites.

In August 1972, at the height of Italy's summer vacation season, a pharmacist from Rome scuba diving off the Calabrian coast close to the inland village of Riace came across what he initially took to be a human arm sticking out of the seabed. Only too aware of the area's reputation for gruesome mob-related murders, he thought that he had discovered a corpse buried in the sand, its decomposing skin turning black. Unlike many of us, who might have swum back to dry land as fast as possible to inform the authorities, our intrepid diver examined his grizzly find a little closer only to discover that the well-proportioned and very realistic male arm protruding from the sand was made of metal. Amazingly, he had just found part of a 2,500-year-old bronze statue of a naked muscular bearded warrior, hero, god, or athlete.

An investigation of the immediate area revealed a second bronze statue, very similar to the first, and both were immediately taken for conservation to the National Museum in Reggio Calabria, the provincial capital. It's not unusual for ancient artworks and artifacts to be recovered from the Mediterranean. The ships of antiquity were superbly built but they were made of wood, and if thrown onto rocks and reefs, they would be holed and sunk. Ancient wrecks litter the rocky costs of Italy and Greece, and they have yielded artworks, treasures, and trading goods—amphorae that were used to transport wine and olive oil.

The archaeologists' initial hypothesis was that the statues were part of a shipment of ancient Greek statues being transported to Rome some time after the Roman conquest of Greece (146–133 BCE). During Roman rule, consuls, generals, senators, and emperors acquired famous artworks from major Greek cities and sanctuaries, including Athens, Olympia, and Delphi, to decorate their palaces, villas, forums, and temples. The two statues could have been taken from a single monument in any of these Greek sites, any time after the mid-second century BCE. However, there was one crucial thing missing to confirm the shipwreck hypothesis: a wreck. Although organic materials such as wood, canvas, and rope will degrade quickly in seawater, once the timbers of a ship are buried in sand, silt, or mud, the microscopic organisms that eat away wood are deprived of oxygen, and the process of decomposition stops. Organic materials many thousands of years old, including baskets, leatherwork, and wood, have survived in relatively good condition after being buried.

Although much of the wreck could have disappeared, swept away by currents, there would have been some trace: the larger timbers, the metal fittings, and the ceramic containers that the crew used to cook and transport food, oil, and water. Even if the wood and metal had been completely degraded, the ceramics would have survived. An alternative ship-bound explanation was that the statues had fallen overboard or had been thrown into the sea during a storm to lighten the load, and the ship either survived or foundered somewhere else. However, it seems unlikely that so valuable a cargo, intended for an illustrious, maybe imperial client, would be packed so poorly that it could fall overboard by accident, or be unceremoniously dumped, especially in clear sight of the coast of southern Italy, and as long as other less valuable objects could be disposed of first.

If the statues were not lost at sea in a wreck or storm, the other explanation was that they had been part of a building that had been engulfed by the sea. The Mediterranean and its surrounding landmasses are subject to earthquakes and volcanic eruptions. For example, a major eruption on the island of Santorini triggered quakes and tsunamis that destroyed the Minoan civilization on Crete in around 1500 BCE; in 79 CE, the southern Italian cities of Herculaneum and Pompeii were buried by the eruption of Mount Vesuvius; and as recently as 1980, Reggio Calabria was struck by a devastating earthquake that destroyed and damaged many buildings in the town. The Greeks who lived and died by the sea built many sanctuaries on the coast, such as the Temple of Poseidon at Cape Sounion in Greece. The theory goes that a coastal shrine or monument could have toppled into the sea in an earthquake or been washed away by a tsunami, thereby explaining the presence of the two statues on the seabed.

Unfortunately, although a sunken building is just as likely an explanation as a shipwreck, it, too, lacks any supporting evidence. Although the coastline is known to have changed since antiquity, if a building had fallen into the sea, its indestructible stones would have remained near the statues, too heavy to be moved by currents like wooden timbers or ceramics. The two statues, however, were discovered on their own, without remains of any kind, and no bases that would have identified them as memorials to living individuals, or as the depictions of mythological heroes or gods.

BROTHERS AT ARMS

It is unlikely that the mystery of how the statues ended up in the sea will ever be fully resolved. Experts have dated them to the mid-fifth century BCE, but they may have been lost soon after their casting or several hundred years later. Although there is no agreement as to their identities, the slightly larger than life-size figures, known simply as Statues A and B, are thought to represent warriors. The position of their hands and arms reveal that they once carried shields and spears, and they wear helmets on their heads. Their nudity, which in some cultures might denote them as vanquished enemies, slaves, or criminals, in ancient Greek art confirms their identification as fighting men. Although Greek men did not fight naked, Greek artistic conventions represented heroes, rulers, and gods naked, in part to differentiate true Greeks from their clothed "barbarian" neighbors and enemies.

Although art historians and archaeologists have produced a great deal of verbiage examining and explaining the differences between the two statues, what immediately strikes the casual visitor to the Reggio museum is the striking resemblance between the two warriors. While their stances and the angles of their heads are different, the appearance and posture of the torso and arms are so similar that many researchers have concluded that they were cast from the same basic model by the lost-wax casting method that allows the same molds to be used, while allowing for variations in detailing and minor postural changes.

Lost-wax casting is a complex multi-step process that creates clay molds for hollow bronze parts that are then soldered together into a finished artifact. The process was used in ancient China to create complex ritual vessels and bells, Buddhas in India, Korea, and Japan, and statues in the Western world from antiquity to the present day. Although the process allows the production of multiple examples of the same artwork, the Riace bronzes, while they share many similarities, have so many differences in posture and detailing that Statues A and B can also be described as original works crafted by master sculptors. The quality of the statues is such that

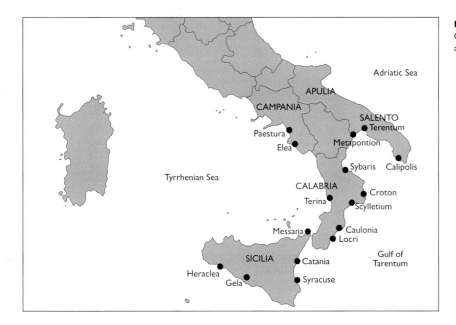

MAGNA GRAECIA
Greek colonies in Italy
and Sicily.

they have been attributed to the great masters of classical Greek sculpture. And while this could mean that the statues originated in Greece, it is also possible that the wax models were taken from Greece to Italy, where local artists used them to create the two Riace warriors.

The exact provenance and authorship of the statues does not reduce their artistic merit. They are extremely rare survivals of fifth-century BCE bronze masterpieces, most of which were melted down for their metal, and are now only known from Roman copies executed in marble. While later Roman copies can show us the quality of the Greek originals, the use of bronze makes a significant difference. Instead of the otherworldly lifeless perfection that marble imparts to statues, the warm tones of bronze bring the figures to life, an impression of reality heightened by the use of other materials: inlaid glass ivory and glass for the eyes, silver for the teeth, and copper for the eyelashes, lips, and nipples.

TOASTING THE KING: PANAGYURISHTE TREASURE
281 BCE

Circumstance of loss: Hoard buried to protect it from invaders

Rediscovery: Uncovered by workmen digging for clay

Historical significance: The rediscovery of the Hellenistic culture of ancient Thrace

Value: $325,000 (gold by weight)

The amphora rhyton from the Panagyurishte Treasure was probably used in fraternization rites, and also a vase related to the mysteries in the cult of the Kabeiroi, as evidenced by the Theban theme on its sides and by the figure of the child Heracles and of the adult Silenus on its base.

The Barbarians of Ancient Europe (2011) by Larissa Bonfante

The rulers of the Odrysian kingdom of Thrace (460 BCE–46 CE) do not feature prominently in the annals of Classical antiquity. However, the discovery of several spectacular hoards of highly ornate gold and silver objects in the twentieth century testifies to the wealth, sophistication, and splendor of their courts. Thrace occupied much of the eastern Balkans, spanning the borders of the modern countries of Bulgaria, Greece, and Turkey. In 512 BCE it became the only European satrapy of the Achemenid Persian Empire from which the Persians launched their two failed invasions of Greece. With the defeat of the Persians by an alliance of city states led by Athens in 479 BCE, Thrace came within the Greek sphere of influence.

Between 347 and 341 BCE, the Macedonian King Philip II (382–336 BCE) campaigned to subdue the whole of the eastern Balkans and annexed southern Thrace into his own kingdom. Philip's much more famous son, Alexander III, known to us simply as "the Great" (356–323 BCE), consolidated his father's Thracian conquests with a campaign in 335 BCE, thereby securing his northern border before he embarked on the conquest of the Persian Empire. In 325 BCE, while Alexander was campaigning in the East, the Odrysian tribes under King Seuthes III (r. ca. 331–300 BCE) rebelled against Macedonian domination.

Alexander's governor restored Macedonian rule in the region, and the Odrysian kingdom remained a Macedonian client state until 279 BCE, when Gauls (who occupied what is now France, Benelux, Switzerland, and Germany) invaded Thrace, Macedon, and Greece. Although quickly expelled from Greece and Macedon, the Gauls remained in Thrace until the end of the third century BCE. When they left, the Odrysians regained their independence, but in 46 CE, the kingdom was conquered by the Romans; it remained a Greek-speaking province of the Roman and Byzantine empires for the next millennium.

In December 1949, three brothers digging for clay outside the central Bulgarian town of Panagyurishte uncovered what they thought was a collection of strangely shaped musical instruments—whistles, bugles, and trumpets. They took the nine shiny metallic objects to the local mayor, who immediately contacted the Plovdiv Archaeological Museum. What the men had found were nine ancient drinking vessels made of 24-carat gold, weighing some 13.5 pounds (6.1 kg): seven rhytons—the wine

"SHINY BUGLES"

© Vassia Atanassova | Creative Commons

DRINKING SET
The gold vessels were used
to entertain royal guests.

glasses of their day—in the shape of horns or human heads, which explained why the workmen had thought they had found wind instruments; an amphora, a flask with two handles in which the thick local wines would be diluted with water and sweetened with honey; and a phiale, a shallow dish-like vessel used to make libations (offerings of wine to the gods or the dead).

The pieces were elaborately decorated with figures taken from ancient Greek mythology, including sphinxes and centaurs, as well as mythological scenes such as the adventures of the hero Herakles (Hercules) and the Judgment of Paris. The style and iconography of the vessels dates them to the fourth century BCE and suggested to some scholars that they had been made by Greek craftsmen for a Hellenized Odrysian king. However, they could just as well have been made by goldsmiths from the Greek colony of Lampsakos in Asia Minor (now Turkey), which was famous for its goldwork in antiquity, or by Thracian craftsmen copying Greek models.

The Odrysian kingdom was established in 460 BCE, a significant date in Greek history. Twenty years earlier, the Persians had attempted to conquer the southern Balkans for the second and final time, determined to subjugate the free Greek city states. In two stunning victories, the Athenians repulsed the Persians and then went on the offensive. The year 460 BCE also marked the beginning of the career of Pericles (ca. 495–429 BCE), the man who was the closest thing fiercely democratic Classical Athens ever had to a ruler. Pericles used Athens' newfound wealth to rebuild the temples of the Acropolis that the Persians had burned in 480 BCE. The buildings we owe to him include the Propylaia (monumental gateway), the Eretchtheion, and the Parthenon. Athens acquired an empire, but unlike the Macedonian and Roman Empires that were based on military might and colonization, Athens' empire was a commercial and cultural enterprise.

Liberated from Persian rule, the Thracians looked to the Greeks as their cultural mentors, though they never adopted Athens' most daring political experiment, democracy. The Odrysian kings and their courts spoke

Greek, and adopted Greek customs and clothing. Although Thrace did not develop an urban culture, its kings built palaces, which combined residential, military, administrative, and religious functions, much like the Mycenaean and Minoan palaces of the Bronze Age. King Seuthes established his palace at Seuthopolis (325–315 BCE), and it is probably there that the gold vessels found at Panagyurishte were used in royal and religious rituals.

As with the Villena treasure (pp. 40–43), the Panagyurishte hoard was found in an area where there were no associated buildings or tombs. But while the Villena gold was found in a ceramic container that gave archaeologists an idea of the date of its burial and the probable identity of the person who had hidden it, the Panagyurishte pieces do not have even this slight archaeological context. As with other hoards, it seems likely that it was buried to protect it from a danger so great that even a fortified stronghold was not thought a safe enough place for it.

If the vessels did belong to Seuthes III or to his heir, Cotys II (300–280 BCE), there are two national emergencies that could possibly explain the burial of the collection of precious gold items. The first was during the Thracian revolt against the Macedonians in 325 BCE, before Seuthes moved his capital to Seuthopolis. However, Seuthes survived the revolt and reigned for another 25 years; therefore, the chances are that the vessels would have been recovered. A much more serious crisis took place two decades later during the reign of his son, Cotys II.

The Thracians, whom the Greeks considered to be *barbaroi*—barbarians living on the margins of the civilized world—were invaded by even more barbaric barbarians: the Gauls, who took and sacked Seuthopolis in 281 BCE. It is possible that the king or some of his courtiers fled from the burning palace, pursued by Gallic tribesmen. Perhaps the escapees feared capture in the vicinity of Panagyurishte and buried the treasures they had managed to bring with them. In the end, the Odrysians never returned to claim the treasure that at the time must have literally been worth a "king's ransom." Slavery, or more likely death, sealed their lips, preserving the golden rhytons of the kings of Thrace for 2,230 years.

TREASURE

Burial goods

Hoards

Shipwrecks

Religious objects or places

Artworks

Gemstones

AFTERLIVING IN STYLE: QIN SHI HUANG'S TERRACOTTA ARMY

210 BCE

Circumstance of loss: Burial of China's first emperor

Rediscovery: Found when farmers were digging a new well

Historical significance: Evidence of ancient China's afterlife beliefs and burial customs

Value: $383,200 (for modern replicas of 8,000 warriors and horses)

Each face has its own expression. Some warriors look serious and determined. Others seem slightly amused, puzzled, surprised, or sad. The soldiers' clay moustaches, beards, and hairstyles all seem different too.

Emperor Qin's Terra Cotta Army (2008) by Michael Capek

In three previous entries on the lost treasures of ancient Egypt (pp. 15–19, pp. 30–35, and pp. 36–39), we came across the civilization of the ancient world that is best known for its belief that "you could take it all with you" when you died. But the Egyptians were far from being unique in the ancient world: According to the Sumerian kings and queens of Ur (pp. 10–14), if you didn't take human attendants with you, you wouldn't enjoy the "afterlifestyle" to which you'd become accustomed during your time on earth. Many Bronze Age cultures followed this rather gruesome example, furnishing their rulers with human and animal companions to accompany them into their versions of royal eternity.

At an early date in human history, however, most cultures substituted living human sacrifices with inanimate statues and models. The tombs of Egypt's pharaohs, priests, and nobles were staffed by servants of different kinds: statues of tomb guardians, effigies of the gods, *ushabti*—mummiform models of the deceased that would serve him or her in the afterlife—and intricate scale models of scenes from the deceased's daily life, complete with human and animal figures, all of whom, it was believed, would become magically animated once the tomb was sealed. Kings, of course, had many more of these "model" servants than nobles, priests, and commoners.

The practice of providing the deceased with lavish and copious grave goods and servants, formerly animate or inanimate, is evidence of a very literal understanding of life after death as a continuation of this life. In the philosophical cults of ancient Greece and Rome, as with the Abrahamic faiths, the preservation of the physical body was not considered vital to the survival of the spirit. In Christianity, Judaism, and Islam, the physical and spiritual planes are completely separate, and the body is only a temporary dwelling place for the immortal soul. Similarly, in Hinduism and Buddhism, which believe in the rebirth of the same spiritual entity in a succession of bodies through the process of reincarnation, the physical form is a shell that can be disposed of and does not need particular attention after death. In these cultures, the body of a deceased person is often cremated, as he or she has already moved on, returning to a new body or moving on to another plane of existence.

A religious positivist might argue that religions evolved from early, more primitive forms of belief in the survival after death of the whole individual— body and spirit—accompanied by elaborate burial rituals and human and animal sacrifices, to more abstract notions of life after death as an entirely spiritual plane of existence. There is one major world culture, however, which combines sophisticated abstract religious and philosophical concepts with a belief in the physical survival of the individual after death. In China, the spirits of the ancestors are held to be in continuous communion with their descendants, and need to be cared for, and, when necessary, placated with rituals and offerings. In modern-day Chinese Daoist practice, offerings including fake money (known as "Hell money") and replica consumer goods and clothing made of paper are burned at the graves of the dead on festival days.

DEAD LIKENESS Ancestor worship is attested to the earliest historical Chinese dynasties, the Shang (ca. 1600–ca. 1046 BCE) and Zhou (ca. 1046–256 BCE). Shang smiths cast elaborate ritual bronzes: weapons, bells, money, food and drink vessels, and sacrificial vessels, all of which have been found in burials. Like the ancient Sumerians, the Chinese practiced the human sacrifice of the slaves and concubines of high-status individuals so that they could continue to serve and entertain their masters in the afterlife. Although they did not practice mummification like the ancient Egyptians, they sought to preserve the body of the deceased by encasing it in a burial suit made of jade, a semi-precious stone associated with incorruptibility and longevity.

Before its unification in 221 BCE, China was composed of a number of smaller states, which shared the same writing system, political organization, religion, and customs. One of these, the Kingdom of Qin, was infamous for the practice of sacrificing slaves, concubines, and high-ranking officials so that they could accompany the king in death. The tomb of one sixth-century Qin dynast contained 186 sacrificial victims. As it was Qin's destiny to unite China in the third century BCE, it is fortunate that Qin abolished this barbaric custom in 384 BCE.

Like other absolute rulers of antiquity, the kings and emperors of ancient China were considered to be far above mere mortals — "Sons of Heaven" — but unlike the divinized pharaohs of Egypt, they were not considered to be gods, either in life or death. After death, pharaohs ascended from their pyramids and underground tombs and became one with the sun god Amun-Ra, to spend eternity steering the barque of the sun on its journey across the heavens by day and through the underworld by night. In the Chinese system, rulers, like the other ancestors, occupied a level of existence between the gods in heaven and humans on earth. While the pharaohs passed beyond the human realm, China's dead never really went away—they remained to watch over their descendants, rewarding them for good behavior and reproving and punishing them if they strayed from the path of righteousness and duty.

If the ancestors of commoners required the constant care and devotion of their descendants, who made regular offerings at their graves and offered prayers at temples and in front of household altars, royal and imperial ancestors required regular devotions and rituals on a national scale. They watched over the well-being of the kingdom, and interceded with the gods on behalf of their former subjects. In Chinese mythology, the earthly hierarchy was mirrored in the afterlife, and in the heavens. Chinese society was like a giant pyramid, with the emperor standing at the apex, over the successive ranks of society, the whole resting on the broad base of the peasantry.

© INTERFOTO | Alamy

DEADLY OBSESSION
Qin Shi Huang's quest for immortality killed him.

There was another ancient Chinese custom that brought royal ancestors into direct communion with their descendants. During the Zhou Dynasty, high-ranking ancestors would join their descendants for feasts and rituals by possessing the body of a "personator" (*shi* in Chinese). Rather than a professional medium, the *shi* was a direct descendant of the deceased, often a young boy. The personator did not play the part of a spirit medium as we understand the role, by actively channeling the words of the deceased. He was a passive spectator who allowed the ancestor to see his descendants, often from behind an elaborate mask in the ancestor's likeness.

MASS-PRODUCED ARMY

Although Chinese dynastic history begins with the Shang in 1600 BCE, China's early kings did not rule a united empire. The Shang, for example, ruled over a small part of what would become the Qin Empire, and the Shang state competed with other Chinese states. The Shang's successors, the Zhou, dominated a larger area of modern China until the eighth century BCE, though for reasons of historical expediency, traditional histories record that they ruled China until the mid-third century BCE. However, in the Zhou Dynasty, between 475 and 221 BCE, during the "Warring States

Period," China was divided into competing states, including the Kingdom of Qin. Zhao Zheng, the future first emperor, Qin Shi Huang (259–210 BCE), became king of Qin as a teenager in 247 BCE. His early life reads like the plot of a Chinese action movie by Ang Lee (b. 1954). Betrayed by his mentor and regent, who was having an affair with the queen mother, the young monarch had to fight for his life on several occasions.

Upon assuming absolute power, the young Zheng set about the efficient and ruthless conquest of his neighbors, starting with the weaker states. In a series of well-executed and bloody campaigns between 223 and 221 BCE he finally overcame his last enemy, the kingdom of Qi. All of the kingdoms that made up Chinese civilization had been unified for the first time in China's already long history. Although Zheng would rule as Qin Shi Huang for just eleven years and his heir for another three before the empire collapsed, he had established a pattern of imperial government that would endure until the beginning of the twentieth century.

Like many Chinese rulers before and after him, Qin Shi Huang had one overriding obsession: immortality. And not immortality in the next life as a god or an impersonated ancestor, but immortality in this life. He expended vast sums on trying to find the "Elixir of Life," and dispatched naval expeditions to discover the "Isles of the Blessed," on which natural springs were supposed to grant eternal life. Needless to say, his quest and expeditions ended in failure. On the advice of the imperial alchemists, he took a compound made of elements that the Chinese believed bestowed, if not immortality, longevity, good health, and extended youth. His fate is a warning to those who think that traditional Chinese medicine, because it is "natural" and "herbal," must be both effective and safe. Unfortunately, what the emperor was given were capsules containing a metallic element that does not tarnish or corrode: quicksilver, or mercury. Mercury, we now know, is a lethal poison, and one that while killing its victim will drive him insane. Qin Shi Huang was probably pretty paranoid to begin with, but his elixir of eternal youth must have turned him into a paranoid schizophrenic.

He died while touring his realm at the age of 49. His prime minister, terrified that news of the emperor's death would trigger a rebellion, hid the emperor's death from everyone apart from his heir and closest attendants. As the emperor's cortege was several weeks away from the capital, the prime minister had wagons filled with fish pulled before and after the emperor's carriage so that people would not notice the smell from the slowly decomposing corpse. To keep up the charade, the dead emperor held audiences and was served meals. When the emperor's rotting body finally reached the imperial capital of Xi'an (now Shaanxi's provincial capital), his death was announced, and his son succeeded as emperor. Like all Chinese sons, the new emperor's first and most important duty was to arrange for his father's burial. An unburied ancestor risks becoming an angry ghost, and the last thing the second Qin emperor would have wanted was the ghost of his formidable father running amok.

The vast tomb complex built for Qin Shi Huang outside Xi'an continues to reveal its extraordinary secrets. The best known, unearthed by farmers digging a well in 1974, is the 8,000-strong Terracotta Army, which was buried in pits about 1 mile (1.5 km) east of the emperor's tomb mound. Although the ranks of generals, officers, archers, infantrymen, cavalrymen, and charioteers (complete with horses and chariots), were made in sections in an early version of an industrial assembly line, each soldier's face, hairstyle, beard, and expression was customized before firing.

The pottery soldiers carried real weapons that appear to have been used in battle. Many were of such quality that they were untarnished and sharp after 1,800 years underground. After they had been made, the warriors were painted in bright lacquer colors, each according to their units and ranks, although most of the lacquer has degraded, leaving the army an earthy monochrome. The army, however, is only one of the tomb complex's wonders; other pits contain musicians, courtesans, and officials—a reproduction in baked clay of the emperor's entire court, with stables, palace buildings, and shrines within a huge double circle of walls.

But the real wonders await a generation of future archaeologists. For the time being, the atheistic leaders of the People's Republic of China have refused permission for the tomb mound containing the emperor's remains to be explored other than remotely. Even they, it seems, fear the wrath of the ghost of China's first and most formidable sovereign. Sounding and imaging techniques have identified a cavernous chamber within the mound, which is dry thanks to an internal (and still functioning) system of drains and dams. High levels of mercury confirm the ancient story that the emperor's tomb contained a vast map of his empire on which the rivers flowed with liquid mercury. If the tomb is indeed undisturbed,

© Bill Tyne | Creative Commons

INVIOLATE
Qin Shi Huang's tomb has never been opened.

the revised edition of this book might feature the treasures interred with Qin Shi Huang himself—maybe his jade burial suit and mask, in which he surveys his vast empire, attended by his inner court reproduced in terracotta.

In post-Maoist China, traditional Chinese beliefs and customs, once banned and repressed by the Red Guard, are allowed to flourish once more. Families pay their respects to their ancestors, and increasingly visit the mausolea of former emperors, not just as tourists but also as loyal subjects. The life-size warriors, while they have traveled in small groups to museums in Europe, Australia, and North America, are best appreciated en masse. Only then can the viewer appreciate the true meaning of Qin Shi Huang's awesome power, which continues to be as great in death today as it was in life two millennia ago.

OZYMANDIAS SYNDROME: ALEXANDER THE GREAT'S SARCOPHAGUS

81 BCE

TREASURE

Burial goods

Hoards

Shipwrecks

Religious objects or places

Artworks

Gemstones

Circumstance of loss: Sarcophagus melted down to be made into coinage

Rediscovery: Destroyed

Historical significance: Loss of the last physical evidence of the ancient world's most famous ruler

Value: Not quite a king's ransom

© Panos Karas | Shutterstock.com

"My name is Ozymandias, king of kings:
Look on my works, ye Mighty, and despair!"
Nothing beside remains. Round the decay
Of that colossal wreck, boundless and bare
The lone and level sands stretch far away.

"Ozymandias" (1818)
by Percy Bysshe Shelley

The pharaohs were considered to be gods in life and in death. Although they were revered and buried with all the pomp, magnificence, and wealth that their successors could afford, with few exceptions, their tombs were broken into and ransacked by robbers, who stripped the carefully preserved mummified body of the king of its gold death mask, amulets, and jewels. Even the greatest pharaoh of them all, Ramesses II (ca. 1303–1213 BCE), had to be rescued and hidden in a humble grave alongside the mummies of other pharaohs to protect him from further desecration.

His sad fate inspired Percy Bysshe Shelley's (1792–1822) poem "Ozymandias" (quoted on p. 67), which ridicules the pompous boasts made on the monuments of mighty kings and conquerors, all of whose names and achievements are soon forgotten—well, almost all. Ramesses, while he might be one of the giants in the annals of ancient Egyptian history, is a B-list monarch when compared to the ruler who was arguably the greatest and most famous in all antiquity, Alexander III of Macedon (356–323 BCE), or "Alexander the Great"—a king, general, and leader of men of such brilliance that his reputation has not dimmed with the passage of over two millennia.

© The Print Collector | Alamy

WORLD-BEATER
Alexander defeating King Darius of Persia.

Although Alexander died at the comparatively young age of 33, his achievements have inspired awe, respect, and envy in would-be world conquerors, from Julius Caesar (100–44 BCE) to Napoleon (1769–1821). Succeeding his murdered father at the age of 20, Alexander began by subjugating the rebellious Greek city states and Thracian kingdoms (see pp. 56–59). Two years later, he embarked on the conquest of the world's largest and most powerful empire, Achaemenid Persia.

In a series of lightning campaigns, he led his armies all the way to the Indian subcontinent to a region that now forms part of the modern state of Pakistan. Having set out to conquer the whole world, Alexander suddenly discovered that the world was a lot bigger than he had originally thought, stretching far beyond India, and not ending at the shores of the great ocean that the Greeks believed encircled the world. Even Alexander's boundless self-confidence and ambition began to fail him, and when his men mutinied, the indomitable Alexander agreed to their demands and turned back.

He arrived in Persia in 324 BCE, and traveled to his eastern capital of Babylon in Mesopotamia. Although he was planning new conquests, he suddenly died of a fever after an all-night drinking session. There were rumors that he might have been poisoned, but the most likely cause of death was malaria aggravated by the many wounds that he had sustained during his ten years of campaigning in the East, combined with his immoderate lifestyle. The death of his closest male companion and some say lover, Hephaistion (ca. 356–324 BCE), may also have contributed to the great man's death. Alexander left an empire stretching from India to Greece and an infant heir who would not long survive his father. His former generals and close companions, known collectively as the Diadochi ("Successors"), fought over his empire and legacy. Central to their claim as his legitimate successors was the honor of burying their former king.

The Macedonian army chose Alexander's half-brother, Philip III Arrhidaeus (ca. 359–317 BCE), to succeed Alexander and escort his body from Babylon to Macedon, where it was to be buried at the royal tombs in the ancient capital of Aigai. It took Philip two years to construct a hearse magnificent enough to transport the mortal remains of a man seen by many as a god. The vehicle was little short of a temple on wheels, its gem-studded roof held aloft by solid gold pillars. Inside, next to a golden throne, Alexander's body was covered in a purple shroud woven with gold. The hearse was so large and heavy that it needed 64 mules to pull it.

Alexander, however, never reached Macedon. One of his generals, Ptolemy I Soter (ca. 367–ca. 283 BCE), who had been made satrap (governor) of Egypt, hijacked the funeral cortege and had Alexander buried in the ancient Egyptian capital of Memphis. But the city of the pharaohs was not destined to be Alexander's final resting place. After his conquest of Egypt in 331 BCE, Alexander had founded the city of Alexandria, on the coast of the Mediterranean, which was destined to become one of the ancient world's greatest cities, famous for its lighthouse—the Pharos—royal palaces, temples, library, and the Sema—Alexander's tomb.

TOMB RAIDERS

Ptolemy I's heir, Ptolemy II Philadelphus (309–246 BCE), who ruled Egypt as the second pharaoh of the Ptolemaic Dynasty, transferred the

© Patrick Neil | Creative Commons

MARBLE MEMORIAL
A stone coffin once thought
to be Alexander's.

body from Memphis to a mausoleum he had specially built in Alexandria. He placed Alexander's body in two sarcophagi made of solid gold, the lids sculpted into the likeness of the king in the style of Egyptian coffins. No trace of the Sema now remains, but historians imagine that it would have been a funerary monument of considerable size and magnificence, equaling or surpassing the tomb of Mausolus (377–353 BCE), itself one of the "Seven Wonders" of the ancient world, and the origin of our word "mausoleum."

Although the Sema's location has not been identified, ancient sources describe the visits of Roman rulers, who came to pay their respects, including Julius Caesar (100–44 BCE), who is said to have sobbed when he saw the great man, not in sadness for the king's fate, but because he could never hope to equal his accomplishments. Caesar's heir, and Rome's first emperor, Augustus (63 BCE–14 CE), came to the tomb after defeating Mark Anthony (83–30 BCE) and Cleopatra VII (69–30 BCE) at the Battle of Actium. Bending over to kiss Alexander's mummy, he is said to have broken its nose. When he was then invited to visit the tombs of Ptolemy's heirs, Augustus declined, saying that he had come to see a king, not to visit the dead. The pilgrimages of Roman emperors continued until the reign of the Emperor Caracalla (188–217 CE), who believed himself to be a reincarnation of Alexander, and who dedicated precious gifts to the Sema.

What none of these visitors saw, however, was Alexander's gold sarcophagi. In 81 BCE, Ptolemy's most reviled successor, Ptolemy IX Soter II (ca. 142–81 BCE), replaced them with a glass coffin. He did so not to allow visitors to see Alexander's remains but because he needed cash to prop up his tottering throne. He melted down the sarcophagi to mint into coins. The people of Alexandria were outraged; Alexander was not just a great king and the founder of the city, he was also worshipped as a god. Ptolemy IX's sacrilege did not go unpunished; he was soon deposed and murdered.

The Sema vanishes from history in the fourth century, when the Emperor Theodosius (347–395 CE) proscribed all pagan cults and closed the remaining temples, though there are no records of Christian zealots attacking and destroying the tomb, which was the sad fate of many of the city's other pagan monuments. Although archaeologists have excavated several sites in Alexandria, including two mosques and a Roman graveyard, none have been conclusively identified as the site of the tomb itself. The city was sacked on several occasions during antiquity and the medieval period, and earthquakes toppled parts of ancient Alexandria into the Mediterranean. If Alexander's extraordinary good fortune continued in death as it had for most of his life, his glass coffin sank to the bottom of the sea, where he will see out eternity without any further disturbance from gawping tourists and envious imitators.

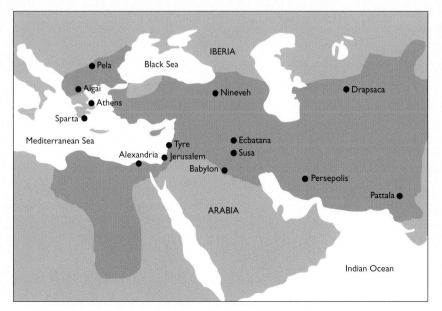

Conquest of Alexander

ALEXANDER'S WORLD
The empire spanned Europe and Asia.

ORRERY 1.0:
ANTIKYTHERA MECHANISM

ca. 70 BCE

Circumstance of loss: Shipwreck off the Aegean island of Antikythera

Rediscovery: Recovered in 1900 by sponge divers, although the mechanism was not understood until the twenty-first century

Historical significance: The world's earliest analog computing device

Value: First known practical application of heliocentrism

In short, the Antikythera Mechanism was a machine designed to predict celestial phenomena according to the sophisticated astronomical theories current in its day, the sole witness to a lost history of brilliant engineering, a conception of pure genius, one of the great wonders of the ancient world.

"The Cosmos in the Antikythera Mechanism" (2012) by Tony Freeth and Alexander Jones

In the past few years, a great deal has been made of the mathematical and astronomical abilities of the Classic Maya who lived in city states in Central America between the third and tenth centuries CE. Their interest (bordering on obsession) in timekeeping led them to develop and combine their very accurate solar and lunar calendars to calculate temporal cycles extending many centuries beyond the survival of their civilization, in order to time the rituals of their complex liturgical year and to date the reigns, buildings, and accomplishments of their god-kings. One of these, known as a *b'ak'tun*, consisting of 394.26 solar years, began on December 21, 2012.

According to many New Age prophets, the momentous first day of b'ak'tun 13, or 13.0.0.0.0 (combining a Maya date with a Christian superstition), would herald the fiery destruction of the world, or, at the very least, a major turning point in the evolution of human civilization. As the rogue "Planet Nibiru" completely failed to crash into the earth and turn our planet into a giant charcoal briquette, we can only hope that a major shift in human consciousness is underway. However, looking at the state of the world since December 2012, it seems questionable that anything occurred at all. In short, the only people who really benefitted from the "Maya Apocalypse" that never was were those canny authors who wrote bestselling books on the coming doom and destruction, all the while secure in the knowledge that they would be spending their royalties on December 22.

The Classic Maya were extremely able astronomers and mathematicians, but materially and technologically their civilization was surprisingly primitive. Although they were superb craftsmen and artists, who succeeded in carving jewels, statues, and masks out of jade, one of the hardest semi-precious stones on earth (see Pakal's death mask, pp. 118–123), they did it with stone tools, as they never extracted, refined, and smelted metals to fashion into tools, agricultural implements, or weapons. They lived in the Stone Age until the arrival of the Spanish in the sixteenth century. The Maya also lacked one of humanity's most basic inventions, the wheel; nor did they have any large draft animals for transportation or agriculture. Despite these shortcomings, their civilization prospered for six and a half centuries in one of the most inhospitable regions of Mesoamerica.

On the other side of the world, in the Balkans, between the fifth and the first centuries BCE, some eight centuries before the high point of Maya civilization, another group of city states located in one of Europe's

HEAVENLY SPHERES
A reconstruction of the front face of the mechanism.

© AFP | Getty Images

most unforgiving environments, developed an extraordinary aptitude for astronomy and mathematics. Although there are many parallels between the Classic Maya and the ancient Greeks — their rich and varied pantheons of gods; their urban, literate cultures that produced great scientific, artistic, and literary achievements and enduring sculptures and monuments; and their political divisions that fostered a vibrant but warlike regional culture of competing powers—there are just as many things that set them apart.

The Greeks, who built their cities on narrow coastal plains hemmed in between the mountains and the sea, lived from the sea as fishermen, maritime traders, and navigators, while for most of their history, the Maya were a landlocked people, who lived in the middle of the rainforest. But perhaps one of the greatest differences between them was in the practical application of their mathematical and astronomical discoveries. Whereas the Maya used their calculations for abstract ritual purposes, the Greeks developed their sciences with very practical ends in mind.

As mariners who crossed the Mediterranean long before the introduction of the magnetic compass to Europe from China in the twelfth century CE, their only means of navigation when out of sight of land was by using the sun by day, and the moon, planets, and stars by night. But the elliptical orbit of the earth around the sun, which causes the sun to rise and set on different points of the horizon as the year processes through the solstices and equinoxes, and the even more complex monthly celestial transits of the moon and planets, meant that navigators needed to know the relative positions of the heavenly bodies on a particular date to be able to calculate their own position on the surface of the earth.

Like later navigators, they must have used written astronomical tables, but they also had extremely sophisticated mechanical devices—described as the first analog computers—with which they could calculate the position of the sun, moon, and the five planets then known against the constellations of the zodiac. This kind of device, known as an "orrery," a clockwork model of the heavens, which plots the positions of the sun, moon, and planets relative to one another and to the constellations, was thought to date from the beginning of the eighteenth century, but as a first-century BCE shipwreck had proven, it was first designed and built by the ancient Greeks in the second century BCE. This ancient orrery, the "Antikythera Mechanism," has revolutionized the understanding of the technological capabilities of the ancient world.

Unlike the Riace bronzes (pp. 51–55), which were discovered with no obvious archaeological context, the Antikythera Mechanism was found amid the debris field of a sunken first-century galley. However, like the Riace find, the wreck was initially mistaken for a scene of carnage, with human and animal body parts strewn over the ocean floor. It soon became apparent, however, that what had first seemed to be rotting corpses half buried in the sand, were in fact parts of bronze and marble statues that had been the cargo of a ship. Historians believe that the galley was carrying Greek artworks and artifacts to Rome, which might have been destined to be part of a triumphal procession held in honor of Julius Caesar (100–44 BCE). Coins found by the French oceanographer and pioneer diver Jacques Cousteau (1910–70) during his 1978 exploration of the wreck date the sinking to between 76 and 67 BCE.

CAESAR'S LOOT

© Getty Images

MARINE EXPLORER
Cousteau's 1978 dive enabled archaeologists to date the wreck.

The discovery of the wreck long predates our understanding of the Anitkythera Mechanism. In 1900, sponge divers sailing back to Greece from the North African coast were forced to seek shelter from bad weather at the Aegean island of Antikythera, just north of Crete. While they were riding out the storm, the captain sent his divers to prospect for sponges in the sheltered waters just off the island. Divers in those days were not equipped with their own airtanks, or lightweight rubber wetsuits, face masks, and flippers; they wore heavy waterproofed canvas suits, with heavy spherical brass helmets, with round porthole-like viewing plates, and heavy lead boots to keep them from floating up to the surface. Air was pumped into the helmet through a long pipe connected to a hand-operated air pump onboard ship. With such primitive equipment, there was always the danger that the diver would suffer from carbon dioxide poisoning and either hallucinate or pass out.

When one diver returned from a 200-foot (60 m) dive with tales of dead bodies on the seabed, the captain thought his crewmate had been poisoned. But just to make sure, he put on a diving suit and went to see for himself. He did not find rotting corpses but Classical Greek, Hellenistic, and Roman statues. With the assistance of the Greek Ministry of Education and the Hellenic Navy, the captain and his crew explored the wreck, recovering many of its treasures, until mid-1901. Unfortunately, the wreck was at a depth that was at the very limits of the diving technology of the day. The deaths of several divers from decompression sickness, known as the "bends," put an end to the wreck's exploration until Cousteau's expedition revisited the wreck with modern scuba-diving gear in the twentieth century.

Among the rare Greek bronzes and Roman marble copies of ancient Classical originals, jewels, pottery, glassware, and coins was a corroded lump of metal and wood of indeterminate function. It was taken with the other artifacts to the National Archaeological Museum in Athens, but it was only in 1902 that a curator finally had time to examine it carefully. What he saw both puzzled and surprised him. Embedded in the corroded mass was a gear wheel, made centuries before mechanical gears were supposed to have been invented.

The initial theory about the largest fragment (Fragment A) of the Antikythera Mechanism was that it was a much later, possibly modern, artifact, that had somehow become mixed up with the debris of the shipwreck. For half a century, the corroded mechanism remained a mysterious oddity in the vaults of Athens' archaeological museum, because there was no technology in existence that could pierce through the layers of corrosion to see what lay within. But gradually, as new scientific techniques emerged, researchers began to unlock the mechanism's secrets. First examined with conventional X-rays in 1951, the mechanism was shown to consist of several interlocked gear wheels mounted on a hand crank that was the device's source of power. Although not clockwork-driven by springs as we know it, the Antikythera Mechanism nevertheless was clear evidence that the ancient Greeks were not just gifted theorists like the Maya, but had advanced engineering skills that would not be equaled or surpassed in Europe for another thousand years.

The last major scientific examination of the mechanism in 2006 (refined by further studies in 2008, 2010, and 2012), which used the latest in computer-aided X-ray tomography, created three-dimensional images at a resolution that enabled researchers to read the ancient Greek inscriptions on the different components, revealing an extremely sophisticated range of functions. The mechanism, which now consists of 82 separate fragments of varying sizes, was surprisingly compact, measuring 13 inches (33 cm) high, by 6¾ inches (17 cm) wide, and 3½ inches (9 cm) thick—about the same size as a small laptop. Made of bronze and originally mounted in a wooden frame, the device consists of 30 known gears, but as it is still incomplete, it is possible that more components (including a possible seven other gears) await discovery in the latest exploration of the wreck with state-of-the-art diving equipment which began in 2012.

The Romans were noted for their military technology and their engineering skills. They were great builders of roads, bridges, aqueducts, and drains, and invented both hot baths and central heating. However, they had little interest in the more abstract sciences. The Greeks, in contrast, were fascinated by the natural world, and they devised practical applications from their theories. The Antikythera Mechanism makes full use of Babylonian and ancient Greek discoveries in astronomy, recreating a "heliocentric"— sun-centered—planetary system, which was only fully accepted in Europe in the sixteenth century during the "Copernican Revolution."

The mechanism had two working faces: The front was like a clock, but instead of 12 hours was inscribed with the 12 signs of the zodiac, corresponding to the constellations visible in the night sky in the Northern Hemisphere. Pointers, like the hands of a clock, indicated the positions of the sun, moon, and the five known planets, as well as the phases of the moon. The rear of the mechanism had two further spiral dials with pointers indicating the stages reached in several important astronomical cycles, including the 18-year Saros cycles, the Exeligmos cycle, used to predict eclipses, the 19-year Metonic cycle, and the 76-year Callippic cycle. The mechanism also came with its own helpful set of instructions—a kind of ancient "help file"—written on one of the doors of the mechanism.

Although no other example of a similar mechanism has ever been found, archaeologists believe that this was not an inspired one-off, as might be the case with the Phaistos disk (pp. 20–24). There are references in first-

FATHER OF INVENTION
Archimedes may have designed the ancestor of the mechanism.

century texts to similar devices, and historians believe that the technological sophistication of the Antikythera Mechanism means that it was already several generations old—Antikythera 3.2 or 4.5, say. As to when it was built, where, and by whom, we have several clues. Once the inscriptions had all been deciphered, researchers dated the mechanism to around 82 BCE and so it was probably lost not long after its manufacture. As there was no standardized list of month names in use in ancient Greece, each city state devised its own month names. Those inscribed on the mechanism were used by the city of Corinth and its overseas colonies, which included Syracuse in Sicily.

Syracuse is significant because the great mathematician, astronomer, and inventor Archimedes (ca. 287–ca. 212 BCE) was a native of the city. Although he died long before the mechanism was made, he could have been the designer of the original Antikythera 1.0. Therefore, the plans for the device could have originated in Syracuse, have been manufactured in Greece, and then been looted by the Romans who were taking it back to Italy. If the mechanism was indeed a creation of Archimedes, the Romans would have had good reason to seize it. In addition to his more theoretical work in astronomy and mathematics, Archimedes invented several ancient WMDs to defend his native city from the Romans. These included an assembly of bronze mirrors that would focus the rays of the sun onto enemy ships, to set fire to them, and a giant crane that could pick ships out of the sea and drop them on the rocks. Despite Archimedes's ingenious designs, the Romans took Syracuse, and the great man was killed by a Roman soldier after refusing, so legend has it, to abandon a mathematical problem he was working on.

HOLY CONFUSION: HOLY GRAIL

ca. 30 CE

TREASURE

Burial goods

Hoards

Shipwrecks

Religious objects or places

Artworks

Gemstones

Circumstance of loss: Disappears after Jesus's arrest

Rediscovery: Not yet found

Historical significance: Physical evidence of life, passion, and death of Jesus Christ

Value: Immortality

"Now," said Sir Gawain, "we have been served this day with meats and drinks we thought on; but one thing beguiled us, that we might not see the Holy Grail, it was so preciously covered. Wherefore I will make here a vow, that tomorrow, without longer abiding, I shall labour in the quest of the Sangrail."

Le Morte Darthur (1485) by Sir Thomas Malory

© Public domain

There are four versions of the Holy Grail, each with varying degrees of abstraction and plausibility. Let us begin with the most concrete, and probably the most accepted version for the past two millennia: The cup that the historical Jesus (ca. 4 BCE–ca. 30 CE) used during the Last Supper in the first act of Holy Communion, when he shared bread and wine with his disciples. According to the gospel of Matthew, Jesus took the cup and said, "Drink ye all of it; For this is my blood of the new testament, which is shed for many for the remission of sins" (Matthew 26:27–28, King James Version). This cup, though popularly known as the Holy Grail, is more correctly the "Holy Chalice"—a chalice being the name of the wine vessel used in church during the Eucharist.

Although the King James Version is a sixteenth-century translation of Greek and Latin scriptures, which themselves may have been based on earlier Aramaic or Hebrew sources, the description of the Last Supper in the Gospels confirms the use of some kind of beaker, cup, or bowl from which Jesus and the disciples drank. However, someone with a skeptical frame of mind might ask, why would someone keep one drinking vessel used at one meal among many? Despite the huge symbolic significance of the Last Supper to later Christian practice and iconography, the disciples at the time did not know that this was to be the final meal they would eat with their teacher.

In the modern context, we are not in the habit of stealing the crockery and glassware from a restaurant just in case someone in the party turns out to be the next Messiah; however, it is likely that Jesus and his disciples, who spent most of their time together on the road, had their own drinking cups, which they used wherever they went. The cup of a first-century carpenter, as Indiana Jones (a.k.a. Harrison Ford, b. 1942) points out in George Lucas's (b. 1944) *Indiana Jones and the Last Crusade* (1989), when he is asked to choose the grail from an assemblage of gold and silver gem-encrusted chalices, would be extremely plain. He picks a humble earthenware cup and survives the ordeal, while the bad guy naturally goes for a gaudy piece of medieval kitsch and gets his just desserts.

The second cup or bowl referred to as the Holy Grail was used to collect Jesus's blood during the crucifixion. Although there is no mention of Jesus's blood being collected in this way in the Gospels, in Luke 19:34, a Roman soldier pierces his side with a spear, causing a deep wound from which gushes forth blood and water. As with the Holy Chalice used at the Last Supper, this Holy Grail might be any waterproof container, but again, as befitted the poverty of Jesus and his family, rather than an expensive item made of precious metal and decorated with gems, it is more likely to have been earthenware, stone, or wood.

Relics were an integral part of Christianity in the medieval period. Compared to the pagan cults that it superseded, Christianity, with its single all-powerful God and simple ritual of sharing bread and wine, must have appeared very abstract and detached from everyday life for people who were used to a multitude of gods and goddesses, as well as spirits of home and place, each honored with sacrifices and their own rituals and yearly festivals. As the Church sought to find its form and place in the pagan world, it borrowed from established cults, helping it to become more familiar and acceptable to converts.

There was no question of co-opting the ancient gods, which were cast out into the outer darkness as demons, but the men and women who had died for the faith — the martyrs, and later saints, of the Church — were held to be especially blessed and closer to God. It was a short step from turning martyrs from ordinary human beings who had earned a first-class ticket to Paradise into holy intercessors between the human and divine realms, with their physical remains providing the means of linking the two. In many cases saints were commemorated in churches built on the sites of the temples and shrines of pagan gods, Christianizing them and taking over some of their attributes, myths, and cult practices.

The most powerful relics of all, of course, would have been the physical remains of Jesus, because he was believed to be the human incarnation of divinity — the *logos* made flesh. However, unlike the saints, after his death, Christ rose from the tomb and ascended to heaven, leaving almost no physical evidence of his earthly life, apart from what were claimed to be phials of his blood and, most bizarrely of all, his preserved foreskin. What made up for this lack of physical remains were the many relics associated with his life, passion, and death: the manger in which he was laid, the crown of thorns, the Holy Sponge, the Holy Lance, the True Cross, his shroud — all credited with miraculous powers — and, of course, the Holy Grail or Chalice.

**TOUCHING
THE
INTANGIBLE**

© Francisco J. Diez Martin | Creative Commons

TOUCHING GOD
A fragment of the True
Cross or a medieval fake?

What is striking about many famous relics of the medieval world is that they appear in Europe during the eleventh century after the First Crusade (1096–99), when an alliance of Western European powers laid claim to the Holy Land. Until 634–638, when Muslim Arab armies conquered Syria and Palestine, the Romans and Byzantines had ruled the province of Judea, endowing it with many shrines and churches that housed the relics of Christ, the Apostles, and the Holy Family, which included the most potent of all, the True Cross on which Jesus had been crucified. The Holy Grail, however, was not one of the relics enshrined and venerated by the Eastern Orthodox Church. It first makes its appearance much later, in Europe, in the twelfth century.

Medieval Christianity developed many practices that would later be seen as little more than idolatry, magic, and superstition by Protestant reformers such as Martin Luther (1483–1546). In the Middle Ages, however, there was a brisk trade in relics. Although some were undoubtedly genuine, there were also unscrupulous clerics and merchants who passed off bones dug up in ancient cemeteries as those of martyrs, and ancient artifacts looted from tombs and archaeological sites as objects used by Jesus and the disciples. For example, at one time there were enough fragments of the True Cross in circulation to make up a forest of crosses, and there is still a complete Crown of Thorns in a Paris church, as well as thorns said to be from the same crown in churches in several other countries. Clearly, many of these relics—especially the more perishable ones, such as the milk of the Virgin Mary, were forgeries. The Catholic Church has quietly disposed of the most obvious fakes, and others have been destroyed in natural disasters, wars, and revolutions, but some, like the Turin Shroud, have survived and remain objects of veneration.

There are two surviving relics, each claimed to be the one, the only, and the true Holy Grail or Chalice, one in Italy and the other in Spain. The first is kept in Genoa Cathedral. Emperor Napoleon I (1769–1821) helped himself to the artistic treasures of his vanquished foes (see Venus de Milo, pp. 93–99) and sent the Genoa Chalice, Il Sacro Catino, to France as part of the spoils from his Italian campaign. The Catino is not a cup but a hexagonal dish 14 inches (35 cm) across and made of a translucent green material that was once thought to be emerald. When the dish broke on its way back to Genoa, the emerald was revealed to be nothing more mysterious or valuable than green glass. Its origin is uncertain, but the dish could have been looted from a mosque in the Holy Land in the twelfth century, or have been booty taken by the Genoese after their capture of Almería in southeastern Spain from the Moors.

Rather than being contemporaneous with Jesus, the Catino is a piece of Islamic glassware made many centuries after his death. Another reason to doubt that it has any relationship with the historical Jesus is that it was a high-status object, and not one likely to have been owned by a humble carpenter and religious teacher who preached the riches of the spirit over material wealth. But to the medieval mind, whose religious iconography of Jesus and the saints saw them clothed in golden, gem-encrusted raiments, the idea that Jesus might have owned a vessel carved from a giant emerald would not seem as improbable as it does to the modern reader.

The second presumed Holy Grail is the prized possession of the Cathedral of Valencia, Spain: El Caliz de Valencia. The Caliz consists of two distinct parts: a base of chalcedony and gold, with two elaborately worked gold handles, and the cup itself, which is carved out of a piece of red agate. The agate cup is about 3½ inches (9 cm) in diameter, and the whole piece, including the base, is 7 inches (17 cm) high. The base has an Arabic inscription but that does not necessarily mean that the two sections are from the same period. In 1960, a Spanish archaeologist dated the agate cup to between the fourth century BCE and the first century CE, and judged it to be of Near Eastern or Egyptian origin. Thus far, however, the date has not been confirmed by scientific testing.

DIVINE SUPPER
The Catholic Church recognizes the Caliz as the Grail.

The Caliz makes its debut in the twelfth-century inventory of a Spanish monastery, when it is referred to as the cup in which "Christ Our Lord consecrated his blood." In the next few centuries, the cup developed a considerable provenance—a backstory explaining how it had come to

© Vitold Muratov | Creative Commons

be in Spain. According to a seventeenth-century account, Saint Peter (ca. 1 BCE–67 CE), the first bishop of Rome, brought the cup with him from Jerusalem, where his successors, the popes, used it to celebrate Holy Communion. During the third-century persecutions of the Church, Pope Sixtus II (d. 258) entrusted the Caliz to one of his deacons, Saint Lawrence (ca. 225–58), who took or sent it to Spain for safekeeping.

In the Caliz's favor is the Church's support for the claim that this is the cup that Jesus used at the Last Supper. The two previous popes, John Paul II (1920–2005) and Benedict XVI (b. 1927), used it to celebrate mass when they visited Valencia. Although John Paul failed to confirm that it was the Holy Grail, the more conservative Benedict used a form of words that indicated that he believed it was the authentic cup used by Jesus. Although the Valencia Caliz is a more plausible grail than the Genoa Catino, it, too, is a high-status object—possibly an antique of considerable value even in Jesus's lifetime, if the fourth century BCE date and Egyptian origin are correct. A pro-Caliz website claims that the Last Supper might have been hosted by a wealthy Christian disciple, which would explain why Jesus used such an expensive artifact, but this sits oddly with the Jesus of the Gospels, who would have given the precious cup to feed the poor and preferred the plainest tableware available.

SMOKE AND MIRRORS

I fear that an entry on the Holy Grail cannot now be written without mentioning the complex web of fictions that culminated in the publication of Dan Brown's (b. 1964) international bestseller, *The Da Vinci Code* (novel, 2003; movie, 2006). Brown claims that his novel is an entirely fictional account of one man's search for the truth behind the grail legend. The Saint Graal, the hero discovers, is a transliteration of the old French sangréal, or "sang royal" ("royal blood"). My excuses to the two people on the planet who have not read the book or seen the movie, as I reveal that the original bearer of the sangréal is Jesus's female disciple and presumed wife, Mary Magdalene who, legend has it, came to live out her days in the south of France. The true heir of Jesus, therefore, is not the pope but the living descendants of Jesus and Mary Magdalene. The grail, then, is not a physical object, but a bloodline.

Michael Baigent, Richard Leigh, and Henry Lincoln, the authors of the non-fictional account of the Jesus bloodline theory, *Holy Blood, Holy Grail* (1982), unsuccessfully sued Brown for plagiarism. But it is at this point that the story takes a bizarre twist worthy of a novel. Baigent et al's evidence was based on documents they found in the Bibliothèque Nationale de France while researching a TV show in the 1970s. The 27-page *Dossiers Secrets d' Henri Lobineau* (*Secret Files of Henri Lobineau*) includes the Genealogy of the Merovingian Kings; a partial history of the secretive "Priory of Sion" and a list of its grand masters, which included such luminaries as Leonardo da Vinci (1452–1519) and Sir Isaac Newton (1643–1727); and a genealogy proving the direct descent of Pierre Plantard (1920–2000) from the last Merovingian king, Dagobert II (ca. 650–79), who in turn, the *Dossiers* claimed, was descended from the descendants of Jesus and Mary Magdalene.

Plantard was a small-time fraudster and a right-wing Catholic monarchist, who deluded himself into thinking he could overthrow the French Republic and become king of France. He and two accomplices forged the *Dossiers Secrets*, which they planted in the Bibliothèque Nationale, where his patsy, the British scriptwriter Henry Lincoln, discovered them. Plantard also made use of a petty clerical scandal in Rennes-le-Château to establish a provenance for the *Dossiers*. He claimed that the parish priest had found the treasure of the Knights Templar (pp. 152–158) in his church in 1891, along with the mysterious *Dossiers*. The sordid truth, however, was that the venal cleric had been defrauding his parishioners.

THE NUMBER ONE *NEW YORK TIMES* BESTSELLER

DAN BROWN
THE DA VINCI CODE

'Fascinating and absorbing... A great, riveting read. I loved this book.'
HARLAN COBEN

© Rod Collins | Alamy

PULP FICTION
The bestselling novel thought to be fact by many.

The story was so compelling and multilayered, with so many leads, that the British investigators were completely taken in, and they repeated Plantard's claims. Dan Brown reproduced many of Plantard's claims in his novel, spicing it up with grail legend, and pitting the Priory of Sion against an equally imaginary group within the Catholic Church, the Council of Shadows, who employ members of the real Catholic charitable organization Opus Dei as their paramilitary wing. Brown's version of the Holy Grail, however, while many would like to believe it as fact, is based on a set of forgeries crafted by a delusional French monarchist, and a series of even flimsier legends and conjectures about Mary Magdalene's possible marriage to Jesus, and her journey to Europe after his death. According to the Greek Orthodox Church, however, Mary Magdalene lived out her last years in Ephesus (now in western Turkey).

Her remains, still venerated as relics, are preserved in a church in the Turkish capital Istanbul (formerly Christian Constantinople).

The fourth and final Holy Grail is the one that features in the Arthurian legends as retold by Sir Thomas Malory (d. 1471) in *Le Morte Darthur* (published posthumously in 1485; see quote p. 79). Although the grail is mentioned as a physical object that is hidden from view beneath a richly embroidered cloth, it is also defined as something that can be achieved. Sir Galahad, the most perfect knight, is said to "achieve the Holy Grail" and to gain immortality. This does not mean he literally lives forever but that, after many tests and travails, he is the recipient of divine grace. The grail, therefore, is a metaphor for salvation, the soul's immortality, which is within reach of all true Christian believers.

TREASURY OF WORDS: THE DEAD SEA SCROLLS

68 CE

TREASURE

Burial goods

Hoards

Shipwrecks

Religious objects or places

Artworks

Gemstones

Circumstance of loss: Hidden around 68 CE during the rebellion against Roman rule

Rediscovery: A Bedouin shepherd discovered the first cave containing the scrolls in 1946; further caves containing scrolls were discovered in 1956

Historical significance: Earliest known versions of the Hebrew Bible on which the Old Testament is based

Value: Word of God

The scrolls and scroll fragments recovered in the Qumran environs represent a voluminous body of Jewish documents, a veritable "library," dating from the third century BCE to 68 CE. Unquestionably, the "library," which is the greatest manuscript find of the twentieth century, demonstrates the rich literary activity of Second Temple Period Jewry and sheds insight into centuries pivotal to both Judaism and Christianity.

"The Qumran Library," from the Library of Congress online exhibit "Scrolls from the Dead Sea" (retrieved March 2013)

We have already examined two treasures connected with the Judeo-Christian religious tradition; the previous entry on the Holy Grail, and the entry on the Ark of the Covenant (pp. 44–50), both items thought to have existed from many textual references but that are missing, presumed irrevocably lost or destroyed. This third entry is a treasure of an entirely different kind, and quite unlike the artifacts made of gold and precious gems that have been featured so far. The Dead Sea Scrolls are closer to the second derivation of the word "treasure"—"thesaurus," meaning a "treasury of words."

© Public domain

BIBLE FRAGMENTS
The Isaiah scroll, one of many biblical books found at Qumran.

The scrolls were discovered near the ancient site of Qumran, located on an arid plateau about 1 mile (1.6 km) northwest of the Dead Sea. The ancient settlement was founded in the late second century BCE and thought to have been destroyed by the Romans in 68 CE. They were found in nearby caves between 1946 and 1956, during a momentous period in the modern history of the region. The first scrolls came to light in the closing years of the British Mandate of Palestine (1920–48), and excavations continued through the difficult early years of the State of Israel.

Ownership of the site and of the scrolls remains a contested issue because Qumran is in an area now known as the "West Bank," claimed by both Israel and the Palestinian Authority to be an integral part of their national territory. After Israel's many victories in its wars against an alliance of Arab states led by Egypt, the Jewish State took over the West Bank (also known as the Occupied Palestinian Territories) and, at the same time, the care and conservation of the scrolls, important fragments of which are now on display at the Shrine of the Book, a specially constructed annex of the Israel Museum in Jerusalem.

The scrolls date from a much earlier but equally politically contested period of Jewish history. When the oldest Dead Sea Scrolls were written, Israel was ruled by the Seleucid Dynasty (312–63 BCE), the heirs of Alexander the Great (356–323 BCE), who were in power until they were expelled by the native Hasmonean Dynasty (140–37 BCE). They, in turn, succumbed to the Romans, who installed Herod the Great (74–4 BCE) as a client king in Jerusalem. Although a small country surrounded by much larger empires, Israel never bore the yoke of foreign domination willingly.

Be it the Egyptians, Assyrians, Babylonians, Persians, Greeks, or Romans, the Israelites constantly rebelled, which cost them dearly materially, but enabled them to develop a religious and national identity whose strength and continuity are unparalleled in the modern world.

A central building block of Jewish identity was the Temple in Jerusalem, first built by King Solomon (r. ca. 970–930 BCE), destroyed and rebuilt in the sixth century BCE, and extensively remodeled by Herod the Great. The Romans destroyed the Second Temple during a revolt against their rule between 66 and 70 CE. As the Temple was never rebuilt, the focus of Judaism shifted to the written word: the Tanakh, the Hebrew Bible, which preserved the history of the Jewish people alongside the tenets, rituals, and festivals of Judaism.

Like the Christian biblical canon, the compilation of the canonical version of the Tanakh, known as the "Masoretic Text," took upward of four centuries (between 200 BCE and 200 CE), with different versions of the text and books accepted or rejected. The modern Tanakh consists of 24 books (a different numbering arrangement from the Old Testament's 39 books) divided into three sections: Torah ("The Instruction/Teaching"), consisting of five books (Genesis, Exodus, Leviticus, Numbers, and Deuteronomy); Nevi'im ("The Prophets"), consisting of eight books (Joshua, Judges, Samuel I & II, Kings I & II, Isaiah, Jeremiah, Ezekiel, and The Twelve Prophets); and Ketuvim ("The Writings"), consisting of 11 books (Psalms, Proverbs, Job, Song of Songs, Ruth, Lamentations, Ecclesiastes, Esther, Daniel, Ezra-Nehemiah, and Chronicles I & II).

Although the Tanakh played such a central role in Judaism after 70 CE, the modern version is based on two relatively late medieval manuscripts: the incomplete tenth-century Aleppo Codex (missing its Torah since 1947, and also now displayed in the Shrine of the Book) and the complete but slightly later Leningrad Codex (1008 or 1009 CE). The discovery at Qumran of numerous caches of both biblical and non-biblical Jewish texts dating from before 70 CE, long before the earliest extant versions of the Masoretic Text, has shed light on the composition of the canonical Tanakh, as well as on the practices of Judaism during the Second Temple Period (516 BCE–70 CE), a period when Christianity was also beginning to emerge as a separate faith.

**WINDOWS
ONTO THE
PAST**

If the question of the ownership of the scrolls remains a contested issue, so is the question of their authorship. Carbon dating and paleographic evidence confirms that the scrolls are not medieval, as had once been suggested, but were composed between the third century BCE and the first century CE. They are written in black ink (with a few in red ink) on a number of different materials: most on parchment made of vellum (animal hides), a smaller number on papyrus, and a few on copper sheets (see final section below). The scrolls had been hidden in 11 caves in large earthenware jars, which, together with the area's dry climate, helped to preserve them. The closest ancient settlement to the caves was Qumran, and the conventional wisdom until the 1990s was that the scrolls had been taken from the library in Qumran and hidden in the caves for safekeeping after the outbreak of the revolt against Roman rule in 66 CE. A second theory has since emerged claiming that the scrolls came from the Temple library in Jerusalem.

© SuperStock | Alamy

POTTERY STACKS
The scrolls survived in sealed earthenware jars.

Two years before the sack of Jerusalem and the destruction of the Temple, Roman troops sent to crush the Jewish rebellion are thought to have destroyed Qumran, maybe because its residents were involved in the revolt, or merely as an act of military terrorism to punish the population at large. Unlike the formidable fortress at Masada, Qumran is not a natural military stronghold. It is on an accessible plateau and has no obvious fortifications. There are several theories about Qumran's function and builders. The French archaeologist and Catholic priest Roland de Veaux (1903–71) excavated the site between 1951 and 1956 and several of the caves in the vicinity. He interpreted the site as the home of a religious community, which he also identified as the origin of the Dead Sea Scrolls. His interpretation has since been challenged, and alternatives include a Roman villa, a Roman fort, and a commercial center.

Among the several buildings de Veaux excavated are pools, associated in Judaism with ritual bathing. Other buildings have been identified as a "pantry," a "library," a "refectory," and a "scriptorium" (a place where manuscripts were copied by hand). The description suggests a monastic community, but Christian monasticism emerged centuries later in Egypt. If de Veaux's interpretation is correct, its inhabitants were not early

Christians but could have been members of a Jewish sect known as the Essenes, whom the Jewish-Roman historian Josephus (37–100 CE) described as living in towns in Roman Palestine and also in a settlement located close to the Dead Sea.

The Essenes were the smallest of the three main sects of Second Temple Judaism, along with the Pharisees and the Saducees. Unlike the worldly, aristocratic Pharisees and Saducees, the Essenes favored an ascetic lifestyle that had much in common with later monastic traditions. They lived communally, sharing property, and some practiced sexual abstinence. Their lives followed a strict ritual calendar, as set down by a "Community Rule," part of which was discovered among the Dead Sea Scrolls.

If the exact authorship of the scrolls is still being debated, their contents have been revealed by the latest in imaging technology and published in facsimile editions and translations. They continue to be the subject of intense analysis by biblical scholars and archaeologists all over the world. Of the 972 documents, 220 are canonical books of the Tanakh, with each book repeated many times over, creating a veritable treasure trove of biblical exegesis. About 80 percent of the scrolls are in Hebrew, with the remainder in Aramaic, Greek, and Nabatean.

The biblical books include 39 versions of Psalms, 33 of Deuteronomy, 24 of Genesis, 22 of Isaiah, 18 of Exodus, 17 of Leviticus, 11 of Numbers, and eight of Daniel. The remaining 752 documents are also mainly religious in nature, including several non-canonical biblical books, biblical commentaries, a history of the Temple, and the Community Rule. Although many of the scrolls are almost identical to the Masoretic Text, several have significant differences, shedding light in the composition of the final text of the Tanakh. The two canonical books found in both Jewish and Christian scripture but missing from the Qumran scroll are the Books of Nehemiah and Esther. Researchers have speculated that Esther's marriage to a Persian king made her unpopular to the compilers of the scrolls, which might explain why she was excluded from their canon.

Although most of the scrolls are either parchment (90 percent) or papyrus (8 percent), around 2 percent are made of sheets of bronze containing only 1 percent tin, making them 99 percent copper. One of these in particular has attracted the attention of treasure hunters rather than biblical scholars

THERE'S GOLD IN THEM THERE JUDEAN HILLS

and professional archaeologists. Simply known as the "Copper Scroll," one of the bronze documents, found in Cave Three in 1952, is not a religious text but a list of 64 secret locations, 63 of which are supposed to be the hiding places of considerable amounts of gold and silver, some weighing several tons. Copper-scroll believers claim that the treasure could have come from the First Temple (destroyed by the Babylonians in 586 BCE) or from the Second Temple before its destruction by the Romans.

Each entry on the list is structured in the same way, starting with a general location in the region, a more specific location, and the nature and quantity of the treasure hidden there. The Hebrew text of several entries concludes with three Greek letters, whose meaning is unknown. The instructions on how to find the treasures, however, are extremely obscure, and none of the hiding places on the scroll has ever been identified. The scroll also contains a tantalizing reference to a second duplicate and more detailed document, which so far has not been discovered.

© Public domain

CRYPTIC CLUES
None of the Copper Scroll's treasures have ever been found.

A paleographic analysis of the Copper Scroll shows that it is stylistically and linguistically different from the other scrolls, although its date overlaps with the later Qumran documents. Additionally, it was found at the very back of the cave, separate from the other scrolls stored there. This has led researchers to argue that it might have been hidden there at a different period than the other scrolls in the cave and might have no connection to them. Regardless of its exact provenance, the scroll's obscure instructions have never been successfully deciphered since its rediscovery (as far as we know). Most archaeologists believe that if the scroll is not some kind of ancient (or, according to some, modern) hoax, the Romans probably found most of the treasures, as they routinely tortured their prisoners to force them to reveal any valuables they might have hidden.

FIRST LADY OF FRANCE: VENUS DE MILO

130 BCE

TREASURE

Burial goods

Hoards

Shipwrecks

Religious objects or places

Artworks

Gemstones

Circumstance of loss: Statue was broken and the fragments left in a niche

Rediscovery: Unearthed in ruins by a Greek farmer and French naval officer on the Island of Melos

Historical significance: The statue played an indirect role in Greece's struggle for independence from the Ottoman Empire

Value: The honor of France

© Galina Barskaya | Shutterstock.com

Voutier sensed from the first glance that he was seeing something extraordinary. This torso was more glorious than anything he could have hoped to find when he set out that morning with the two sailors and a few picks and shovels.

Disarmed (2003) by Gregory Curtis

The discovery in the spring of 1820 of the *Venus de Milo*, a statue of the Greek goddess of love and lust Aphrodite (known to the Romans as Venus), on the small Aegean island of Milos (Milo in French), came at key points in the histories of both Greece and France. In 1815, the French Emperor Napoleon I (1769–1821) was deposed for the second and final time after his defeat at the Battle of Waterloo, and was replaced by King Louis XVIII (1755–1824), brother of the last absolute monarch of France's Ancien Régime, Louis XVI (1754–93). During his rule as First Consul and then Emperor, Napoleon conquered most of Europe, starting with the still divided states of the Italian Peninsula. Like many conquerors before and since, and like the Romans and Italians had done themselves for millennia, Napoleon helped himself to the artistic treasures of conquered territories, which in Italy included many masterpieces of Greco-Roman sculpture, such as the *Medici Venus* from Florence and *Laocoön and His Sons* from the Vatican in Rome.

HOT ART
One of the ancient artworks
stolen by Napoleon.

Napoleon gave these and many other looted Classical treasures to the Musée Napoléon in the Palace of the Louvre in Paris, as a symbol of France's and the emperor's greatness, and also to associate the newly founded French Empire with the glories of its ancient Roman predecessor. Although there had been an intervening French Empire during the reign of Charlemagne (742–814), not to mention great kings, such as Louis XIV (1638–1715), the former was a "barbarian" from the "Dark Ages," and the latter the founder of France's hated absolute monarchy that Napoleon himself had helped to overthrow. Both were part of the dark, obscurantist, pre-Enlightenment, pre-revolutionary history of France that had been discarded politically in 1789, and culturally by Neo-Classicism, both of which looked back to Classical antiquity. While the French Revolution had tried to revive the ancient Roman Republic and Greek ideals of democracy, Napoleon turned to the all-powerful Roman consuls and emperors as his political models.

Like all other would-be world conquerors, Napoleon overextended himself, just as Adolf Hitler (1889–1945) would in 1941, by launching an attack on Russia in 1812. The destruction of the Grande Armée in the terrible winter retreat from Moscow and the combined forces of Europe arraigned against him led to his military defeats in 1814 and 1815. The treasures that he had looted from the great collections of Europe were crated up and returned to their original owners, leaving the Louvre's grand halls bereft of the greatest masterpieces of Greco-Roman sculpture, which had to be replaced with plaster casts. Napoleon's successor, the aged Louis XVIII, could do little to restore France's greatness either politically or culturally.

As France entered a period of decline, at the other end of Europe, another country was emerging from centuries of foreign domination and obscurity. Although Classical Greece (sixth–fourth centuries BCE) had dominated the Mediterranean world culturally and commercially, it was too divided ever to dominate it politically or militarily. In the fourth century BCE, the Greek city states submitted to the Macedonian Empire, and in the second century BCE, they became subject to the ever-expanding Roman Republic. After the fall of the Western Roman Empire in 476 CE, Greece, though often the victim of barbarian raids, remained part of the Byzantine Empire for another millennium. The Peloponnese, the southernmost part of Greece, formed part of a much reduced Byzantine Empire until the fall of the capital Constantinople to the Ottoman Turks in 1453.

© Public domain

IMPERIAL THIEF
Napoleon used looted art to glorify France.

While the Ottoman state continued to expand into Eastern and Central Europe, Greece, along with the other European provinces of the empire, prospered. The empire was technologically and socially the most advanced state of its day, and acted as a large free-trade area that anticipated the European Union. Ethnically and religiously diverse, it was at the same time remarkably tolerant. Unlike other Islamic empires, it did not forcefully convert its subject populations, preferring persuasion and the advantages to be gained to win over converts to the religion of the Prophet Muhammad (ca. 570–ca. 632). But after three centuries of continuous expansion, the Ottoman Empire, too, faltered and entered an extended period of decline, during which it would earn the name, the "sick man of Europe." As the West developed new technologies and reached distant markets by sea, the Ottoman Empire stagnated, turned into itself, and began to disintegrate.

Badly led, corrupt, and looking back to its glorious past, the empire, or Sublime Porte, became increasingly repressive and conservative, triggering rebellions in its far-flung provinces that it repressed with growing savagery.

In 1821, the Greeks began an 11-year war of independence that would end with the creation of the Kingdom of Greece with the help of Britain, France, and Russia. Initially, the three European powers, while many of their citizens were sympathetic to the revolutionaries, wanted to preserve the status quo. Europe was still recovering from two decades of wars with France, and the socio-political upheavals that the French Revolution had wrought on the Continent.

With both the Revolution and Napoleon defeated, and the French monarchy restored, albeit as constitutional monarchy on the English model, England and Russia did not want to see the Continent set aflame with a new war in the Balkans. The Ottoman Empire's European provinces were tempting prey for her neighbors, Austria-Hungary and the Italian states, and if Greece managed to break away, Britain, France, and Russia feared what might become of the rest of the Balkans, which were then, as now, the fuse that could detonate a wider European conflict.

VENUS ARISING FROM THE DIRT

A year before the Greeks began their rebellion against Ottoman rule, a French naval vessel called in at the small Aegean island of Milos. Now a tourist destination, the island was then an undeveloped backwater of an impoverished province of the Ottoman Empire in Europe. The island's population, a few thousand strong, was oppressed by the Sultan's government in Constantinople and by the "primates," its Greek representatives on the island. The island typified the downfall and oppression of Greek civilization. Once an outpost of Hellenistic culture, Milos was strewn with ruins that the local farmers plundered for building material, or if the marble blocks were not suitable to build walls, crushed to make lime plaster.

A decade earlier, between 1801 and 1812, the British ambassador to the Sultan's court in Constantinople, Lord Elgin (1766–1841), had arranged for statues and architectural members from the ancient buildings on the Acropolis in Athens to be shipped to London. The ancient structures were in a terrible state of disrepair, especially the Parthenon, which had been severely damaged by an explosion during the Venetian siege of the city in

1687; many of the building's sculptures were in danger of being used as building materials or sold to foreign tourists by venal Ottoman officials. Elgin (and now the British Museum in London that owns and displays the marbles) claimed that he acted to save the sculptures that would have otherwise been lost forever.

Stolen, acquired legally, or saved from destruction, Classical works were leaving Greece in growing numbers, destined for the palaces and museums of Paris, London, Saint Petersburg, and Munich. Ottoman officials cared little for Greece's pagan heritage, and were easily bribed, and the Greeks themselves had not developed the sense of national pride that would lead them to agitate vociferously for the return of the Elgin Marbles in the twentieth century. In 1820, the French felt a particularly pressing need to acquire their own Greek antiquities, to fill the holes left in the collections of the Louvre after Napoleon's defeat and to keep up with the acquisitions made by the British.

It was Olivier Voutier (1796–1877), a young ensign on the French ship that had docked at the Island of Milos, who was destined to rescue France's honor. Something of a classicist and amateur archaeologist, Voutier came ashore with two sailors equipped with shovels. He chose to dig among the ruins of a Greek theater, whose stone seats were still partially visible. Voutier and his men had already found fragments of marble statues when the young ensign noticed a local farmer staring into a niche he had partly excavated a few feet away. The man had been looking for stones he could use as building material, but the large, oddly shaped fragments of marble that he had found in the niche would have been useless; hence, he was already filling it back in when Voutier, curious to see what the man had found, paid him to continue digging.

What appeared were two fragments of a large statue of a woman, the draped folds of her clothing frozen as they were slipping down to her hips, revealing her naked torso. Further digging revealed a third piece that connected the two large pieces, enabling the statue to stand without support. The niche also yielded fragments of an arm and a hand holding an apple, and pieces of two herms (monoliths with the head of the god Hermes and male genitalia). Voutier was struck by the beauty of the female statue and was certain that he had discovered a lost Greek masterpiece.

© Shakko | Creative Commons

CLASSICAL PIN-UP
The naked Aphrodite was an iconic ancient female image.

In the days that followed, Voutier showed his discovery to the local French consul, whom he tried to persuade to buy the statue for France, and to a young officer from another French ship that had called in at the island, Jules Dumont d'Urville (1790–1842). Both Voutier and d'Urville tried to persuade their captains to take the statue to Constantinople, but they countered that their ships were too small, and transporting the statue might risk damaging it further. Dumont d'Urville's ship arrived in Constantinople first, and he persuaded the French ambassador to the Sublime Porte, the Marquis de Rivière (1763–1828), to acquire the statue for France. Dumont d'Urville was sent back to the island to collect the statue, only to find that the Greek primates had reneged on their deal with the French and were about to ship the statue to Constantinople as a present for the sultan.

© Public domain

SLEIGHT OF HAND
The Venus de Milo once held an apple.

Rather than face the wrath of the French Navy, and no doubt with bribes changing hands, the primates entrusted the statue to Dumont d'Urville, who transported it to the French port of Toulon. Rivière, ever the astute politician, presented the statue to the king, who later gave it to the Louvre.

Dumont d'Urville had already correctly identified the statue as Aphrodite, the Greek goddess of love, better known at the time by her Roman name, Venus. The hand and apple that had been found with the statue were a direct allusion to the Judgment of Paris, when the Trojan prince was asked to judge who was the most beautiful among the goddesses Athena, Hera, and Aphrodite, and award the winner a golden apple. Aphrodite won, a decision that proved disastrous for Prince Paris, as it led to the outbreak of the Trojan War and the destruction of his native city. The exact age and authorship of the statue were much debated, with the most extravagant claiming that she was the work of the fourth-century BCE Athenian sculptor Praxiteles, whose other works included the world-famous *Aphrodite of Knidos* (lost but known from later copies).

The attribution, however, flew in the face of one important piece of evidence: the plinth that had first been taken to be part of another statue but that fit so perfectly that it must have been part of the original. The inscription on the plinth read: "Alexandros son of Menides, citizen of Antioch on the Maeander made this." The city of Antioch on the Maeander did not exist in the fourth century BCE, and if Alexandros was the sculptor, then the statue was the product of a much later phase of Classical art, the Hellenistic period. Today, the statue is dated to around 130 BCE, after the Roman conquest of Greece. This, however, did not match the extravagant praise of the Louvre's experts and curators, and the plinth with its embarrassing inscription mysteriously vanished before the statue was presented to the king and French public.

With a minor historical sleight of hand, the *Venus de Milo* had singlehandedly (not bad, for a girl without arms) restored the pride of a nation and of one of the world's great museums. In the two centuries since her arrival in France, she has undergone several restorations, which were later much criticized and undone. Unlike ancient statues discovered during the Renaissance, such as the *Laocoön*, whose missing arm had been replaced, the *Venus de Milo* was left without her upper limbs, establishing a new convention for the display of ancient works of art. The missing plinth, however, has never been found. In addition to restoring French honor, the *Venus de Milo*, true to her roots, also played a part in the liberation of her homeland. As tangible evidence of Greece's former cultural greatness, she helped sway public opinion to the Greek revolutionaries who were beginning their fight to restore Greece's independence, culture, and language, just as the statue was attracting the crowds and plaudits of Paris.

BRONZE AGE SAINTS: CHAUSA TREASURE

ca. 300 CE

Circumstance of loss: Buried sometime after the year 300 CE

Rediscovery: Found in a field in 1931

Historical significance: First Jain hoard to have been unearthed in the Ganges Valley

Value: The first religion

The discovery of a hoard at Chausa in 1931 pushes the history of bronze casting in that state to at least the first century BC. That bronze casting continued to flourish in the region during the Gupta period is known from literary and artistic evidence.

Indian Sculpture **(1989)**
by Pratapaditya Pal

Certain readers might believe that Christianity is among the oldest extant religions, but its two millennia are dwarfed by the possible 4,000–5,000 years that are claimed by the adherents of Jainism, which they suggest was founded during the Valley civilization (3300–1300 BCE). The Indus Valley, or Harappan (from the ancient site of Harappa), civilization flourished in what is now Pakistan during the Bronze Age, when it was among the first urban civilizations to develop on earth, alongside ancient Egypt, and Sumeria ("Ram in the Thicket," pp. 10–14), with whom it had trading links. Compared to these two civilizations, the culture of the Indus Valley is still little understood because its script has yet to be deciphered.

NAKED SAINT
Rishabha, founder of Jainism.

The Harappans lived in large barrack-like brick cities with no large buildings, such as temple or palace complexes; that, and the lack of high-status goods and burials, has led many archaeologists to conclude that Harappan society was communitarian, egalitarian, and maybe, even democratic. They left behind a rich artistic legacy of terracotta, soapstone, and bronze statuettes, and thousands of carved seals, many of which show figures in positions reminiscent of yoga *asana* (postures), and also in the standing Jain meditation posture known as *kayotsarga* in which the *tirthankara*, the Jain equivalent of Buddhas (enlightened humans who help others achieve enlightenment) are often depicted.

The Indus Valley civilization disappeared almost at the same time as the Bronze Age Collapse (1200–1150 BCE) that saw the end of many urban cultures in the eastern Mediterranean, and possibly for the same reason: invasion by "barbarian" nomads. In the Mediterranean, the invaders, the "Sea Peoples," came by boat, but in ancient India, they came overland on horseback from Central Asia. How much of Indus Valley culture survived and was absorbed in the Hindu Vedic culture that succeeded it is still a fiercely debated question in the archaeology of the subcontinent. However, it is possible that the basic tenets of Jainism were established during the Harappan period, making Jainism the oldest surviving religion on earth.

Like Hinduism and Buddhism, Jainism teaches that souls are bound to endless cycles of life and death by karma, from which they can be liberated through self-control and the strict practice of *ahimsa*—non-violence.

The latter precept entails the most scrupulous avoidance of taking life, or of causing harm to any living thing, including insects and microorganisms, as well as certain plants, such as seeds and tubers, which are seen as sources of life. Jains follow the teachings of 24 enlightened teachers, the tirthankara, who taught their devotees prayers, rituals, and techniques to achieve *moksha*, or liberation from the cycle of birth, death, and rebirth.

THE BURIED TIRTHANKARA

In the nineteenth and early twentieth centuries, Western cultural positivism saw religions as progressing from the animistic worship of natural objects and phenomena (trees, rocks, the sun, storms), to more abstract conceptualizations of gods and goddesses in polytheistic religion and philosophy, until civilization attained a greater understanding of morality through the worship of a single god. This is a conceit of Western scholars who looked at the evolution of their own cultures and religions as the models followed by all other regions of the world. Religion on the Indian subcontinent, however, followed a quite different course—almost a reverse progression from Europe. If Jain claims are correct, and their faith goes back to the Indus Valley civilization, one of the first world religions was a highly sophisticated belief system based on a single godhead and ethical principles that went far beyond those of the "Religions of the Book."

In ancient India, Jainism attracted many converts, including several powerful rulers, who ruled their kingdoms according to Jain principles of non-violence—a stark contrast to the jihads and crusades of Islam and Christianity. Jainism, despite its longevity, did not go unchallenged. In India it was overtaken by Buddhism, which emerged in the sixth century, and later by various Hindu cults. Although these religions preached tolerance, non-violence, and peaceful conversion, there were also instances of persecution and forced conversions. However, much worse was to come with the Muslim invasion of India that began in earnest in the eleventh century. Islam forbids the making of human images as idolatrous, and the Hindu, Buddhist, and Jain temples of India must have appeared to them like idolatry on steroids. They did not appreciate the subtleties of Jain philosophy, and they slaughtered Jain monks, demolished Jain temples, smashed Jain statues, and burned Jain libraries.

In 1931, farmers discovered a hoard of 18 Jain bronzes near the village of Chausa, Bihar State, in northeast India. Without any associated archaeological context, such as a burial or building, it is impossible to date exactly when, why, and by whom the pieces were buried. Even their date of manufacture is a matter of conjecture, some saying that the pieces are first or second century BCE, others claiming that they may be as late as the sixth century CE. I have opted for a middle-range date of around 300 CE, supported by John Cort's 2009 study *Framing the Jina*. Although this is long before the Muslim invasion, the bronzes may have been buried to protect them from desecration, perhaps at the hand of Hindus.

The hoard contains a *Dharma Chakra*, the Wheel of Life, a symbol shared by Buddhism and Jainism, supported by two *yakshi* (mythical female beings) standing on *makara* (mythical animals); a *Kalpavirksha*, a sacred wish-fulfilling tree; and 16 statues of the tirthankara, including Rishabha (traditionally fl. 7190 BCE), who is considered to be the founder of Jainism and of the mythical Ikshvaku Dynasty.

Rishabha is portrayed naked standing in the kayotsarga meditation pose, which remains the convention with Jain images of the tirthankara. Although not particularly ancient when compared to Jainism itself, the Chausa hoard represents some of the earliest extant sacred Jain bronzes from Bihar, which was also later famous for its production of Buddhist bronzes.

© Jarno Gonzalez Zarraonandia | Shutterstock.com

CIRCLE OF LIFE
The Dharmachakra is an important Jain symbol.

TREASURE

Burial goods

Hoards

Shipwrecks

Religious objects or places

Artworks

Gemstones

SILVER SERVICE: NEPTUNE DISH

ca. 410 CE

Circumstance of loss: Buried to protect it and never recovered

Rediscovery: Found by farmers plowing in a field in 1942

Historical significance: Confirmation of sophistication and wealth of Roman Britain

Value: $7,678 (in silver bullion)

The artistic and technical quality of the silver objects is outstanding, and though we do not know who owned them, it was probably a person or family of considerable wealth and high social status.

"The Milden Hall Treasure" (www.britishmuseum.org, retrieved March 27, 2013)

It took some time for the Romans to turn their full attention to the British Isles, but when they finally did decide to conquer the island frontier of northwestern Europe, they came in force, and they came to stay. In 55 and 54 BCE the great Julius Caesar (100–44 BCE), when he was engaged in the conquest of Gaul (now France), had led two smaller expeditions across the Channel. His second expedition installed pro-Roman rulers in southeast Britain but did not gain any territory for the Roman state, which was already fully engaged in absorbing the mutinous Gallic tribes.

After several abortive invasion attempts, the most bizarre of which was led by the mad, bad Emperor Caligula (12–41 CE), who, instead of taking his army across the Channel to subdue the Britons, had his men attack the sea and collect seashells, it was left to Caligula's successor, the lame, stuttering Claudius (10 BCE–54 CE) to launch (but not lead) a full-scale invasion in 43 CE. The Romans took a further four decades to pacify modern-day England and Wales, but they never conquered Caledonia (Scotland) or Hibernia (Ireland). In the Roman provinces of Britannia, however, the Romans built cities, roads, aqueducts, temples, bathhouses, and villas, inaugurating over three centuries of Pax Romana.

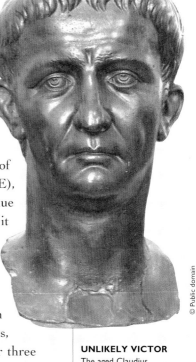

© Public domain

UNLIKELY VICTOR
The aged Claudius
conquered Britannia.

By the beginning of the fifth century, however, the western half of the empire was in deep crisis. Civil wars and barbarian invasions had fatally weakened the empire's defenses, and the shift of the empire's power base east to Constantinople, the new Christian capital, also acted to demoralize and weaken the Roman west. In 410, there were two momentous events in the west: The Visigoths sacked Rome, the first time the city had fallen in eight centuries, and the legions left Britain to fight in a continental campaign. The Roman Empire in the west itself only had another 66 years left, as its traditional demise is dated to the year 476 with the abdication of the last officially recognized western emperor.

Britain would share the fate of many of the empire's western provinces, experiencing a full-scale "barbarian" invasion — by Saxons, Angles, Jutes, and Frisians, who migrated across the North Sea from modern-day Holland, Germany, and Denmark. However, Roman civilization did not collapse overnight in Britain. The cities were fortified against the invaders, but the country houses of the super-rich were impossible to defend and had to be abandoned. With bands of barbarians marauding around the countryside, the owners of many fine villas buried their gold and silver treasures, hoping to retrieve them when the legions returned and restored order. The legions never came back, and Roman civilization slowly faded from the island.

THE NOT-SO-WILD NORTHERN FRONTIER

Up until fairly recently, many archaeologists did not think that the outer limits of the Roman Empire, such as the province Britannia, shared the same high culture and standard of living as the richer, more central provinces of Italy, Iberia (Spain), and Gaul. Britain was seen as a less developed military, industrial, and commercial outpost, conquered for its natural resources, in particular its tin and iron ore. While this was probably true for the lives of the soldiers stationed on the Caledonian frontier on Hadrian's or the Antonine walls, built to keep the marauding Picts (Scots) out of Roman Britain, the discovery of high-status buildings, such as the

DOLCE VITA
Hadrian's Wall marked the limits of Roman civilization.

Fishbourne Palace in West Sussex and the Thermal Baths in the city of Bath, and of several Roman hoards containing objects that would not have been out of place at the imperial and senatorial tables of Rome and Constantinople, has recast late Roman Britain as a place of high art and culture.

© Colipicto | Shutterstock.com

In 1942, at a time when Great Britain was embroiled with another continental "empire," the German Reich, two farmers plowing a field in Mildenhall, Suffolk, unearthed a collection of metal objects, whose origin and value they did not recognize. It was only after the war, in 1946, that they reported the find to the authorities, which declared the "Mildenhall treasure" to be a "treasure trove." What the two men had stumbled across was the most outstanding collection of Roman silverware found anywhere in the late-Roman world. The treasure consists of a complete service of Roman tableware decorated with elaborate mythological motifs: two large serving platters, two small decorated serving plates, a deep fluted bowl, a set of four large bowls, two small bowls, two pedestalled dishes, a deep flanged bowl with a domed cover, five ladles with dolphin-shaped handles, and eight long-handled spoons.

The most outstanding piece from the treasure is the "Neptune" or "Great Dish," so called because it has the head of the sea god Neptune at its center. Made by a master silversmith somewhere in the Mediterranean region in the fourth century, the solid silver dish measures 23⁴/₅ inches (60.5 cm) in diameter and weighs 18 pounds (8.25 kg), and would have been a splendid centerpiece for any grand feast, and on prominent display when not in use. The platter is covered in fine engraved and chased decoration set in two circles around the bearded head of the sea god.

The inner circle, bordered by scallop shells, consists of sea nymphs riding mythical marine creatures: a seahorse, triton, sea stag, and sea dragon. The outer frieze features Bacchus himself, holding a bunch of grapes and a staff known as a thyrsus and resting his foot on a panther. The god of wine and revelry, who was a favorite theme for Roman tableware, presides over dancing and drinking in his honor. The participants include Heracles, already so drunk that he has to be held up by two attendants, the goat-legged god Pan, and various satyrs, devotees, and musicians.

Although the decoration on the dishes is pagan, the spoons bear the Christ monogram "Chi-Rho," composed of two Greek letters X and R, suggesting the owner was probably a wealthy Christian. A further clue as to its origin is in the inscription "property of Eutherios" in Greek, scratched into the base of two of the smaller dishes. Eutherius was an official serving the last pagan Roman emperor, Julian the Apostate (331–63 CE), who tried to restore the ancient cults of Rome and challenge the dominance of the Church. One theory is that several or all of the dishes were a gift from Eutherius to a senior Roman officer based in Britannia, who after his retirement from the army, rather than building himself a villa in Gaul, Italy, or Greece, preferred to settle in the rolling hills of the Suffolk countryside.

TREASURE

Burial goods

Hoards

Shipwrecks

Religious objects or places

Artworks

Gemstones

"FIFTY SHADES OF GRAY": SUTTON HOO SHIP BURIAL

ca. 624 CE

Circumstance of loss: Burial of an Anglo-Saxon ruler

Rediscovery: Private archaeological excavation in 1939

Historical significance: Illustrates the sophistication of early Anglo-Saxon England

Value: "Barbarian" Anglo-Saxon England revealed

Mound 1 commemorates a fighting-man, whether pagan or Christian we do not know. I concur that Raedwald is a suitable contender, but do not put out of bounds some one of his immediate successors or their senior colleagues. Conversion did not, after all, affect the practice of laying the dead to rest fully clothed and supplied with weapons.

The Age of Sutton Hoo (1992) edited by Martin Carver

Ever since the Italian poet Petrarch (1304–74) first named it the "Dark Ages," the period from the fall of the Western Roman Empire in the late fifth century CE to the coronation of Charlemagne (742–814) as the first Holy Roman Emperor in Rome in 800 has not had a good press from historians. In *The History of the Decline and Fall of the Roman Empire* (1776–89), Edward Gibbon (1737–94) dismissed the whole period as so much "rubbish" hardly worth bothering with. It was as if those three centuries were some kind of dreadful aberration between classical antiquity and the Middle Ages, during which nothing of interest took place, no great art was produced or great literature written.

The idea that the Dark Ages was a period of illiterate barbarism, however, has been comprehensively revised. Rather than being "dark," the three centuries of what is now known more neutrally as the "Early Middle Ages," were merely "overcast," or maybe, to jump on a very fashionable bandwagon, "Fifty Shades of Gray." For one thing, classical civilization did not disappear from the Mediterranean world. Although Roman rule collapsed in Western Europe, to be replaced by a hotchpotch of barbarian kingdoms, the Eastern Roman Empire, with its capital in Constantinople (now Istanbul), continued to exist and to influence the West culturally, religiously, and militarily. Second, while the civilian administration disappeared, the Church, with its own bureaucratic structure of provinces, dioceses, and parishes, took up many of the functions of the imperial government, maintaining social order, literacy, and education.

Many of the "barbarians," who hastened the demise of the Western Empire, the Franks, Goths, and Vandals, had formerly been *foederati*, allies of the Roman state, employed as mercenaries, or invited to settle within the empire's borders to boost its falling populations. The Visigoths who sacked Rome in 401 CE, for example, had fought for Roman emperors, who had treated them so badly that they finally turned against their former allies and paymasters. Many barbarians had already forsaken their tribal gods for Christianity. The Visigoths, for example, were Arian Christians, a sect considered heretical in the empire, but Christians nevertheless, which meant that when they sacked Rome, they spared the Vatican, churches, shrines, and monasteries. The Visigothic ruling elite was to a degree literate and many had adopted Roman ways. They would have gladly integrated into Roman society had they been treated as equals by the Roman

GRAVE MARKER
The Anglo-Saxons built earth
mounds over burials.

population, but they were alienated by being treated as second-class subjects of the emperor who could never be as good as full Roman citizens, who were often of barbarian origin themselves, civilized in earlier conquests.

It was not the case, however, that all barbarians were equally well inclined toward Rome. While some tribes were Christian and allies of the empire, others were pagan and had no love for Roman rule or Roman ways. The Germanic and Scandinavian tribes that crossed the North Sea to Britain—the Saxons, Jutes, Angles, and Frisians—were pagans and inimical to Rome. They first came to English shores as raiders to plunder the coastal settlements, and then, after 410, when the legions had left never to return, they came to conquer and settle. They were not unopposed, however, and it took them several hundred years to take over the whole of England, destroying the last remnants of Roman civilization, and pushing the original Britons south and across the sea to Brittany, west into Wales, Cornwall, and Ireland, and north into Scotland.

The invaders established kingdoms in England, leaving us modern place names that speak of their ancient origins: East Anglia, the kingdom of the Angles, and the Saxon kingdoms of Sussex, Wessex, and Middlesex. The Church, which had been established in Britain in the first century, and survived in Ireland and Scotland, was not about to abandon England to paganism. In 597, Saint Augustine (d. ca. 604), the Apostle of the English, and the first Archbishop of Canterbury, arrived in England to reclaim the British Isles for Catholic Christianity.

The missionary drive was not entirely unopposed, however, and in the first decades of the seventh century there was a pagan backlash, when Christian clerics and missionaries were expelled from the kingdoms of Kent and Essex, which reverted to their old pagan ways. It is to this period of political and religious uncertainty between the different Anglo-Saxon kingdoms that made up the "Heptarchy" (seven realms) that we owe one of the most remarkable burials ever discovered in the British Isles, at Sutton Hoo, Suffolk, in East Anglia, kingdom of the East Angles.

Mention the term "ship burials," and many readers will imagine Viking longboats carrying the body of a dead chieftain, ablaze as it sails into the sunset. However, this has more to do with Hollywood imagination and SFX than real Norse burial customs. Although Norse chieftains were indeed sent to their eternal rest in ships—and real vessels in which they would have sailed, raided, and fought during their lifetimes—the longships were not set alight on the waters but buried in pits, and then topped by earthen mounds (known as barrows or tumuli). In Norse practice, the body was often cremated, which may have given filmmakers the idea for the flaming ship sailing into eternity.

Several of the peoples who migrated to Britain in the sixth century were of Norse-Germanic stock, and they brought with them burial practices from their original homes. The Angles came from what is now the northernmost state of Germany, Schleswig-Holstein, on the Baltic Sea, which was long the subject of a claim by Germany's immediate northern neighbor, Denmark. The dispute between the Danes and Germans during the nineteenth century, which became known as the "Schleswig-Holstein Question" was the Israeli–Palestinian conflict of its day, prompting the British premier Lord Palmerston (1785–1865) to exclaim in exasperation: "Only three people [...] have ever really understood the Schleswig-Holstein business—the Prince Consort, who is dead—a German professor, who has gone mad—and I, who have forgotten all about it."

The second Anglo-Saxon ruler to convert to Christianity was Rædwald (r. ca. 599–ca. 624), king of the East Angles, baptized around 605 at the court of King Æthelberht of Kent (ca. 560–616), who had been converted by Augustine a few years earlier. According to early British histories, his conversion brought him great military and political success: He became the fourth *bretwalda*, meaning "supreme ruler," or "high king." This was not equivalent to the current title of king or queen, which implies that the monarch rules over a united kingdom. Rædwald was a paramount king who received the fealty of all the other Anglo-Saxon rulers on the island. Nevertheless, the position entailed great power, prestige, and wealth.

SAILING INTO ETERNITY

© Mhardcastle | Creative Commons

WARRIOR BLING
The king's elaborate solid gold buckle.

The Anglo-Saxon graveyard at Sutton Hoo consists of 17 mounds, some of which had been opened and looted, but several of which were intact. The most impressive of the burials was discovered during a private archaeological dig, sponsored by the landowner, in 1939, but as soon as the importance of the find was revealed, it was taken over by a team of professional archaeologists. What became known as "Mound 1" contained the undisturbed burial of an Anglo-Saxon ruler thought to be King Rædwald of the East Angles and Anglo-Saxon England's fourth *bretwalda*.

ENGLAND'S TUTANKHAMUN

As with the discovery of Tutankhamun's (ca. 1341–ca. 1323 BCE) intact burial in 1922, there is a twofold value of the Sutton Hoo find: the material value of the treasures recovered, of course, and the historical value of their survival that revealed the arts, technologies, beliefs, and burial customs of a people who might be known from a few disparate items that survived the depredations of time, war, and looters. What was revealed at Sutton Hoo was far from confirming Edward Gibbon's disparaging notion that nothing of interest could ever be reclaimed from England's Dark Ages. Far from being dark, or even in "shades of gray," as I jokingly implied in my introduction, the courts of Anglo-Saxon England shone with the luster of gold, silver, and semi-precious gems; their lords wore gold brooches and belt clasps inlaid with garnets, to fasten textiles imported from Scandinavia, Gaul, and the Near East. These were far from being uncouth barbarians isolated from the greater world.

King Rædwald had been interred in an oak longboat 89 feet (27 m) long and 14 feet (4.4 m) wide, which would have been rowed by 40 oarsmen. Although the body had been dissolved by the acidic soil of the mound, the position of the burial goods and traces of phosphates in the ground indicated that the king had been interred and not cremated, as was the case in earlier pagan burials at the site. The fact that he had been buried, and the presence of two silver spoons with Greek inscriptions reading "Paulos" (Saint Paul) and "Saulos" (the Old Testament Saul), along with ten silver bowls made in the Eastern Roman Empire, suggests that this was a Christian burial, strengthening the identification of the deceased with the Christian Rædwald, yet with enough pagan elements to suggest that he was a convert and not born and raised a Christian.

Along with these Christian trappings were the helmet, armor, weapons, and jewelry of a mighty Anglo-Saxon king. The helmet and sword with its garnet cloisonné pommel were particularly magnificent. Made of intricately worked iron and bronze plaques fitted to an iron skull cap, the helmet also has a full facemask and long cheek pieces, complete with eyebrows picked out in garnets and a bronze mustache. The metal face that looks at us from a distance of almost 1,400 years is not so much frightening as severe and regal. His clothes were fastened with a great niello-inlaid gold buckle, and his cloak fastened with hinged gold-and-garnet shoulder clasps. A leather purse, with an intricate gold, garnet, and horn lid, which hung from the king's belt, contained 37 gold coins from different Frankish (French) mints, three blank gold coins, and two small gold ingots—money to pay the ferryman who would take the king to the afterlife, a pagan belief that had survived the coming of Christianity, and which was further evidence of Rædwald's pagan origins.

In addition to the king's personal accouterments, the burial chamber was packed with things that he might need in the afterlife: a mail coat—one of the few surviving from the period—several hanging bowls, including one elaborately decorated with champlevé enamels, a feather cushion, an iron ax, wooden platters, an Egyptian or Levantine bronze bowl, an Anglo-Saxon lyre in a beaver-skin bag, and many textiles—blankets, cloaks, and wall hangings—some of local manufacture, others imported from Scandinavia and the Near East.

© geni | Creative Commons

ROYAL VISAGE
The king's helmet had a fierce facemask.

TREASURE

Burial goods

Hoards

Shipwrecks

Religious objects or places

Artworks

Gemstones

THE KHAN'S GOLD: PERESHCHEPINA TREASURE
ca. 670 CE

Circumstance of loss: Hoard or burial of Kubrat, Khan of "Great Bulgaria"

Rediscovery: Found by accident in 1912 when a boy playing by a river fell into the hole where the treasure was buried

Historical significance: Evidence of the second wave of barbarian migrations

Value: $1,122,300 (in silver and gold bullion)

Bulgar groups appear in the late Roman sources as early as the late 400s. During the early 630s, an independent Bulgar polity was established in the steppe corridor to the east of the Sea of Azov under the rule of Kubrat. Later Byzantine chroniclers called that polity "Great Bulgaria."

The Other Europe in the Middle Ages (2008)
edited by Florin Curta and Roman Kovalev

When asked about the "barbarian invasions," my Western European readers will immediately think of the Germanic and Scandinavian tribes that migrated into the Roman Empire beginning in the fifth century CE, creating kingdoms that would one day become the regions and countries of modern Europe, whose names record their tribal origins: the Franks—France; the Angles—England and East Anglia; the Saxons—Saxony, Sussex, and Essex; and the Lombards—Lombardy. As was discussed in the previous entry, however, the term "invasion" needs to be qualified. Although there were barbarian incursions that were destructive raids for slaves and plunder, often the tribes had been employed as mercenaries by the Romans, and invited to settle in border provinces that had become depopulated. In this case the term "migration" is more appropriate.

The reasons for the mass migrations that continued for several centuries are not well understood. One theory suggests climate change as a possible driver for the mass movements of population to the west and south. Another well-supported theory is that the Central Europeans were displaced by people from further east—in other words, a barbarian "domino effect." The Franks, who settled in the Roman provinces of Gaul, came largely peacefully, and created a hybrid Romano-Gaulish-Frankish culture. The Anglo-Saxons (see previous entry) migrated to Britain after the Roman military had left, so rather than conquer in the conventional sense of the term, they came to fill a power vacuum.

The Western barbarian migration, however, was only the first wave of a phenomenon that lasted centuries and involved many different peoples. The second wave did not impact very much on Western Europe; hence, it does not form part of our historical consciousness in the same way as it does further east in Eastern Europe and the Balkans. The most significant of these peoples were the Avars, Khazars, and Bulgars, of Central Asian Turkic stock, which had been moving westward, probably displaced by other Asiatic tribes such as the Huns. As they moved west, they reached the borders of the Eastern Roman or Byzantine Empire, whose capital in Constantinople (now Istanbul) had taken over from Rome as the center of the civilized Christian world.

In the seventh century, however, the Byzantine Empire was not the self-confident world-conquering state that it once had been. Under the Emperor Justinian I (ca. 482–565), for example, the Byzantines had succeeded in reconquering large portions of the former Western Roman Empire, and in 627, Heraclius I (ca. 575–641) annihilated Byzantium's long-term enemy, Sassanian Persia. What the Byzantines could not have foreseen was the sudden emergence on the world stage of a completely new power that would transform the early medieval world: militant Islam. In the generation after the Prophet Muhammad's (ca. 570– ca. 632) death, Muslim armies conquered Syria (637) and Egypt (639), two of the empire's richest provinces, and in 674, they besieged the capital itself. It was only with the greatest difficulty that the Byzantines, sometimes allied with the Turkic tribes of the Black Sea and Caucasus, and sometimes at war with them, held the Arab armies at bay, and began to recover some of their lost territory and former self-confidence.

BULGAR KHAN AND BYZANTINE PATRICIAN

The Bulgars, whose name is commemorated in the Balkan nation-state of Bulgaria, originated from the open steppe north of the Black Sea and Azov Sea, in what is now the southern part of the Republic of Ukraine. It was there that Khan Kubrat (r. ca. 632–665) established the empire dubbed "Great Bulgaria" by his Byzantine contemporaries. Although Great Bulgaria did not survive its founder, it was a prelude for a much more successful and long-lasting First Bulgarian Empire in the former Byzantine Balkans in the heartland of the Odrysian kingdoms (see pp. 56–59).

Kubrat followed the pattern established by other barbarians in finding refuge at the court of a Roman or Byzantine emperor. When Heraclius was at the height of his power, and lauded as the new Julius Caesar (100–44 BCE) for his victory over Persia, he hosted Kubrat at his court in Constantinople, though whether he was an adult refugee from an internecine feud, or a child hostage sent to assure the good behavior of his father, is not entirely clear. According to the Byzantine chronicles of the time, he was baptized and given the aristocratic Byzantine rank of *patrikios* (patrician).

True to his alliance and his personal friendship with Alexius, Kubrat never made war on his Byzantine mentors and allies. When Kubrat died in 665, Alexius was also long dead, and the Byzantine Empire was being buffeted by Arab advances across the whole Mediterranean region. His own realm, divided between his warring sons, would fall to the Khazars soon after his death, but it endured long enough for one of his sons to give his father a burial befitting the ruler of an empire.

In 1912, a shepherd boy playing by a river near the Ukrainian village of Malaya Pereshchepina fell into a hole. When he was pulled out, his rescuers discovered a cache of 800 gold and silver objects, representing one of the largest treasures ever unearthed from the migration period. Opinions are divided whether the find represents evidence of a burial or a hoard, but the presence of a signet ring bearing Kubrat's monogram makes the former interpretation likely. As with the Sutton Hoo ship burial, the body could have decayed, but the archaeologists of the day did not have the scientific techniques that could have confirmed the existence of human remains from trace elements in the soil.

The find consisted of precious objects of Byzantine, Sassanian (Persian), Avar, Sogdian, Turkic, and Bulgar origins, consistent with a treasure collected as royal gifts and war booty over a long period. The gold items weighed over 45 pounds (21 kg) and the silver, some 110 pounds (50 kg). Among the gold artifacts were two 12-piece drinking sets, consisting of rhytons and serving vessels that the khan would have used when entertaining his guests. There was also a Byzantine dish with a Christian motif, and a Sassanian dish with a portrait of Shapur the Great (309–79).

Like the Anglo-Saxon burial at Sutton Hoo, the cache contained weapons fit for a powerful ruler, including swords and daggers, whose hilts and scabbards were elaborately worked and studded with gemstones; gold and silver accessories that the khan would have worn on his person, including a torque (neck ring), an earring, seven bracelets, and seven rings with inlays of amethyst, sapphire, tiger-eye, garnet, natural crystal, and emerald, and a massive gold belt buckle worn by Byzantine patricians weighing 14 ounces (400 g). Finally, the hoard included a necklace of gold Byzantine coins, ranging in date from the sixth to the mid-seventh centuries, to the reign of Alexius's successor Constans II (641–68), whom Kubrat would probably have met while he was living in Constantinople.

RIVER OF GOLD

TREASURE

Burial goods

Hoards

Shipwrecks

Religious objects or places

Artworks

Gemstones

THE VERY HUMAN ALIEN: PAKAL'S DEATH MASK

683 CE

Circumstance of loss: Burial of King Pakal of Palenque in the Temple of the Inscriptions

Rediscovery: Discovered in the king's intact burial chamber in 1952

Historical significance: Reveals the technological and artistic skills of the Maya

Value: Human skill

In short, the sarcophagus lid portrays Pakal ascending out of the maws of the underworld [...] Behind the king, who is portrayed as the deity Unen K'awiil in the position of being born into the otherworld, rises the World Tree, surrounded by the ether of the flowery otherworld, indicated by the many jewel-like emblems of k'ulel.

"The Tomb of K'inich Janaab Pakal" by Stanley Guenter

I recently caught the repeat showing of several episodes of the 2012 season of the History channel's *Ancient Aliens*. It assembles, in a truly breathtaking manner, the most half-baked pseudo-archaeological theories, ancient myths and legends from around the world, frauds long ago exposed, conspiracy theories, and deliberate misrepresentations of the historical facts, the whole punctuated by the constant refrain of "As ancient astronaut theorists believe...". The show romps through world history and archaeology making spurious connections between cultures thousands of miles and thousands of years apart, in a way that must make all serious archaeologists and historians apoplectic with barely controlled rage and must sometimes drive them to attack their TVs with blunt instruments.

Having watched the Maya doomsday prophecy episode (remember December 21, 2012 — the End of the World?), I treat the show for what it is: pure fiction and entertainment. As a teenager, I remember my enjoyment as I read Erich von Däniken's (b. 1935) equally fantastic books about the supposed contacts between our ancestors and aliens. One of the most absurd theories of the likes of von Däniken and other "ancient astronaut theorists" links the ornate, steep-sided, stepped temple platforms built by the Maya with the broad-based, undecorated Egyptian pyramids that were built as tombs. Apart from the striking differences in style, building techniques, decoration, and function, what really separates the Great Pyramid of Khufu (r. 2589–2566 BCE) in Giza and Pakal's Temple of the Inscriptions in Palenque completed around 683 CE is that they were built 3,239 years apart. We are much closer to the Classic Maya who lived a mere 1,500 years before us; therefore, we should investigate the Maya's secret influence on the building of the San Francisco Transamerica Pyramid!

The Classic Maya were a people who lived in an area that is now occupied by the southern Mexican state of Chiapas, and the countries of Guatemala, Honduras, and Belize. Between 250 and 900 CE, they famously built a civilization in Yucatán, an inhospitable region of Central America, which remains an undeveloped area of rainforests prone to yearly droughts, whose thin soils support less than half a million inhabitants. At its height, it is thought that Classic Maya civilization sustained a huge population of ten million; however, this was at considerable cost to its long-term survival.

Although the Maya overcame water shortages and droughts by building extensive networks of cisterns to store water during the dry season, ultimately, they could not provide enough food to feed their growing populations. One by one, the great ceremonial centers, studded with temple and palace complexes, were destroyed in wars over water, food, and land, or were abandoned when their citizens rebelled against their divine kings, or when everything ran out. The Maya migrated north, to establish a second, Post-Classic civilization that survived until the coming of the Spanish conquistadors in the sixteenth century.

TEMPORARILY MISLAID BUT NEVER LOST

The fantasy connection between the Old and New Worlds that explains the existence of tall pyramid-shaped structures in Egypt and Central America began in the eighteenth century, when European explorers speculated about the origins of Central American ruins, many of which had been known since the time of the Spanish Conquest. Looking at the Maya of their time, who were impoverished, uneducated, oppressed, and had been forcibly converted to Catholicism, their culture all but eradicated in the name of the one true god, Europeans refused to believe that these were the descendants of the builders of the Classic Maya cities. They suggested contacts with the Egyptians, Babylonians, and the lost tribes of wandering Israelites (a people not known for their pyramids, however).

DIVINE LORD
Bust of Ajaw Pakal of Palenque.

© Irafael | Shutterstock.com

The suppression of the Native American origins of the Maya sites suited the colonial administration that did not want its native population reminded of their glorious and warlike past. This colonialist, racist slur on the Maya has since morphed into ancient astronaut claptrap, which is equally racist—not just to Native Americans but to the entire human race, who were deemed incapable of developing their skills in mathematics, astronomy, art, and architecture, without a helping pseudopod from passing extraterrestrials.

While it is true that the locations of several Maya sites had been forgotten and were rediscovered by European explorers in the twentieth and twenty-first centuries, to say that the whole of Maya civilization was lost is going much too far. At worst, it was purposefully mislaid by a racist colonial administration. A full account of the history of the rise and fall of Pre-Classic, Classic, and Post-Classic Maya civilization is beyond the scope of this book. Its focus is on very special objects—treasures— that, given the right context, can teach us a great deal about the lives and beliefs of the people who made them.

Among the greatest sources of information available to archaeologists are burials, which give a secure context and date to objects that might otherwise be rediscovered in isolation, like the many hoards featured in this book. One of the most important Central American burials discovered thus far is the undisturbed grave of K'inich Janaab Pakal (603–83), *ajaw* (divine king) of the Classic Maya city of Palenque in Southern Mexico.

WRITTEN IN STONE

Pakal's burial chamber is unusual because it was discovered within the Temple of the Inscriptions. Although described as a pyramid, the temple is actually a broad-stepped platform, measuring 89 feet (27.2 m) high, 197 feet (60 m) wide, and 139 feet (42.5 m) deep, on top of which stands a temple 37 feet (11.4 m) high, 83 feet (25.5 m) wide, and 34 feet (10. 5 m) deep. Although burials were not uncommon within Maya plazas and temple complexes, the way these were constructed meant that burials were secondary to the true function of the building and often added after construction or during remodeling. In this they were quite distinct from Egyptian pyramids, whose function was exactly the same as an earth barrow or tumulus: to enclose and mark a high-status burial.

When they rebuilt or expanded the sacred centers of their cities, the Maya did not demolish a preexisting temple and level its base to start the new building from ground level but built on top of it, producing an architectural layer-cake effect. Temple buildings were probably considered too sacred to demolish and discard; hence, they too were ritually "killed" and "interred" within succeeding structures, which, over time, grew taller and more impressive. Archaeologists have long been aware of this practice, which explains why the Temple of the Inscriptions, which had been first seen by Europeans as early as 1567, was not investigated to see if it contained a tomb. The temple, however, is untypical in a number of ways. Pakal built it from scratch as his personal funerary monument, starting construction in 675, eight years before his death.

The king died before its completion, and soon after his death he was sealed into the unfinished burial chamber with a cache of rich offerings. His heir, however, continued to work on the external and internal decorations of the temple above the tomb, completing the scheme several years later. The temple owes its name to the second-longest extant hieroglyphic inscription in the Maya world, which records about 180 years of the city's history, of which 68 years had been under the stewardship of Pakal (amazingly without a single mention of alien visitors). In other words, the Temple of the Inscriptions was both a mausoleum and record in stone and stucco of the history of Palenque and its ruling dynasty. Sculpted bas-reliefs and stucco panels depict Pakal and his heirs in the guise of the patron deities of the city, in whose form, it was believed, he would be reborn after death.

Maya beliefs about the afterlives of their kings were as complex as those of the Egyptians about their pharaohs, but the Maya did not preserve the body of a deceased ruler as a mummy. The king's earthly body had served its purpose, and though it was buried in a splendid tomb, it was not supplied with the range and quantity of burial goods offered to a deceased pharaoh. Pakal would rise from the underworld and become an incarnate god who would watch over his native city as he had in life. His spirit, however, was somehow tied to his mortuary temple, because the burial chamber, although the 82 feet (25 m) access stairwell had been blocked with tons of rubble, was

TRANSFORMATION
Pakal rises from the
Underworld as the
Maize God.

equipped with a "psychoduct," a narrow tube-like passage through which the king's spirit could leave the tomb to be reborn as a god, and maybe also to be in contact with his descendants.

ESCAPING THE JAWS OF THE UNDERWORLD SERPENT

It took archaeologist Alberto Ruz (1906–79), who discovered a mysterious stairwell descending into the interior of the temple, almost four years to remove the rubble that blocked it, reaching an intact limestone door at the bottom. What he found beyond the door astonished him, because it was one of the first royal burials to be excavated from this type of building. He described it as a "huge magic grotto carved out of ice, the walls sparkling and glistening like snow crystals." The most famous discovery was the massive limestone sarcophagus, whose lid represents the deceased Pakal.

The conventional interpretation of the image, in keeping with many other depictions of Maya rulers in both life and death, is that the king is pictured as an incarnation of the Maize God, curled up in the fetal position and emerging from the underworld, represented by the open mouth of a giant snake, with the world tree above him leading into the sky. The "Truth-is-out-there-but-the-government-hushes-it-up" version is that Pakal is an alien riding a spacecraft back to his home planet. Strangely, however, among the many thousands of bas-reliefs of kings from the Classic Maya period, this is the only one that has been interpreted in this way.

The burial chamber was filled with rich offerings, including jade and shell ornaments, brightly painted ceramic plates and vessels, and a stucco head of the king. Pakal lay undisturbed within the huge sarcophagus, his body adorned not with gold as was the custom in Egypt and Peru, but with a jade mask made of 200 separate pieces, with jade and shell earplugs, jade pendants, necklaces, bracelets, and rings. In his right hand, he held a squared piece of jade, and in his left a jade sphere.

Mesoamerican jade is jadeite, which is an extremely hard mineral that is difficult to work, especially without the aid of metal tools. Maya craftsmen showed their skill and ingenuity by creating objects such as Pakal's death mask using tools made of jade, bone, wood, leather, and cord. The most prized jadeite was a deep green color, which symbolized longevity, as the material does not degrade with age, and has the green of new plant growth. Hence, the gemstone represented Pakal's immortality and his imminent rebirth as a god.

© John Mitchell | Alamy

LIVING STONE
Green jade symbolized
life and rebirth.

TREASURE

Burial goods

Hoards

Shipwrecks

Religious objects or places

Artworks

Gemstones

MERCIAN ENIGMA: STAFFORDSHIRE HOARD

ca. 700 CE

Circumstance of loss: Buried by its owner to protect it

Rediscovery: Found by an amateur metal detectorist in 2009 in a field

Historical significance: Largest Anglo-Saxon hoard ever found

Value: $5 million

The Staffordshire hoard is evidence that Mercian kings preyed on each other, a fact in keeping with what is known about the struggle for supremacy in the region before Offa. The hoard includes Christian objects, showing Christian rulers fought each other and plundered sacred objects from each other's churches and treasuries.

Anglo-Saxon Keywords (2012) by **Allen Frantzen**

We first visited England in 624 CE, to explore the Anglo-Saxon ship burial of Sutton Hoo (pp. 108–113), dated from a period in the British Isles when Christianity fought to re-establish itself after a 200-year pagan interlude. This visit takes us to the late seventh century when, in theory, the whole of the island had been converted. Yet while all the kingdoms of Britain were officially Christian, there were pagan remnants among the population that would not be reconciled with the church for generations. Among the last kingdoms to abandon paganism was Mercia, situated in what is now the heartland of England, the Midlands. The name Mercia indicates that the kingdom was on the borders, or "marches," of Anglo-Saxon England.

Mercia formed part of what is traditionally known as the "Heptarchy," the seven kingdoms of Anglo-Saxon England, along with Northumbria to the north, and Kent, East Anglia, Essex, Sussex, and Wessex to the south. More recent historical scholarship has recast this rather simple political map of Anglo-Saxon England by adding several other kingdoms, which, although much smaller and sometimes absorbed by their larger neighbors, nevertheless played a significant role in English history. In addition to these Anglo-Saxon rivals, to the west and north were the descendants of the "first Britons," the Scots, Irish, Cornish, and Welsh, who maintained their independence, in the case of Scotland and Ireland, for centuries after the union of England and Wales in the thirteenth century.

During the reign of Rædwald of East Anglia (r. ca. 599–ca. 624), one of the most likely candidates for the deceased king honored at Sutton Hoo, the southern kingdoms were in the ascendant, and their kings held the title of *bretwalda* (high king) of the Anglo-Saxons; by the eighth century, however, there had been a shift of power northward, to the kingdoms of Mercia and Northumbria, which jockeyed for supremacy for the next century. In 633 the pagan King Penda of Mercia (r. ca. 630–55) fought and lost against the Christian king and bretwalda Edwin of Northumbria (585–633), but in 633, Penda defeated and killed his northern rival. In 655, it was Penda's turn to face defeat and death at the hands of another Northumbrian, King Oswig of Bernicia (ca. 612–70). The two kingdoms continued to fight, involving their Anglo-Saxon and Welsh neighbors, through the next century, but neither ever managed to overcome the other.

If the history of the Heptarchy is beginning to resemble the plotline of George R. R. Martin's (b. 1948) *A Game of Thrones* (novel, 1996; TV series,

2011), it's because, like many other fantasy epics since *The Lord of the Rings* (novels, 1954–55; movies, 2001–2003), it is in part inspired by the epic Anglo-Saxon poem *Beowulf*, composed between the eighth and eleventh centuries, which combines the political and military exploits of kings and warriors with supernatural dealings with witches and monsters.

Ultimately, both Mercia and Northumbria fell prey to the Norse, popularly known as the Vikings. Although some of the original Anglo-Saxons were themselves of Norse (Danish) descent, they had been separated from their Scandinavian cousins for centuries, had become Christian, and had developed their own language, Old English, and a distinct Anglo-Saxon cultural identity. The Vikings plundered coastal settlements and monasteries from the late eighth to the mid-ninth centuries and later occupied large parts of Mercia, East Anglia, and Northumbria, an area that became known as the Danelaw (886–954). The final act in the saga of Anglo-Saxon England, which had begun in the early fifth century with the departure of the Romans, was the death of the last Anglo-Saxon king, Harold Godwinson (ca. 1022–66), who was defeated and killed at the Battle of Hastings ("Bayeux Tapestry," pp. 136–139) by the first Norman king of England, William I, the "Conqueror" (ca. 1028–87).

MILITARY BLING

The quick history lesson above is an attempt to give a context to the Staffordshire hoard—the largest cache of Anglo-Saxon gold and silver yet discovered—found in 2009 by an amateur treasure hunter with a metal detector when he was surveying a recently plowed field in the village of Hammerwich, near the town of Lichfield, Staffordshire. The record find consists of 3,500 fragments of many hundreds of different objects, to which another 81 smaller fragments were added after an investigation of the site in 2012. The artifacts have been tentatively dated to between the sixth and eighth centuries, and are of local manufacture, though the raw materials—11 pounds (5 kg) of gold, 2.9 pounds (1.3 kg) of silver, and 26 garnets—would have come from Europe and maybe even Asia.

Apart from two crosses, one bent out of shape, and a gold strip inscribed with a Latin quote from the Old Testament: "SURGE DNE DISEPENTUR INIMICI TUI ET FUGENT QUI ODERUNT TE A FACIE TUA" ("*Surge Domine et dissipentur inimici tui et fugiant qui oderunt te a facie tua,*" "Rise up, Lord; may Your enemies be scattered and those who hate You be driven from Your face."), the remainder of the objects are what would today be described as "military bling"—decorations made for weaponry and other accessories worn by high-status warriors. The hoard contains no eating and drinking utensils or items of female jewelry.

Of particular note among the artifacts are gold and silver decoration that would have adorned helmets and weaponry, in particular swords. The iron sword was the Anglo-Saxon warrior's weapon of choice, and high-status swords would have been richly ornamented. The hoard contains no sword blades, but it does boast the largest and finest collection of Anglo-Saxon gold and silver sword pommels, hilt plates, and a hollow gold sword pyramid, weighing 0.56 ounces (15.88 g), decorated with cloisonné garnets and blue glass. Once one of a pair, the pyramid would have been attached to a "peace band," a leather strap tied around a sword hilt to prevent a warrior from drawing his sword in anger—a primitive form of safety catch.

LUCKY SEVEN
Mercia was one of the Anglo-Saxon Heptarchy.

The questions that researchers have been asking about the hoard since 2009, are: "Why?," "From where?," and "By whom?" With little or no archaeological context, it is extremely difficult to reconstruct the date, circumstances, and function of the hoard's burial. Unlike the Villena treasure (pp. 40–43), there is no ceramic container that could be used to date the deposit, and unlike the Pereshchepina treasure (pp. 114–117), there are no handy signet rings identifying the probable owner. In this respect, it is much more like the isolated, anonymous deposit made at Panagyurishte (pp. 56–59).

The first clue to the origins of the objects is where they were found. In the Anglo-Saxon period, Staffordshire would have been in the western part of the Kingdom of Mercia, and the Lichfield was one of the kingdom's leading Christian centers. The second significant clue is that the hoard was buried on the south side of Watling Street, the main thoroughfare of Anglo-Saxon Britain and formerly a paved Roman road, which started in Kent, passed through London, and terminated in south Wales. In the ninth century it formed the boundary between Anglo-Saxon England and the Danelaw.

The date of the contents and location of the hoard rule out Viking involvement. The Vikings began raiding the northeast coast of Britain in 793, and it took them another 77 years to reach the eastern part of Mercia. The western location of the hoard, on the main road to Wales, suggests Anglo-Saxon or Welsh raiders fleeing along Watling Street with their booty. There is a passage in *Beowulf* that describes the stripping of decorations of swords of vanquished enemies to depersonalize them. Alternatively, the ornaments could have been taken from a treasury in Lichfield along with the Christian crosses. A pursuing Mercian force might have been on the point of overtaking them, and rather than risk losing the treasure, the raiders may have buried it to be collected later.

Alternatively, the hoard might have been the treasure of a Mercian king, who was fleeing after being defeated. Yet a third possibility is that the cache was a votive offering made by pagans. This could explain why one of the crosses was bent out of shape. But other historians have argued that this is far too great an amount of treasure to be offered to the gods, and that even Christians might have bent the large ornamental cross so that it took up less room when being transported and hidden.

Whatever its exact origins and functions, the Staffordshire hoard gives us yet another example of the superb technical skills and artistic virtuosity of the Anglo-Saxon craftsmen of the "Dark Ages." Like the treasures of Sutton Hoo, it reveals an age, which though much more violent and militaristic than the previous period of *Pax Romana*, was perfectly capable of appreciating and creating beautiful, high-status objects.

SACRED WASTE HEAP: MOGAO LIBRARY CAVE

ca. 1030

TREASURE

Burial goods

Hoards

Shipwrecks

Religious objects or places

Artworks

Gemstones

Circumstance of loss: The library cave was sealed at the beginning of the eleventh century either because it was full or to protect the contents from destruction

Rediscovery: A Chinese Daoist monk restoring the caves found the entrance in 1900

Historical significance: The most important collection of Buddhist and lay manuscripts from China and Central Asia dated from the sixth to eleventh centuries

Value: £220 sterling in 1907

The Library Cave, as it would come to be known, is one of the greatest treasure troves of information ever found. Sealed in the early eleventh century, it contained up to fifty thousand documents—no one is sure of the exact number.

Cave Temples of Mogao (2000) by Susan Whitfield and Neville Agnew

We have featured several important religious treasures in earlier entries: from Judaism ("Ark of the Covenant," pp. 44–50; "Dead Sea Scrolls," pp. 87–92), Christianity ("Holy Grail," pp. 79–86), and classical paganism ("Venus de Milo," pp. 93–99), as well as bronzes associated with what is thought to be the world's oldest extant religion, Jainism ("Chausa hoard," pp. 100–103). This entry features the third major world faith to emerge from India after Hinduism and Jainism, Buddhism, founded in the sixth century BCE by Siddhartha Gautama (ca. 563–ca. 483 BCE), the Buddha—a relative latecomer on the Indian religious scene. But in world terms, Buddhism long predates the current most populous religions: Christianity and Islam.

Buddhism, like Jainism, was once considered a heterodox sect of Hinduism with which it shares many beliefs and practices. All three faiths have similar notions of the endless cycle of life, death, and rebirth through which souls must pass, subject to the unbreakable law of cause and effect, karma. Although the three faiths vary in their understanding of the nature of the soul and of godhead, all three offer to their followers a means of escaping reincarnation as an animal or human by teaching them how to settle their karmic accounts for good. This enables humans to attain enlightenment and continue to the next stage of spiritual development.

Whereas Hinduism is a complex amalgam of religious cults, gods and goddesses, philosophical schools, and ascetic and spiritual practices, Buddhism offers a much more straightforward explanation of the human condition and a single path to achieve enlightenment through moral precepts, supplemented by meditation. Although the teachings of the Buddha, the "Four Noble Truths" and the "Eightfold Path," appear very simple, they are based on an extremely sophisticated understanding of human psychology and equally challenging metaphysical concepts about the nature of reality and divinity. These are set out in the Buddhist sutras, which again are deceptively short texts. Buddhism, for all its claim to simplicity, has generated thousands of pages of commentaries since the fifth century BCE, first in India, and then in the highly literate cultures it encountered on its way eastward.

Originating in northern India, Buddhism first established itself in native land. From 322 to 185 BCE, the Maurya Dynasty succeeded in uniting the greater part of the Indian subcontinent, including most of the present-day

Republic of India, and parts of Pakistan and Bangladesh, with only the southern tip of India and Sri Lanka as independent client kingdoms. After a particularly bloody campaign against the Kingdom of Kalinga in eastern India, the Emperor Ashoka (304–232 BCE) converted to Buddhism and promised to rule according to Buddhist precepts of universal compassion to all living beings and non-violence.

He propagated the faith in India, erecting Buddhist monuments all over his vast empire, including the famous iron pillars, one of which has survived rust-free in Delhi for over two millennia. He also engaged in a massive program of public works: building roads and irrigation projects, hospitals, public inns, and universities. In a country that was then as it is still now riven by ethnic, religious, and caste differences, Ashoka treated all his subjects equally. Like the first Christian Emperor Constantine (ca. 272–337 CE) would do centuries later, Ashoka convened a council of the Buddhist *Sangha* (community) in 250 BCE. He also saw it as part of his mission to spread Buddhism throughout the world, and he dispatched missionaries west to the Mediterranean, north to Central Asia, south to Sri Lanka, and east to Burma.

Ashoka's missions to the West did not bear fruit. Although missionaries traveled to the courts of Alexander the Great's (356–323 BCE) successors in Persia and the Near East, they do not seem to have made any lasting converts. The missions to the north, south, and east, however, were far more fruitful. Sri Lanka and Burma were converted and from there Buddhism was disseminated throughout Southeast Asia. Central Asia also welcomed Buddhism, which would remain the area's religion until the coming of Islam in the medieval period. From Central Asia, the missionaries followed the Silk Road to China, where Buddhism was granted imperial patronage in 67 CE, and with it, the establishment of the first Buddhist temple in China in the then imperial capital of Luoyang in Henan Province.

Although at first Buddhist iconography in East Asia followed Central Asian models that were influenced by both Indian and Hellenistic art, it quickly became completely acculturated. It was in East Asia that Buddhism was to know its greatest flowering, and it remains the main religion of Tibet and Mongolia, and an important religion in China, Korea, and Japan. East Asia developed its own distinct schools of Buddhism, notably *Chan* (*Son* in Korea and *Zen* in Japan), Lotus school, and Pure Land Buddhism.

Chinese Buddhism has given the world some of its most extraordinary religious architecture and monuments: colossal statues carved out of cliff faces and natural and manmade caves, decorated with vividly colored murals and filled with thousands of statues of Buddhas, Bodhisattvas, and other supernatural beings from the Buddhist pantheon. The most famous of these, the Mogao Caves, also known as the Dunhuang Caves, are located near the Oasis of Dunhuang, Gansu Province, northwestern China, which was an important staging post on the overland trade route that linked China with the Western world.

Qin Shi Huang (259–210 BCE), the master of the buried Terracotta Army (pp. 60–66), was the first emperor of a united China. His dynasty, however, barely survived him, and within two years of his death, the first Chinese empire was overthrown by rebellions that quickly developed into civil wars between rival claimants to the throne. His son had just enough time to bury his father before being deposed. The real beneficiary of Qin Shi Huang's conquests was Liu Bang (later Emperor Gao; ca. 250–195 BCE), who defeated his rivals and established China's longest-lasting dynasty, the Han (206 BCE–220 CE), whose four centuries are roughly contemporaneous with the heyday of the Roman Republic and Empire.

In the second century BCE, Emperor Han Wudi (r. 141–87 BCE) expanded west into Central Asia, moving against the nomadic Xiongnu, who had created an empire in what are now Mongolia, Siberia, and Manchuria, which threatened the survival of the Han state. In 121 BCE Wudi's armies defeated the Xiongnu, and in 111 BCE the Chinese established Dunhuang as a garrison town to protect the new western provinces of the empire, and as a staging post for further conquests of the Tarim Basin. The pacification of the region opened up one of the most important networks of overland trade routes in world history, known collectively as "the Silk Road," thus called because silk and other Chinese manufactures were transported along it to the Mediterranean. The Silk Road started in Xi'an, had two main routes through Central Asia, with two branches heading south into India, then crossed Persia and the Near East, where it terminated in the Roman city of Syrian Antioch (now in Turkey not far from the modern Syrian border).

The Silk Road was much more than a trade route; it served as a major conduit for the transmission of ideas. Among the most far-reaching intellectual exchanges that it facilitated was the transmission of Buddhism from Central to East Asia in the first centuries CE, just when Buddhism was beginning to lose influence in India. For the Chinese, the oasis of Dunhuang represented a wild frontier town and the outer limits of the "Middle Kingdom" beyond which there were only uncivilized "barbarians," but to the peoples of Central Asia, it represented the gateway into one of the oldest, most advanced, and wealthiest civilizations on earth.

Between the fourth and fourteenth centuries, Buddhist monks excavated hundreds of cave temples around Dunhuang, the most famous being the 492 Mogao cave temples, situated 16 miles (25 km) southeast of the oasis. The caves were not small, isolated hiding places like the caves in which the Dead Sea Scrolls had been hidden to protect them from the Romans; these were large temples, with grand ceremonial gateways and façades, and colossal statues of the Buddha, all splendidly decorated with brightly colored murals.

CAVE OF WONDERS

During the late Tang Dynasty (618–907), Buddhism reached the peak of influence in China but at a great cost to its long-term survival. Native Confucians and Daoists engineered a nationalist reaction against Buddhism, describing it as an imported religion. As a result, the Buddhist clergy lost many of their privileges, and the Chinese *Sangha* suffered a persecution at the hands of the imperial government in 845. Although Buddhism survived in China, it never recovered the influence and wealth that it had enjoyed during the early Tang Dynasty, when Dunhuang knew its greatest period of expansion, with the building of new temples funded by imperial and aristocratic patronage.

BARGAIN HUNTER
Pelliot acquired priceless manuscripts for a few hundred dollars.

The Mogao temples, distant from the centers of Chinese civilization, did not suffer persecution or damage, but after Islam overtook Central Asia, and direct maritime routes replaced the overland Silk Road to the West, Dunhuang quickly lost its commercial and cultural importance. By the beginning of the twentieth century, most of the temples had been abandoned, and many had filled with sand and debris. In the late nineteenth century, a local

© Gamma-Keystone via Getty Images

LIBRARIAN
Wang worked to preserve
the caves and their treasures.

Daoist priest, Wang Yuanlu (ca. 1849–1931), appointed himself abbot and caretaker of the temples. In 1900, while restoring Cave 16, Wang noticed a sealed door that led into another cave, Cave 17, which would become known as the "Library Cave." While the Qumran caves that held the Dead Sea Scrolls yielded less than a thousand documents, this single cave was packed with around 50,000 ancient manuscripts dating from 402 to 1002, as well as textiles, banners, statuettes, and ritual paraphernalia, all crammed together so tightly that there was barely room for two men to stand in the remaining space.

The Library Cave manuscripts are mostly written in Chinese, but there are also documents in other Central Asian languages, including the earliest known texts in Tibetan, as well as Khotanese, Turkic, Uyghur, and Sogdian. Many of the manuscripts were previously unknown or were thought to have been lost. They provided unique insight into the religious and secular life of China and the Central Asian kingdoms in the first millennium. As in Qumran, most of the manuscripts are religious works, with the majority being Buddhist, including important sutras and the earliest known printed versions of the *Diamond Sutra*, dated 868, as well as learned Buddhist commentaries, monastic workbooks, and prayer books. The find revolutionized the understanding of the historical development of Chan (Zen) Buddhism and of mainstream and esoteric Tibetan Buddhism. Texts from other faiths were also found in the cave, including Confucian, Daoist, Nestorian Christian, Jewish, and Manichaean manuscripts.

In addition to the religious texts, the cave also held many lay documents covering an astonishing variety of topics, including books of Chinese folk songs; musical and dance notation; a manual for the board game *go*; classical Chinese poetry; official and local histories; dictionaries; and textbooks on geography, medicine, astronomy, mathematics, and divination. The manuscripts record the political and cultural life of the time, providing first-hand evidence of the secular concerns of the region and a rare glimpse into the lives of ordinary people.

There are two main theories about why the cave was sealed sometime after 1002. The Hungarian-born British explorer Aurel Stein (1862–1943) believed that the cave was used to store sacred texts and ritual paraphernalia that could not be burned or discarded as ordinary trash. This would have included handwritten copies of the sutras that had been replaced by printed versions, as well as copies worn out from overuse. A related theory was that the cave was used as an archive over several centuries and was sealed off when it became full. The French Sinologist Paul Pelliot (1878–1945) disagreed with Stein and saw the cave as a hiding place when the rising power of the Western Xia Dynasty (1038–1227) threatened Dunhuang in the 1030s. An earlier invasion threat by Muslims who had destroyed the Central Asian Buddhist kingdom of Khotan in 1006 could also have prompted the monks to seal off the cave to prevent the destruction of the manuscripts.

Wang, though revered for finding the Library Cave, is also reviled for selling tens of thousands of manuscripts to Stein and Pelliot, as well as to Japanese and Russian explorers. In his defense, Wang had spent seven years trying to persuade the Chinese authorities to fund the conservation of the caves and their precious contents, and only when this was not forthcoming did he agree to sell to Stein and Pelliot. He sold around 14,000 manuscripts to Stein for £120, and another 10,000 to Pelliot for £90, earning a grand total of £220, which though a considerable sum at the turn of the century in Central Asia, was nowhere near their true value.

As with the Dead Sea Scrolls, there is an ongoing dispute over their ownership, ranging the European and Japanese institutions that own many of the rarest pieces against the Chinese government, which claims that they were stolen and demands their return as priceless cultural artifacts belonging to the Chinese people. Pending a decision on the fate of the scrolls, the International Dunhuang Project, established in 1994 under the aegis of the British Library in London, is working to conserve, catalog, and digitize the huge collection of ancient manuscripts found in Mogao and other sites in the Dunhuang region.

MULTILINGUAL
The cave held texts in many languages, including Hebrew.

© Public domain

TREASURE

Burial goods

Hoards

Shipwrecks

Religious objects or places

Artworks

Gemstones

MEDIEVAL COMIC STRIP: BAYEUX TAPESTRY

1105

Circumstance of loss: Feared lost in a fire in 1105

Rediscovery: Reappeared in an inventory of the Cathedral in 1476

Historical significance: A first-hand account of the Norman Conquest of England

Value: One of the world's best propaganda coups

A long, narrow hanging that is suspended around the nave on the Feast of Relics, on which are embroidered a number of figures and inscriptions depicting the Conquest of England.

Description of the tapestry in the 1476 inventory of the treasures of Bayeux Cathedral (www.normandie-heritage.com, retrieved April 22, 2013)

The English proudly boast that, compared to their continental neighbors, they have seldom been invaded and occupied by foreign invaders. While this holds true for most of the second millennium CE, during the first, the British Isles experienced major invasions and migrations, starting with the Romans, followed by the Anglo-Saxons and the Norse—and not forgetting the Welsh, Picts (Scots), and Irish, who regularly invaded and raided Anglo-Saxon lands. Although the Anglo-Saxons were forced to cede eastern England to the Norse Danelaw (886–954), they held on, sandwiched between the Norse and Welsh. The political and military disasters of the ninth and tenth centuries forced the Anglo-Saxons to make common cause as never before, establishing something close to a united kingdom (small "u" and "k") of England, anticipating the later United Kingdom (capital "U" and "K"), which would include England, Wales, Scotland, and Ireland.

© Public domain

DISTANT COUSINS
William of Normandy was of the same Norse stock as the Anglo-Saxons.

The political situation in England in the eleventh century was extremely complex. There were several claimants to the throne, reflecting the cultural diversity of the islands. The Norse, who had once ruled an empire that included Scandinavia and large parts of the British Isles, claimed the Crown; the Anglo-Saxons who had been rallied by Alfred the Great (849–99), were ruled by the childless Edward the Confessor (ca. 1003–66); and there was another claimant in the person of William, Duke of Normandy (ca. 1028–87), who had persuaded Edward to name him as his successor. When Edward died, one of the leading Anglo-Saxon earls, Harold Godwinson (ca. 1022–66) was chosen to succeed him, but both the Norse and the Normans immediately contested his accession.

The Normans, whose power base was Normandy, a northern French peninsula that points like an accusing finger toward the British Isles, were also originally of Germanic-Norse stock. They had come as raiders in the early tenth century and settled in northern France, where they had become Christian and rebellious feudal vassals of the French king. However, their origins made them distant cousins of the Anglo-Saxons, who themselves had migrated to England from Germany and Denmark in

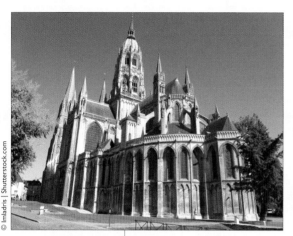

© Imladris | Shutterstock.com

HOUSE OF GOD
The tapestry was used to decorate Bayeux Cathedral.

the fifth century. When Harold was crowned king, William prepared to invade to make good his own claim. But just as the Normans made ready to attack from the south, King Harald Hardrada of Norway (ca. 1015–66) led his own invasion across the North Sea to northeastern England.

Harold led an English army north, defeated and killed Harald and put an end to the Norse claims on the English throne for good, but was immediately forced to march south to face the Normans. The fateful battle between Harold and William took place on October 14, 1066, at Hastings on the Kent coast. At first, the Anglo-Saxons on the higher ground had the advantage over the heavily armored Norman knights, but when Harold was fatally struck in the eye by an arrow, his army was routed. William I was crowned at Westminster Abbey, hailed as "the Conqueror of England."

ONE IN THE EYE FOR LES ANGLAIS

To say the "French" beat the "English" at the Battle of Hastings is a historical anachronism, because there really wasn't any such thing as a French or English national identity at the time. In a sense, both the Anglo-Saxons and the Normans were interlopers in the lands they had settled in England and France. If there were any real "English" and "French," they were the Celtic peoples who had been pushed to the margins of both countries: the Bretons, the Cornish, and the Welsh. But as the Normans completed the conquest of England, it was the Anglo-Saxons who portrayed themselves as the dispossessed "English," and a century later, it would be the Normans' turn to become the "English" when they fought the Welsh and Scots.

Central to the Norman claim to legitimacy was a unique piece of medieval propaganda known in Norman French as the *Telle du Conquest*, better known as the Bayeux Tapestry, which tells the story of the conquest from the death of Edward to the coronation of William. Commissioned by William's half-brother, Bishop Odo of Bayeux (ca. 1035–97), for his new cathedral church, Notre-Dame de Bayeux, consecrated in 1077, the tapestry is actually a giant piece of embroidery hand-stitched with eight colored woolen yarns onto nine linen panels sewn together, and measuring a total of 231 feet (70 m) long by 20 inches (50 cm) wide.

History's first "comic strip" features 49 trees, 41 ships and boats, 37 castles and buildings, 505 species of animals, including dogs, mules, and horses, a cast of 626 assorted kings, courtiers, clerics, and warriors, and the first Western depiction of a comet. Such an ancient artwork comes with its fair share of unsolved mysteries, such as a scene of a priest striking a woman (an early English royal scandal?), and the presence of ribald naked men in the tapestry's border. There are also rumors of a missing panel that came after the coronation scene, as well as heavy-handed restorations that several scholars have interpreted as attempts to edit the narrative to suit the propaganda needs of later ages. Although the tapestry was made for a Norman cathedral, it was probably stitched in the south of England, probably in Winchester or Canterbury. In an age when few laymen could read, the tapestry was an inspired piece of royal propaganda, depicting the official Norman version of the conquest.

The tapestry has had an eventful existence since 1077. It was feared destroyed during the siege of Bayeux of 1105, when part of the cathedral burned down and when a possible last panel might have been destroyed. However, the tapestry resurfaces in a fifteenth-century inventory (see quote above, p. 136), when it was used on feast days to decorate the knave of the cathedral. It survived the Hundred Years War (1337–1453), the French Wars of Religion (1562–98), during which Protestant zealots destroyed the tomb of William the Conqueror, and was almost lost twice during the French Revolution (1789–1803), the first time in 1792, when soldiers leaving for the front wanted to use it to cover their supply wagons, and the second time when it was almost cut up to provide decorations for a float used in a revolutionary festival in 1794. In 1803, Napoleon I (1769–1821) ordered the tapestry to be displayed in the Louvre Museum in Paris to gain support among the French population for his planned invasion of England. Finally, before returning to be displayed in its hometown of Bayeux, the tapestry narrowly escaped being looted by the retreating Germans in 1944.

© Getty Images

LAST SUPPER
King Harold feasting before his fateful defeat at Hastings.

NATIONAL TREASURES: IMPERIAL JAPANESE REGALIA

1185

Circumstance of loss: Presumed lost during a sea battle

Rediscovery: One or more of the items may have been recovered after the battle

Historical significance: The regalia was used to legitimize the imperial succession

Value: Legitimacy

When Amaterasu's grandson was sent down to earth to become the first emperor, she presented him with three gifts, to this day regarded as the Japanese Imperial Regalia, namely a bronze mirror, a sword, and a curved jewel.

Understanding Japanese Society (2013) by Joy Hendry

In the West, the traditional representation of a reigning monarch has the king or queen wearing a crown—either a plain gold circlet, or a more elaborate gem-studded creation like the Imperial State Crown that is used in the coronation of British monarchs. The symbolic link between monarchy and the crown is so strong that "The Crown" stands for the royal family and the monarchical system of government as a whole. Hence, in the United Kingdom, members of the queen's government are known as "ministers of the Crown." In European usage, the crown forms part of the royal regalia, which includes other items symbolic of regal power such as a sword, an orb, and a scepter. By its association with monarchs believed to reign by "divine right," the items of the regalia themselves become objects imbued with enormous symbolic and religious power. When the succession to the throne is contested, possession of the regalia can be seen as ensuring the legitimacy of a particular claimant.

Imperial or royal regalia does not always include a crown. Although the ancient Greeks and Romans had kings and emperors, they did not crown them. In ancient Rome, the color purple, the most expensive dye known in antiquity, was reserved for imperial and senatorial use, and though Roman emperors wore crown-like diadems and tiaras, what really symbolized their legitimate imperial status was being *porphyrogenitus*, "born in the purple." China and Japan followed ancient Rome in reserving a color for imperial use, though in East Asia, it was not purple but yellow, the color of gold and power, and in Daoist metaphysics, of the center of the universe. The concept of a special kind of headgear reserved for a monarch originated in ancient Persia (now Iran), and slowly made its way west, first to the Hellenistic kingdoms that succeeded the Macedonian Empire of Alexander the Great (356–323 BCE), then to the Byzantine Empire, and from there, to the medieval kingdoms of Europe.

Before Japan's defeat in the Second World War in 1945, and the drafting of her U.S.-inspired postwar constitution, which defines the emperor as the constitutional "symbol of the state and of the unity of the people," the Japanese believed that their emperor was not merely appointed by the Shinto gods of Japan but reigned because he was a direct descendant of the Sun Goddess Amaterasu-Omikami—in other words, that he had divine status. The emperor was said to reign in an unbroken line of succession from the first Japanese ruler, Amaterasu's grandson, Ningi-no-Mikoto, whom she had sent to earth to teach the Japanese the arts of civilization and the cultivation of rice. In order to aid him in his task, the goddess gave Ningi the *Sanshu no Jingi*, the Three Sacred Treasures of Japan: the sword *Kusanagi-no-Tsurugi*, representing martial valor; the mirror *Yata-no-Kagami*, representing wisdom; and the jewel *Yasakani-no-Magatama*, representing benevolence, which became the imperial regalia, presented to Japanese rulers at their accession, and symbolizing their legitimacy.

THE IMPOTENT GOD

Although the Japanese accorded their emperor divine honors, and he was, in theory, an absolute monarch, for most of Japanese history, the emperors reigned in their ceremonial capital of Kyoto but did not rule. The real task of government was first usurped by aristocratic regents, the Fujiwara clan, who married their daughters to young emperors, whom they deposed if they showed any signs of independence, and later by a succession of feudal samurai warlords, to whom the emperor graciously granted the title of shogun (military leader), after they had defeated all their rivals. From the point of view of the dynasty, the arrangement was beneficial in that it ensured its survival, but with the emperor as the impotent and sometimes impoverished ceremonial head of state and high priest of the Shinto religion. When other more hands-on dynasties in Asia and Europe lost power, they were inevitably replaced.

The Japanese claim that the emperors have ruled in "a line unbroken since time immemorial," however, does not really stand up to rigorous historical scrutiny. There were several usurpations and breaks in the line of succession, which were patched over by imperial marriages and adoptions, or simply by historical sleights of hand. During the Nanboku (Southern and Northern Courts) period (1336–92), there were two rival Japanese emperors. Although the northern emperor was the more legitimate, the southern emperor had the military support of the shogun; therefore, it was his line that was recognized as legitimate and from which the current imperial family is descended. The Southern Court's control of the imperial regalia was a significant factor in assuring its acceptance by the Japanese.

The authenticity of the Three Sacred Treasures used to legitimize the southern emperor in 1392, however, is itself in doubt. Two centuries before, during the Genpei War (1180–85), two powerful samurai clans, the Minamoto and the Taira, each with an imperial claimant in tow, slugged it out to see who would become the first of Japan's shoguns and place their imperial candidate on the throne. The conflict ended in the naval battle of Dan-no-ura (1185), which took place in the Shimonoseki Straits between the two main Japanese islands of Honshu and Kyushu. The Minamoto won a decisive victory over the Taira. Rather than risk being captured by the Minamoto, many of the Taira warriors, the surviving members of the imperial family, including the child Emperor Antoku (1178–85), threw themselves into the sea along with the imperial regalia.

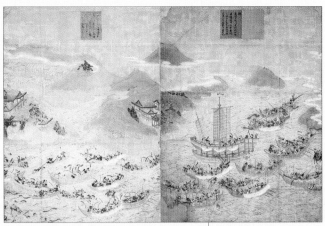

© Public domain

LOST AT SEA
The regalia were thrown into the sea during a naval battle.

Depending on which account you follow, the sword and mirror were lost to the waters, or were recovered by divers after the battle, and the jewel, too, was lost or was saved, when the lady-in-waiting who was carrying it was prevented from jumping into the sea. The treasures were then entrusted to different shrines in Japan. There are no drawings, photographs, or written descriptions of the Three Sacred Treasures, nor have they been seen by anyone apart from their priestly guardians and the reigning emperor, to whom they are presented during the enthronement ceremony. One artist's impression of the *Sanshu no Jingi* is based on artifacts found in ancient royal burial mounds in Japan and Korea. In this version, the mirror is of a circular bronze type made in Japan's ancient and classical periods as high-status court and shrine artifacts; the sword, a straight-bladed bronze or iron weapon; and the jewel, a kidney-shaped piece of polished jade. The treasures were last used in the coronation of Emperor Akihito (b. 1933) but were hidden from view, shrouded in elaborate boxes and coverings.

THE GREAT TABOO: GENGHIS KHAN'S TOMB

1227

Circumstance of loss: Genghis Khan was buried in a secret location and the workmen who had built the tomb were all killed

Rediscovery: The tomb may have been found in 2009 (discovery is yet to be confirmed)

Historical significance: Burial of the most influential man of the thirteenth century

Value: Preserving the world

© Hemis | Alamy

From the time of the Khan's death in 1227 up until 1991, the 90 square miles that make up the Forbidden Zone were as off-limits as any place in the world. Shortly after he died, the Khan's surviving commanders ordered a group of 50 particularly battle-hardened families, collectively known as the Uryangqai of the Woods, to occupy this land and kill any trespassers.

"Conjuring Genghis Khan" (2009) by Luke Dittrich

When *Star Trek* (the original series) wanted to portray human exemplars of good and evil in "The Savage Curtain" (episode 77, first aired in 1969), they pitched Abraham Lincoln (1809–65), representing the best of humanity (along with James T. Kirk and Mr Spock, of course), against the founder of the Mongol Empire (1206–1368), Genghis Khan (ca. 1160–1227), who incarnated the worst, along with an assortment of made-up sci-fi super-villains. Certainly, even by the standards of an extremely violent age, the Mongols were not particularly *nice* people—not the kind of folks you'd want to invite to your barbeque unless disemboweling the guests and making a pyramid out of their severed heads was part of the entertainment for the day.

© Public domain

CONQUEROR
Genghis Khan led the Mongols to world domination.

The greatest conflict in human history before the early modern period was not between different nation states, ethnicities, or religions, but between two different lifestyles: nomadic pastoralism and settled agriculture. A by-product of farming, which in good years produced large surpluses, was urban civilization. Hence, the settled farmers of the Neolithic Era (10200–3600 BCE) sowed the seeds (literally, as well as metaphorically) for the flowering of the great urban civilizations of the Bronze Age (3600–1200 BCE). However, we saw in the entry of the "Mask of Agamemnon" (pp. 25–29), that civilization in the eastern Mediterranean experienced its first "Dark Ages" between 1200 and 1150 BCE, when the nomadic "Sea Peoples" annihilated many settled Bronze Age cultures. The second European "Dark Ages" (476–800 CE) were triggered by the migrations of Germanic, Scandinavian, Slavic, and Turkic tribes into Western, Eastern, and Southern Europe.

Yet these were a mere rehearsal for the greatest clash between nomadic pastoralists and settled peoples that would take place in the thirteenth century, and lead to the creation of the world's largest land empire, when Genghis Khan finally succeeded in uniting the Mongolian tribes and subjugating their immediate neighbors, the Sinicized Western Xia (1038–1227) and the Jin Dynasty (1115–1234). The Mongols were among the many nomadic tribal confederations of the great steppes of Mongolia, who were usually engaged in petty intertribal feuds—a chronic disunity that was welcomed and actively encouraged by the settled peoples of China and Central Asia whom they would have otherwise threatened.

The Mongols were "born in the saddle." The horse was first domesticated in Central Asia, and the vast grasslands of the Mongolian steppes were natural horse country. They moved with their flocks, seeking out the best pastures in the hills in the milder months and going south in the winter. In addition to caring for their livestock, they hunted wild game with the bow, which they could fire with great accuracy from the saddle. Their endless internecine feuds also gave them a lot of target practice, and their lifestyles made them extremely hardy, impervious to the cold and heat, and capable of riding many miles in one day, skills that they would exploit militarily with terrible effect.

In 1206, Genghis Khan united the feuding Mongolian tribes, creating a highly mobile army of superb mounted bowmen. Although the Chinese had already developed gunpowder weapons, these were extremely primitive, inaccurate, and took a long time to load. Although they initially frightened the nomadic tribesmen—more because of the noise and smoke they produced than their power to injure or kill—the Mongols' bows were far more accurate and deadly, and a skilled Mongol archer could loose a dozen arrows in the time it took a Chinese bombardier to reload his firearm. For a century and a half the Mongols appeared invincible. Under Genghis Khan they disposed of nomadic rivals, and quickly overran Central Asia, northern China, and eastern Persia. His successors would bring terror, death, and destruction in Eastern Europe, and the conquest of the Islamic Abbasid Caliphate and the destruction of its capital Baghdad in 1258.

RAIDERS OF THE IKH KHORIG

As befits such a larger-than-life figure as Genghis Khan, there are several versions of his death. The first and least glamorous claims that he died of an illness, probably pneumonia, and the second that he died fighting or as a result of injuries sustained in battle against the Western Xia. The third, and most intriguing, is that a Western Xia princess, whom he had taken captive after destroying her people, managed to hide a knife on her person. As the khan was about to rape her, she castrated him, and he later died from the wound. Following the custom of his tribe and the khan's own wishes, the body was then taken back to Mongolia, to the place of his birth where it was buried, again according to Mongol custom, in an unmarked grave.

It is surprising that Indiana Jones (a.k.a. Harrison Ford, b. 1942) was never dispatched to discover the tomb of the world's greatest conqueror, as it remains one of the great, unsolved mysteries of archaeology. As to what it might contain, there are no clues in period sources. He might lie in nothing more than the clothes he died in, with his weapons by his side, or he might be buried with heaps of looted treasure. His followers went to great pains to hide the whereabouts of his tomb. The workmen who excavated it were all put to death, as were the soldiers who had guarded and killed them. One story says that the khan was buried with a baby camel, as it is believed that a mother camel would always be able to find the place were its dead offspring was buried. When the mother camel died, however, the location of the tomb was lost forever.

Another legend recounts that a river was diverted over the site of the tomb, ensuring that it would never be disturbed. It is likely that the khan's remains are near his birthplace in Mongolia. Genghis's heirs declared a 90-square-mile (240 km²) region of the Khentii Mountains, the Burkhan Khaldun, to be *Ikh Khorig*, "Great Taboo" or "Forbidden Zone," guarded by tribesmen who were sworn to kill trespassers. The area has only been open to archaeologists since 1992, and several researchers have claimed that they have discovered the site of the khan's palace and tomb. The latest claim, by Albert Lin, identified the potential location using satellite and remote-sensing imaging techniques. Discovering and opening the tomb might be extremely ill advised, however, as one Mongol legend claims that this will trigger the Apocalypse—the end of the world.

UNMARKED GRAVE
Following Mongol custom, the khan was buried in an unmarked grave.

PORCELAIN SHIP: NANHAI ONE

ca. 1230

Circumstance of loss: Shipwreck in the South China Sea of a laden cargo ship

Rediscovery: Found intact by divers in 100 feet (30 m) of water

Historical significance: A treasure trove of export wares from the Song Dynasty, and evidence of the "Maritime Silk Road" with the West

Value: $35 million

Experts also predict that the value and influence of the final unveiling of the ship "Nanhai No. 1" will match the discovery of the terracotta statues at the tomb of Qin Shihuangdi in Xi'an.

The Maritime Silk Road (2006) by Li Qingxin

We return to China, which we first visited for the entry on Emperor Qin Shi Huang's (259–210 BCE) 8,000-strong army of terracotta warriors (pp. 60–66), and then for the cache of 50,000 manuscripts found in the Mogao Library Cave (pp. 129–135). When it comes to treasures, it seems, the Chinese do not go in for half measures, burying or losing them in thousands, when other cultures leave no more than dozens or hundreds. In 1987, salvage divers looking for an eighteenth-century wreck off the coast of Hailing Island in the South China Sea made a once-in-a-lifetime discovery: a wooden ship, standing upright 100 feet (30 m) below the surface of the water. Although the whole ship was covered in a layer of silt, the timbers of the hull were hard and sound, and the vessel, which must have been swamped by high waves during a storm, was otherwise intact.

The 3,800-ton (3,447-metric-ton) vessel, dubbed the *Nanhai* (South China Sea) *One* by archaeologists, is the largest merchant vessel of its kind to have been found, measuring 100 feet (30.4 m) from stem to stern, with a beam of 32 feet (9.8 m), and 11 feet (3.5 m) from the keel to gunwhales. When she sank near the Pearl River estuary, she was loaded with a precious cargo destined for foreign markets, amounting to 60,000–80,000 different artifacts, also believed to be mostly undamaged inside her once watertight holds. Shipwrecks, ancient and modern, are not uncommon in the busy waters of the South China Sea, but what makes this submarine discovery unique is the age of the ship, dating from the latter half of the Song Dynasty (960–1279), which is approximately eight centuries old. For a wreck of that age to be so well preserved is little short of miraculous.

Chinese history has exhibited three distinct phases: periods of expansion and openness to the outside world under self-confident Chinese dynasties; periods of growing isolation and paralysis, when the empire turned inward or was torn apart by civil wars; and periods of decline and conquest by Central Asian nomads, such as the Mongol Yuan Dynasty (1271–1368), the descendants of Genghis Khan (see previous entry). There have been four expansive phases prior to the current one under the Communist government: the Han Dynasty (206 BCE–220 CE), when the overland Silk Route was established with the West; the Tang Dynasty (618–907), when the Chinese expanded westward into Central Asia and developed the oasis of Dunhuang; the subject of the current entry, the Song Dynasty (960–1279); and finally, the Ming Dynasty (1368–1644).

The Song Dynasty is divided into two periods: the Northern Song (960–1127), who ruled all of China, and the Southern Song (1127–1269), when the western and northern parts of the empire were occupied by the nomadic Western Xia (1038–1227) and Jin Dynasty (1115–1234), who were both later wiped out by the Mongols. Although the Southern Song Dynasty lost the traditional birthplace of Chinese civilization, the dynasty is recognized as one of the nation's high points, when the Chinese excelled in every field of human endeavor, from the arts, industry, agriculture, banking, and commerce to military technology, mathematics, and the pure and applied sciences. We owe to the Song the invention of the world's first paper banknotes, the magnetic compass, gunpowder, and movable type. Due to constant pressure from foreign enemies, the Song developed the world's first arsenal of gunpowder weapons, including the first primitive handguns, bombards, and landmines, and created the first permanent navy.

Symbolic of Song China's openness to the outside world was the flourishing trade it engaged in from south Chinese ports westward along the "Maritime Silk Road." Large merchant ships like the *Nanhai One* sailed to ports in Southeast Asia, India, Sri Lanka, East Africa, Yemen, and southern Iraq, from where Chinese merchandise was taken overland to the great Islamic markets of Iraq, Egypt, and Syria, for resale at fat profits to the countries of Christian Europe. The twelfth-century Arab geographer and cartographer, Al-Idrisi (1099–ca. 1165), active during the Southern Song period, wrote that the Chinese merchants brought iron, swords, silver, silk, velvet, and porcelain, which they traded for pearls, coral, agate, frankincense, spices, turtleshell, rhino horn, ivory, and cotton.

The *Nanhai One* was leaving her homeport in China when she foundered just off Hailing Island. In 2007, rather than attempt to excavate the wreck in situ, and risk disturbing it and damaging it and its contents further, the entire ship was lifted from the seabed in a specially designed stainless-steel container that fitted around and under the ship, like the jaws of a giant grab dredge. The ship now lies submerged within the "Crystal Palace" in 52 feet (16 m) of seawater kept at the same temperature as the sea where the wreck was found, in the Maritime Silk Road Museum on Hailing Island, Yangjiang, Guandong Province. The continuing exploration and excavation of the ship is one of the highlights for visitors to the museum as marine archaeologists can be seen at work on the wreck through the glass

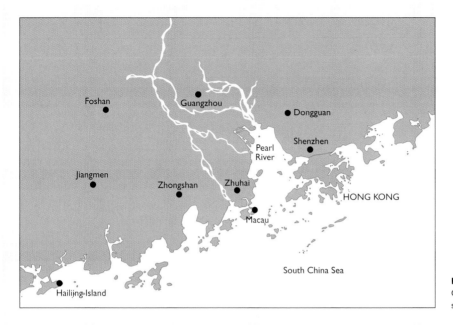

Foshan

Guangzhou

Dongguan

Pearl River

Shenzhen

Jiangmen

Zhongshan Zhuhai

HONG KONG

Macau

South China Sea

Hailijng Island

PEARL RIVER
China's medieval trade superhighway.

walls of the Crystal Palace. So far archaeologists have retrieved about 4,000 artifacts, including a waist chain made of four twisted gold strands, 286 pounds (130 kg) of silver ingots, 200 pieces of Song porcelain, and about 6,000 Song copper coins.

Song porcelain is particularly sought after for its superb quality, translucent glazes, and minimalist design, which appeals to contemporary tastes much more than the patterned polychrome Ming porcelain that was the height of fashion in the West in the nineteenth century. Due to its great age and fragility, the best Song wares are extremely rare and thus fetch very high prices at auction. At a sale held at Sotheby's, New York, in March 2013, a Northern Song Dynasty Ding bowl, which measured 5 inches (12.7 cm) in diameter, and which was expected to sell for $300,000, sold for $2.2 million. The *Nanhai One* is estimated to contain between 60,000 and 80,000 items of cargo, much of it porcelain made for the export market. Although the cargo is unlikely to hold many items as fine as the $2.2 million bowl, even a conservative valuation of $500 per piece of porcelain, multiplied by 70,000, gives us the not inconsiderable sum of $35 million.

ONWARD CHRISTIAN BANKERS: THE TREASURE OF THE KNIGHTS TEMPLAR

1312

Circumstance of loss: Rumored to be hidden just before the order was dissolved

Rediscovery: Not yet found

Historical significance: Beloved of conspiracy theorists, the order has spawned a great deal of pseudo-archaeology and pseudo-history

Value: The secrets of life, death, and the universe

The blow to the Order was struck with great rapidity and skill [… on] Friday, October 13th, 1307, every member of the Temple Order then in France was cast into prison. By these same instructions all their property was seized and retained by Crown Officials.

Knights Templar (2003) by A. Bothwell-Gosse

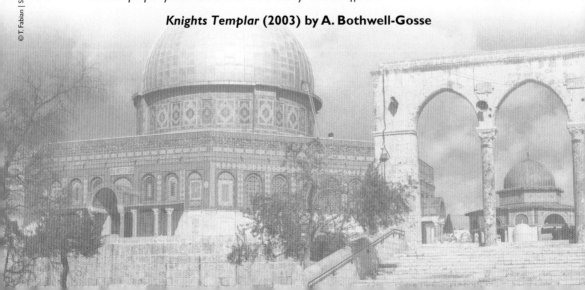

In the past decade there has been a noticeable "escalation" in the range of pseudo-history, pseudo-science, and pseudo-archaeology. In my youth, books and TV shows featured a single "unsolved mystery"—the lost continent of Atlantis, the Maya collapse, or "flying saucers," for example— but now the trend is to interweave disparate phenomena, historical events, civilizations, artifacts, sacred locations, myths and legends, with the bizarre fantasies of the inspired, deluded, or plain insane, to create complex layered narratives that purport to explain what is really going on in the world but is always "hushed up by the government."

It doesn't seem to trouble this generation of conspiracy theorists that we have hundreds of governments on the planet (yes, folks, amazingly the Federal Government doesn't run the whole world), many of which are at each other's throats and would never cooperate, and are, in any case, completely incapable of "hushing up" even the most minor misdemeanors of their leaders and agencies; therefore, what realistic chance would they have of keeping quiet about something as earth-shattering as visits from extraterrestrials? (Of course, that's what they want you to think.)

There are several features of the modern world that might explain this phenomenon, starting with the decline in organized religion, as the British writer G. K. Chesterton (1874–1936) so trenchantly observed, "When people stop believing in god, they don't believe in nothing—they believe in anything": fairies, crystals, pyramid power, angels, and little gray men with bug eyes who like to make crop circles in the south of England, rummage around in human underwear, and vivisect livestock (everyone needs a hobby). Second, is the extraordinary complexity of the modern world, very little of which makes any sense, and a vast conspiracy, at least, is easy to understand. It was so much easier in the days of the Evil Empire when you knew who the baddies were and that the only good red was dead. Now they manufacture our cars and cell phones and lend us money to buy them. Third, is the weirdness of real science in the age of the Higgs boson, dark matter, and the Large Hadron Collider. Fourth, is the superb quality of sci-fi and fantasy TV shows and movies, whose special effects blur the difference between reality and fiction. Finally, of course, is that it makes writers and cable channels a lot of money.

To write a bestselling "unsolved mystery" book, you need to combine the following ingredients: a secretive medieval order, the Temple of Solomon, the Holy Grail, rumors of occult knowledge, and vast amounts of treasure, which should earn you at least three weeks on the *New York Times* bestseller list. Unfortunately, several pseudo-historians have done it already and have reimagined the story of the Knights Templar, or to give them their full Latin name, *Pauperes commilitones Christi Templique Salomonici* ("Poor Fellow-Soldiers of Christ and of the Temple of Solomon"), who were an order of medieval crusading knights founded in the Holy Land in 1119 and dissolved "with extreme prejudice" in Europe in 1312.

TEMPLARS INC.

In our first visit to Jerusalem (pp. 44–50), we left it a smoking ruin in 70 CE, on top of which the Romans built the pagan city of Aelia Capitolina, dedicated to the father of the gods, Jupiter Capitolinus. After the Emperor Constantine (ca. 272–337 CE) ended the persecution of Christianity, he had the pagan temples demolished and rebuilt Jerusalem as a Christian city, which, because of its associations with the life of Jesus of Nazareth (ca. 4–30 CE), soon became Christendom's most important pilgrimage site, and was literally defined as the center of the world. In 325, Constantine consecrated the Church of the Holy Sepulcher, supposedly over the sites of Jesus's crucifixion, burial, and resurrection. Apart from a brief period of Persian rule between 614 and 629, Jerusalem remained in Christian hands until the Arab conquest of Syria and Palestine (634–38).

After Mecca and Medina, Jerusalem is the most sacred site in Islam. It is believed that it was from Jerusalem's Temple Mount that the Prophet Muhammad (ca. 570–ca. 632) undertook the *Isra* and *Miraj*, the Night Journey to Heaven. Because Islam recognizes Jesus as a prophet (though not as the son of god), along with Moses, the "religions of the Book"—Christianity and Judaism—were not treated as harshly as other faiths, such as Hinduism and Buddhism. Nevertheless, Christians and Jews who refused to convert paid special taxes and faced limitations to their civil and legal rights. In the early centuries of Muslim rule, most Christian places of worship were respected, but the church on the Temple Mount was demolished to make way for the Dome of the Rock (685–91) and Al-Aqsa Mosque (705). The Jews, excluded from the city during Byzantine rule, were allowed to return and build a synagogue, though there was no question of their being allowed to build on the Temple Mount itself.

At the beginning of the eleventh century, this tolerance gave way to persecution, and the Christian churches of Jerusalem were demolished.

This caused consternation and outrage in Western Europe. Although Jerusalem and the other sites associated with Christ's birth, life, ministry, and martyrdom had been under Muslim rule since the seventh century, at that time the countries of Europe were in no state to intervene. The future nations of Western Europe were still then in the process of elaborating their political, social, religious, and national identities; much of northern and central Europe was still pagan; and Italy and the papacy depended for its survival on Byzantine funds and arms. By the end of the eleventh century, however, Europe was more settled and self-confident, and the Roman Church had declared its independence from the empire and Eastern Orthodox Church.

In 1095, Pope Urban II (ca. 1042–99) answered an appeal from the Byzantine Emperor Alexius I (1056–1118), whose territory in Asia Minor (now Turkey) had been overrun by the Seljuk Turks. Although what Alexius asked for was a mercenary force to help him re-establish his rule, what he got instead in 1096 was a full-scale crusade, led by members of the Western European nobility, who intended to recover the Holy Land and carve themselves out new kingdoms and principalities in the wealthy countries of the Levant. As the Muslim world was disunited, the First Crusade succeeded in all its objectives, establishing Latin states in Syria and Palestine, known collectively as the Kingdoms of Outremer.

The conquest of the Holy Land, however, was a particularly bloody and violent episode. Among the worst atrocities carried out by the crusaders was the massacre of Jerusalem's Jewish and Muslim population when the city fell in 1099. Unlike the Muslim rulers of the city who had reopened the Christian places of worship and allowed pilgrims to visit the Holy Land, the crusaders were ruthless in their suppression of both Islam and Judaism. The foundation of the Latin and Roman Catholic Kingdom of Jerusalem (1099–1292) was steeped in Jewish and Muslim blood.

But even a generation after the conquest of Outremer, the country outside the fortified strongholds of the crusaders was infested with bandits who robbed and slaughtered European pilgrims who were traveling from the port of Jaffa (modern-day Tel Aviv-Yafo) to Jerusalem and Bethlehem. In 1119, a French knight, Hugues de Payens (ca. 1070–1136), petitioned King Baldwin II of Jerusalem (1060–1131) to allow the establishment of an order of knights that would protect pilgrims and the holy sites.

The king agreed and gave the new order premises on the Temple Mount, the location of the First and Second Temples, in buildings that had formerly been Islamic places of worship. Not being historians or linguists, the crusaders believed that the Dome of the Rock and Al-Aqsa Mosque were part of the original Jewish Temple. They converted the Dome into a church and the Al-Aqsa Mosque into the royal palace. Although the Templars were given quarters in the palace, they chose as their emblem the Dome of the Rock, and incorporated the "Temple of Solomon" in the name of the order.

The Templars, whatever conspiracy theorists might claim, were not unique or particularly secretive. There were over 30 orders of Christian knights created between the eleventh and sixteenth centuries, three of which predated the Templars. Their organization and aims were broadly similar: They were set up as the military wing of the Roman Catholic Church, to protect pilgrims in Europe and the Holy Land and to spread the word of God, by the sword wherever and whenever necessary. Like monks, the knights took vows of poverty and chastity, but unlike their clerical brethren, they did not "turn the other cheek" as long as they were capable of hacking the enemy's head off. Most of the orders were dissolved between the late Middle Ages and the early nineteenth century, but a few survived into the modern period as charitable institutions or monastic orders.

The Templars were unusual, however, in their enormous early success. In part this was due to the location of their HQ and the name that identified them so closely with Jerusalem and the Holy Land, but it was also because of their great business acumen. Although the brethren had taken vows of individual poverty, this did not stop them from making huge amounts of money for the order itself. The Templars have been described as the world's first multinational corporation. They pioneered international banking by taking deposits in Europe from pilgrims and knights traveling to the Holy Land, and issuing them with letters of credit that could be redeemed with the order in Jerusalem. They also owned farms, vineyards, and a trading fleet, which earned them considerable sums.

The Ayyubid sultan of Egypt and Syria, Saladin (1137–93), retook Jerusalem in 1187, and Acre, the last stronghold of the Kingdom of Jerusalem, in 1192, destroying the last remnants of Outremer, and forcing the withdrawal of the Templars to the Island of Cyprus. Although the order's *raison d'être* had been eliminated, it continued to trade and amass wealth, and to act as a bank for the royal houses of Europe. Lending to commoners was relatively safe, but lending to medieval monarchs was always a risky business—you might lose both your money and your head!

One hundred and twenty years after the fall of Jerusalem, the Templars were still based in Cyprus—then as now a tax haven—and were still trying to persuade the crowned heads of Europe to launch a crusade to retake Jerusalem, which had briefly been in Christian hands in the mid-thirteenth century, but had been lost after a decade. Fabulously wealthy and exempt from any civil jurisdiction and taxation as a religious order, the Templars owned property and land all over Europe. They continued their banking activities, lending vast sums to Philip IV "the Fair" of France (1268–1314), who was constantly in debt, paying for his father's and his own wars against the Spanish and English. In 1306, he arrested and exiled the French Jews so that he could seize their considerable assets. Despite his sequestrations of other people's money and property, Philip was always on the lookout for more cash. If there had been credit-rating agencies in the fourteenth century, Philip would have merited "junk bond" status.

In 1307, Philip summoned the Grand Master of the Templars, Jacques de Molay (ca. 1244–1314), ostensibly to plan a new crusade. De Molay arrived with 150,000 gold florins and several hundredweight of silver to fund the enterprise. What he encountered, however, was deceit and treachery. Philip, who had borrowed heavily from the order, had decided that instead of paying them back, he would seize their wealth in France and encourage his fellow monarchs in Europe to do the same. He had de Molay arrested and instructed his officials to arrest all the Templars in France. He accused the brethren of blasphemy, idolatry, and sodomy in their initiation rituals, and extracted confessions by torture.

The Templars appealed to the pope, Clement V (1264–1314), who, though unwilling to move against an order that had served the church for three centuries, was in the king's power and therefore proved ineffective in his attempts to protect the knights. Whenever the Templars were brought

CRASH AND BURN

© Public domain

BETRAYED
The last grand master of the Templars, Jacques de Molay.

before the Church courts or representatives of the pope, they recanted the confessions obtained under torture and pleaded their innocence. But after seven years, the king got his way and de Molay and many other French Templars were burned at the stake as heretics who had recanted; the order was dissolved, and its surviving members and its holdings not already seized by the royal governments of Europe were transferred to other religious orders.

PETTY THIEF
King Philip coveted the order's vast wealth.

And what of the fabled "treasure of the Templars"? I can say categorically that it did exist; in fact, it was the cause of their downfall. But there was nothing occult about it: they owned land, houses, estates, castles, churches, vineyards, a fleet of merchant ships, reliquaries made of precious metals and gems, and a great deal of gold and silver bullion given as donations, left to them as legacies, and earned from their many business activities.

There is no reason to invoke the missing treasure of the Temple of Solomon, including the Ark of the Covenant, hidden within the Temple Mount, to explain the Templars' wealth, nor is there any substance to any of the tales that they were the keepers of the Holy Grail. We saw in that entry (pp. 79–86) that the much-discussed "cursed treasure of the Templars" of Rennes-le-Chateau was in fact the proceeds from a petty clerical scandal. Another inspired fabrication is the story that the Templars anticipated Christopher Columbus (1451–1506) by 180 years and managed to escape with their treasure and occult secrets to America. Although the Templars had a fleet of merchant ships, these were small, flat-bottomed coastal vessels used to transport wine, and would not have made it across the Atlantic. Apart from the treasure that Philip extracted from the Templars through betrayal and torture, the only money that has been made from them is by modern authors claiming to reveal their secrets.

PLAGUE GOLD: SRODA TREASURE

1348

TREASURE

Burial goods

Hoards

Shipwrecks

Religious objects or places

Artworks

Gemstones

Circumstance of loss: Pawned to Jewish bankers who died in the Black Death or in an anti-Jewish pogrom

Rediscovery: When houses in Sroda Old Town were being demolished

Historical significance: A window onto the medieval Holy Roman Empire

Value: $50 million (2001 valuation)

Little less considerable find from the town of Sroda Slaska. In 1988, a veritable royal treasure was salvaged from the municipal garbage dump, out of the waste of houses demolished in the medieval town center.

In Laudem Hierosolymitani (2007)
edited by Igris Shagrir et al

© Public domain

PAWNBROKER
The jewels were left as
security for a loan.

It would be a dream come true: You're making improvements to your home and when you're pulling down an outhouse or extension, you stumble across an old crock, which you throw into the dumpster, but when it breaks open, you discover it contains a hoard of antique gold and silver coins and jewelry. This is not far off what happened to construction workers renovating a medieval house in Sroda Slaska in 1985. The Lower Silesian town of Sroda, population 8,800, is 20 miles (32 km) west of Wroclaw in southwestern Poland. Many of my readers will be familiar with the history of Poland during the Second World War, when so much of the country was deliberately laid waste by the Nazis and Soviets; they will wonder how the town's medieval center escaped destruction, when the historic centers of Warsaw and of most of Poland's cities were reduced to piles of rubble. What ensured Sroda's survival, was that before 1945, Lower Silesia was part of Germany, and the town was known as Neumarkt in Schlesien.

The first find that came to the attention of the authorities was a ceramic vessel containing some 3,000 fourteenth-century Prague *groschen* minted for Wenceslas II (1271–1305), king of Bohemia and Poland, each weighing about 0.12 ounces (3.5 g) of high-quality silver. Three years later, workers demolishing another house in the old town came across an even bigger cache of coins, including gold florins (originally a coin struck in Florence in the mid-thirteenth century, but widely adopted across Europe). At this point, amateur archaeologists and treasure hunters decided it might be worth investigating the rubble removed from this and the earlier demolition sites and dumped at a municipal landfill. There were further discoveries of coins and reports of jewelry, some of which disappeared, no doubt to be sold on the black market, before the authorities sealed off the area and turned it over to professional archaeologists. In an effort to recover the missing pieces, the Polish government has since offered to buy any precious items found in Sroda to add to the permanent exhibit at the Sroda Museum.

As we have seen time and time again with hoards, the lack of archaeological context usually makes it very difficult to identify the owner of the hoard, as well as when and why it might have been hidden, and also, why its owner never recovered it. The coins and precious items found in Sroda would represent a veritable fortune in any period. In the 2000s, the treasure was valued at $50–100 million. In the fourteenth century, the owner of such fabulous wealth could only be an extremely important nobleman, king, prince, or, of course, a banker. In this case, however, historians believe that they have identified the original owner of the jewels, the banker to whom they were entrusted, and how he met his end. The mid-fourteenth century was an extremely turbulent period politically, socially, and militarily, but it is also remembered for one of the greatest natural disasters of the medieval period, the Black Death (1348–51), an outbreak of bubonic plague (*Yersinia pestis*) that killed between one-third and one-half of Europe's population.

FIT FOR A QUEEN

The jewelry recovered includes four gold filigree pendants; two rings, one with dragonheads, and another with a crescent-moon-and-star motif, and the star item of the collection, a crown "fit for a queen." The crown is made up of detachable rectangular gold panels, decorated with enamels and set with sapphires, garnets, spinels, aquamarines, natural glass, and pearls. The panels are topped with eagles holding rings in their beaks, and are joined together with pins in the shape of florets. Another important jewel is a circular brooch, the largest known example of a medieval ring brooch, its center decorated with a chalcedony cameo of an eagle surrounded by garnets, pearls, and sapphires. The brooch would have been used to fasten ceremonial robes at the shoulder. In addition to the jewels, 39 gold and around 4,000 silver coins were recovered.

The eagle-and-ring motif on the crown, symbolic of the marriage bond and good fortune, suggests that it was commissioned for a royal wedding, most likely between Charles IV (1316–78), king of Bohemia and king of the Romans from 1346, Holy Roman Emperor from 1355, and king of Burgundy from 1365, and the first of his four wives, Blanche de Valois (1316–48), whom he married in Prague in 1329. It is unlikely that the royal couple hid the jewels in a commoner's house in Sroda, although the town was in the Duchy of Wroclaw, which was part of Charles's domain.

When we think of an emperor, we probably imagine the all-powerful Roman *imperator*, the Byzantine *basileus*, the Russian czar, or a Chinese son of heaven, who exercised absolute authority over their subjects. However, the medieval office of Holy Roman Emperor, established in 800 by

FINAL ACCOUNT
The treasure was lost during
the Black Death.

Charlemagne (742–814), was elective. There were seven "prince-electors:" three senior churchmen, and four temporal rulers from within the empire. Rather than an absolute ruler, the Holy Roman emperor was the "first among equals," and his position was attained through negotiation, bargaining, and bribery. In order to ease his path to the imperial throne, Charles would have required considerable funds. Historians believe that in around 1348, he borrowed a large sum from a Jewish banker called Moishe in Sroda, leaving his wife's crown and other jewels as security to be redeemed when the loan was repaid.

Unfortunately for all concerned, the Black Death, which had been devastating the Byzantine Empire since 1347, reached Central Europe in 1348. Moishe suddenly disappeared from the historical record; either he was a plague victim or was murdered in one of the anti-Jewish pogroms that took place in the region during the Black Death, because the Jews were blamed for spreading the plague. Whatever his fate, the banker had carefully hidden the royal jewels and a considerable sum in gold and silver coins before his death, secreting them so well in the fabric of his house that they remained undiscovered for 640 years.

LOST IN THE NIGHT: MOCTEZUMA'S TREASURE

1520

TREASURE

Burial goods

Hoards

Shipwrecks

Religious objects or places

Artworks

Gemstones

Circumstance of loss: Fell into Lake Texcoco during the retreat on the *Noche Triste*

Rediscovery: A piece of the treasure may have been recovered in the twentieth century

Historical significance: An early example of the plundering of Native American cultures, and the destruction of their artistic and religious heritage

Value: The wealth of the Aztec Empire

The greater part of the treasure, the baggage, the general's papers, including his accounts, and a minute diary of transactions since leaving Cuba—which, to posterity, at least, would have been of more worth than the gold—had been swallowed up by the waters.

**The History of the Conquest of Mexico (1843)
by William H. Prescott**

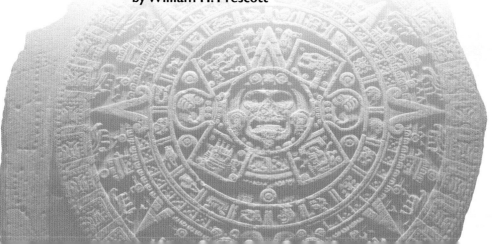

© Public domain

SELF-FULFILLING PROPHECY
Moctezuma believed that the end of the world had come.

This entry is the first of several on the wealth of the Americas, so much of which was plundered by Europeans, only to be lost in battles, civil wars, and shipwrecks. As every schoolchild knows, "In fourteen hundred and ninety two, Columbus sailed the ocean blue," in search of a westerly passage to the East Indies—the spice islands of Java and Sumatra (Indonesia), Cathay (China), and Xipangu (Japan), where, it was said, gold was as common as base metal, and could be picked up off the ground.

Christopher Columbus (1451–1506) was not an explorer who embarked on the perilous crossing of the Atlantic because he was curious to discover hitherto unknown regions of the globe; he was a hardheaded businessman who had promised a great deal to his patrons, the Catholic monarchs of Castile and Aragon (Spain). Gold and spices were the lure that drove European navigators south, east, and west, to bypass the Muslim stranglehold on the eastern trade after their capture of Constantinople and the last remnants of the once-mighty Byzantine Empire in 1453–54. The Portuguese led the way in the fifteenth century, sailing south along the coast of Africa and west into the Atlantic. Although they colonized the Azores, they concentrated their efforts on the eastern passage to the Indies: the long, arduous journey around the Cape of Good Hope (South Africa) and across the Indian Ocean, which they first achieved in 1499. From there, they would sail on to Southeast and East Asia, being the first Europeans to reach Japan.

Contrary to popular legend, Columbus did not have to persuade his patrons that the world was round. That the earth was a sphere was known since antiquity, to the educated, at least. He followed Greek and Roman geographers in their calculations of the probable size of the globe, and like them, massively underestimated the distance between Spain and East Asia. Instead of sailing all the way to China, in four voyages between 1492 and 1503, Columbus discovered the West Indies and Central and South America, giving Spain a vast new colonial empire. It took the Spaniards less than a generation to subjugate and then liquidate the Native American population of the Caribbean, and to discover that they had very little gold. However, as they began to explore the coasts of Central America, they heard of a much wealthier inland empire. In 1519, Hernán Cortés (1485–1547) set out with around 1,000 infantry and 100 cavalry, equipped with steel armor and weapons, crossbows, and about a dozen primitive firearms to conquer one of the great empires of the day.

Had the conquistadors known that they faced an empire of between five and ten million people, with around 300,000 men under arms, they might have turned back, even though the Aztecs were armed with Stone Age obsidian weapons, bows and arrows, slings, and throwing sticks, and their war tactics were designed to capture enemies for human sacrifice rather than maim or kill. The Aztec Empire—though confederation might be a better description—occupied most of modern Mexico with its capital at Tenochtitlan (now Mexico City), situated in the middle of the Lake Texcoco, and linked to the lakeshore by eight causeways. The empire was a fairly recent creation, the Aztecs having achieved dominance in the Valley of Mexico only in the fifteenth century. Like several empires of the ancient Near East, they ruled at a remove, extracting tribute from conquered peoples but leaving their rulers and elites in place. Their rule was constantly challenged by rebellions, and there were important independent enclaves within the empire—all of which was exploited by the astute Cortés.

Although the Spanish had superior technology, they also benefited from two factors: powerful native allies who despised the Aztecs, and Aztec beliefs, legends, and superstitions. Like the Maya, the Aztecs had a cyclical notion of time, believing that events recurred with the repetition of each calendar cycle. Cortés's arrival coincided with prophecies of the return of the god Quetzalcoatl (the feathered serpent, portrayed as a pale-skinned, bearded man) and of the destruction of the Aztec Empire. No one was more pessimistic than the Aztec ruler, or *tlaotani*, literally "speaker," Moctezuma II (ca. 1466–1520). Moctezuma's first mistake was to try to bribe Cortés with lavish gifts, including gold artifacts, not to come to Tenochtitlan, but these only spurred the conquistador on.

DOOMED EMPEROR

Once established in the capital, Cortés turned the tables on his host, taking Moctezuma hostage and demanding a vast amount of gold to ensure his safety, which was duly delivered. The Aztecs were skillful goldsmiths, who manufactured gold jewelry, ornaments, and statuary, but they did not value the metal particularly other than as an artistic material as they did not have a monetized economy that used gold as currency as in the Old World.

The Aztec economy was based on tribute and barter, and the closest thing they had to a unit of portable currency was the cocoa bean. Probably to the amazement and puzzlement of their unwilling hosts, the Spanish melted down the huge heaps of beautifully crafted objects that had been brought to them to ensure Moctezuma's well-being, turning them into shapeless lumps of gold, using whatever was at hand as molds.

By 1520, the citizens of Tenochtitlan had had enough of the Spaniards, their native allies, and the ruler who seemed incapable of resisting the foreigner's greed, crimes, and attacks on Aztec religious practices. They rebelled, laying siege to Cortés in Moctezuma's palace. When the king tried to appeal to his subjects to allow the Spaniards to leave, they pelted him with stones, fatally injuring him. Fearing that he would be trapped and killed, Cortés planned to slip out of the city under cover of darkness on the night of June 30–July 1, 1520, remembered by Spanish chroniclers as the *Noche Triste* (Night of Sorrows).

The Aztecs were waiting for them and had cut the bridges on four of the causeways connecting the city to the lakeshore. Weighed down by their share of Moctezuma's treasure, about 450 of Cortés soldiers were captured or killed during the ensuing retreat that quickly turned into a rout. The rest of the treasure—including Cortés's and the king of Spain's shares—were lost to the muddy waters of Lake Texcoco. The city would fall in a bloody siege the following year, and it is unlikely that the Aztecs ever bothered to recover the melted-down lumps of gold. After the conquest, Lake Texcoco was drained and Mexico City was built over the ruins of Tenochtitlan.

In 1981, the Mexican press speculated that a tiny fraction of the treasure had been found when a construction worker dug up a 4-pound (1.8 kg) lump of gold, worth $81,000 at current bullion prices, molded to fit inside a conquistador's breastplate. It is impossible to put a price on the looted Aztec gold, but, in any case, the bullion would only represent a fraction of the real value of the thousands of artifacts, artworks, and jewels that the conquistadors destroyed.

GOLD LAGOON: TREASURE OF LAKE GUATAVITA

1537

TREASURE

Burial goods

Hoards

Shipwrecks

Religious objects or places

Artworks

Gemstones

Circumstance of loss: Religious offerings made in Lake Guatavita

Rediscovery: Gold was recovered from Lake Guatavita by several expeditions between 1545 and 1929

Historical significance: The origin of subsequent El Dorado legends

Value: $300 million

In the sixteenth century, seeking a golden kingdom in what would later be South America made sense. After all, in the early part of the century three had already been found, conquered, and looted.

Sir Walter Ralegh and the Quest for El Dorado (2000)
by Marc Aronson

© Public domain

SUN KING
The Spaniards strangled the
Inca Atahualpa.

A decade after Hernán Cortés (1485–1547) had destroyed the Aztec Empire (see previous entry), another Spanish conquistador and Cortés's distant cousin, Francisco Pizarro (ca. 1471–1541), achieved a similar success in the Inca Empire of Peru. He came with even fewer men than Cortés but employed the same terror tactics, kidnapping, ransoming, and finally murdering the Inca ruler Atahualpa (1497–1533). The Inca valued gold far more than the Aztecs, because they associated the metal with their main deity, the Sun God Inti. The bulk of the gold for Atahualpa's ransom came from Inti's principal temple in the Inca capital of Cuzco, the Qurikancha, whose walls and floors were said to be covered in sheets of pure gold, and that housed gold statues of the gods.

The conquistadors melted the Inca jewels, statues, and artworks and reshaped them into ugly metal ingots to be minted into coins and sent back to Spain, but there never seemed to be enough gold to satisfy their greed. They continued their explorations and conquests in South America, drawn further into the interior by tales of El Dorado, "the golden man," said to be the ruler of a fabulous city of gold, which was waiting to be discovered in an as yet unexplored region of the continent. It is thought that Native Americans embellished the stories to direct the Spaniards toward the territories of other peoples. However, there was some basis in fact for the story of a man who was literally covered in gold, in the accession ritual of the Zipa, one of the two rulers of the Musica Confederation of Colombia.

In 1638, a Spanish chronicler wrote a retrospective account of the ceremony that took place in the Laguna de Guatavita, a circular lake almost 1 mile (1.6 km) in diameter, formed inside a meteor or volcanic crater, located 39 miles (63 km) north of the modern capital of Colombia, Bogotá. Like many other pre-Columbian Central and South American rulers, the Zipa combined both temporal and religious powers. After he underwent a period of seclusion, meditation, and fasting, the new ruler marked his accession by a ceremonial journey across the sacred Lake Guatavita, carried on a royal barge made of rushes, furnished with gold fittings, banners, and incense burners, and carrying members of the Musica nobility all splendidly attired in gold and feathered headdresses, with offerings of gold and emeralds.

The nobles stripped the Zipa naked and covered him in a sticky gum over which they sprinkled gold dust, turning him into a living El Dorado. At the center of the lake, the Zipa and the other dignitaries on the barge made their offerings to the gods of the lake. In1969, farmers from the village of Pasca found the famous gold representation of the ritual made between 600 and 1537 CE in a ceramic container hidden in a cave.

In 1537, a Spanish force massacred the Musica who cared for Lake Guatavita, and in 1540, they conquered the Musica Confederation and brought an end to their culture and religion, and to the real ritual behind the El Dorado legend. Although the conquistadors found a great deal of gold, they quickly learned that the Musica had no goldmines of their own and obtained the precious metal through trade. In 1541, Francisco Pizarro's half-brother Gonzalo Pizarro (1502–48), hoping to match his kinsman's conquest of the Inca Empire, together with Francisco Orellana (1511–46), led an expedition to discover El Dorado and the *País de la Canela*, "the Land of Cinnamon," combining two medieval obsessions: gold and spices. The expedition crossed the Andes and descended into the

FATAL QUEST

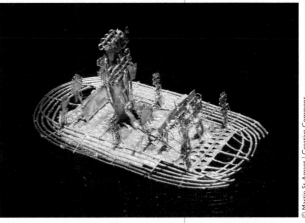

© Martin St-Amant | Creative Commons

GOLDEN MAN
A Musica ritual was the origin of the El Dorado myth.

Amazon basin, but a year after setting out, running out of provisions and with mounting casualties, Pizarro decided to turn back, ordering Orella to continue along the river with 50 men. Although he would never find El Dorado, Orellana was the first European to navigate the whole length of the Amazon River, arriving at the Brazilian coast in the summer of 1542.

Pizarro and Orellana's was not the only expedition that set out to discover El Dorado. In 1528, the Spanish king and Holy Roman Emperor Charles V (1500–58), who was deeply in debt to the German bankers of Augsburg, awarded them the concession to Venezuela, known as Klein-Venedig (Little Venice), the only German colony in South America. In 1540, the German governor of Klein-Venedig, Philipp von Hutten (1505–46), led another fruitless search for El Dorado into the interior of the province. Attacked by Native American tribes, he was forced to retreat. The English explorer and adventurer Sir Walter Raleigh (ca. 1554–1618) also sought the fabled golden city of Manoa El Dorado on the shores of Lake Parime in Guyana. The lake, which featured on maps of South America until the eighteenth century, has never been found and is now believed to be fictitious, or a reference to another lake in Brazil that had drained naturally because of tectonic activity.

In addition to the many failed expeditions to find El Dorado, attempts were made to recover the Musica offerings made at Lake Guatavita. The earliest took place in 1545, when the Spanish governor of Columbia tried to drain the lake with a chain of buckets. The prospectors recovered gold artifacts amounting to about $100,000. A second attempt to drain the lake in 1580, by cutting a notch into the rim of the crater, managed to lower the water level by 65 feet (20 m) and allowed the recovery of more gold, but it also caused a catastrophic landslide that killed many of the laborers working at the site. In 1801, the German explorer and geographer Alexander von Humboldt (1769–1859) valued the contents of the lake at $300 million, ensuring that the lake would attract a new crop of treasure hunters.

The final attempt to recover the treasure of Lake Guatavita was in 1898 by the British-sponsored Company for the Exploitation of the Lagoon of Guatavita. The British dug a tunnel under the crater and drained the lake completely, exposing a 4-foot (1.2 m) deposit of mud and slime. The company recovered some gold artifacts, which were later sold at Sotheby's auction house in London for about £500 (at 1898 prices), before the mud dried in the sun and set like concrete, preventing any further exploration. The company filed for bankruptcy in 1929, ending one of the most fabulous treasure hunts in history, which had cost thousands of Native American and European lives.

WELL OF GOD: TREASURE OF THE SACRED CENOTE

1546

TREASURE

Burial goods

Hoards

Shipwrecks

Religious objects or places

Artworks

Gemstones

Circumstance of loss: Offerings made to the gods cast into the Sacred Cenote

Rediscovery: Recovered by dredging and diving

Historical significance: Collection of artifacts spanning from the Late Classic Maya to the Spanish conquest of Yucatán

Value: Access to the Underworld

Like caves, cenotes were regarded as providing access to the Underworld and were places of ritual importance. This is underscored by the offerings recovered from the muddy bottom off the larger of the cenotes in Chichen Itza, now known as the Sacred Cenote.

Handbook to Life in the Ancient Maya World (2002)
by Lynn Vasco Foster

© e X p o s e | Shutterstock.com

© Joseph Calev | Shutterstock.com

CITY OF THE WELL
Chichen Itza owes its
existence to several
nearby *cenotes*.

The last of the great pre-Columbian civilizations to submit to Spanish rule was the Maya of Yucatán. As we saw in the entry on Pakal's death mask (pp. 118–123), the Maya experienced two major ecological collapses: one at the end of the Pre-Classic period (ca. 200–50 CE) and the second at the end of the Classic Period (ca. 800–900 CE). Each time, the Maya were forced to abandon their cities and to migrate to new areas. At the close of the Classic period, the surviving Maya elites moved from the Petén region of Guatemala northward, toward the coast of Yucatán, where they established new population centers, and built cities whose architecture and iconography were influenced by the powerful empires of the Valley of Mexico. Although the Maya kingdoms of Yucatán were never part of the Aztec hegemony, they maintained regular trading and diplomatic contacts.

The city of Chichen Itza in northern Yucatán came to prominence in the Late and Terminal Classic periods (600–900 CE) and became one of the largest and most powerful cities of the Post-Classic era (900–1540s), becoming the regional power center in the first quarter of the second millennium. Around 1250, however, the city experienced some sort of collapse. Although elite activities, such as the carving of inscriptions and the building of new temples and palaces ceased altogether, Chichen Itza continued to be occupied and to be used as a religious center by the Maya until the Spanish conquest. The city's El Castillo (The Castle) temple pyramid is a highlight of the Maya Trail, and after the steep-sided pyramids of Tikal in the Petén, Guatemala, is one of its most iconic buildings.

The Maya chose the site of Chichen Itza, which translates as "At the mouth of the Well of the Itza," because nearby there were several cenotes: deep water-filled circular sinkholes in the limestone skin, which resemble oversized wells. In an area prone to droughts, with few lakes and rivers, cenotes provided access to underground rivers. Because of their importance to the survival of the Maya, they also became sacred places.

The most important cenote of the Maya period was called *Chen Ku* ("Well of God") in the Itza language, and is now also referred to as *El Cenote de*

Sacrificios ("Cenote of Sacrifices") and *El Cenote Sagrado* ("Sacred Cenote"). The cenote is 197 feet (60 m) in diameter, with a 50-foot (15 m) vertical drop from ground level to the surface of the water, and a further 42 feet (13 m) of water to the muddy bottom. A 985-foot (300 m) *sacbe*, or ceremonial highway paved with limestone plaster, led from the center of Chichen Itza to the edge of the cenote, denoting its importance as a cult center. The Maya believed that the cenote was one of the entrances to Xibalbá, the Underworld, where it was possible to communicate with the gods and the ancestors.

The Maya, having learned from the defeat of the Aztecs, were far more successful at resisting Spanish incursions. They repulsed two invasions by the first governor of Yucatán, Francisco de Montejo (ca. 1479 –ca. 1553) in 1530 and 1535. It was his son, also called Francisco de Montejo (1502–65), who pacified most of the peninsula by 1546, though an independent Maya kingdom survived in the dense jungles of the Petén until the seventeenth century. The Spaniards established themselves in Chichen Itza, which they renamed Ciudad Real, but the Maya recaptured it before the final conquest of the area. By 1588, the city, its temples and the Sacred Cenote had been abandoned and were part of a cattle ranch. The site would not regain prominence until the "rediscovery" of the Maya in the mid-nineteenth century by European and American explorers.

© The Art Archive | Alamy

CAST-OFFS
Precious offerings and human sacrifices were made in the Sacred Cenote.

WELL OF SOULS

For six centuries the Maya threw offerings into the Sacred Cenote. These consisted of the most precious material known to the Maya, jade, the mineral jadeite, from which they carved personal ornaments and statuettes; and gold and copper artifacts—materials that were imported from other parts of Mesoamerica, which suggests that pilgrims came great distances to make offerings to the cenote. The mud at the bottom also preserved objects made of perishable materials, including wooden weapons, scepters, statuettes, tools, and jewelry, as well as textiles. Items made of pottery, stone, and bone, and shells were also recovered, and many of the offerings were intentionally damaged, indicating that they were being ritually "killed" as a form of a sacrifice. There was also evidence of human sacrifice. The cenote was thought to be the home of the rain god Chaac, to whom young men were sacrificed in order to assure the coming of the rains.

Like Lake Guatavita, the Sacred Cenote was explored several times in an attempt to recover the gold and other offerings. Unlike Lake Guatavita, however, this was done under archaeological supervision, beginning in 1904, by the American consul and amateur archaeologist Edward H. Thomson (1857–1935), many of whose finds are now displayed at the Peabody Museum in Cambridge, MA. He began his two-decade explorations of the cenote with a simple dredge consisting of a bucket-and-pulley system. According to Thomson's journals, once they had cleared the cenote of debris, they managed about 16 to 18 hauls a day. In 1909, Thomson decided to use a diving suit to explore the cenote. Although the visibility was very poor, and the cenote was full of shifting rocks and trees, he managed to recover gold, copper, and jade artifacts from the mud that had accumulated in the cracks in the cenote's limestone bottom.

There were two further expeditions to investigate the contents of the Cenote Sagrado in the twentieth century, sponsored by the Mexican National Institute for Anthropology and History. The first, in 1961, recovered several important artifacts, including a bone sheathed in gold, a sacrificial knife with a wooden handle covered in gold leaf, and wood, jade, and onyx ear ornaments, now on display at the Museum of Archeology and Anthropology in Mexico City. The second expedition, led by archaeologist Ramón Piña Chán (1920–2001) in 1967 attempted to drain the water from the cenote and when this failed, to clarify the water to allow a more detailed examination of the bottom. Unfortunately, this was only partially successful, as the water quickly became murky again. The Maya gods and ancestors, it seems, are unwilling to give up the offerings that were made to them over the centuries.

KING IN THE PARKING LOT: REMAINS OF RICHARD III

1612

Circumstance of loss: The exact location of the tomb was lost in 1612

Rediscovery: Found by archaeologists in a parking lot in Leicester

Historical significance: The truth about one of the most famous kings of England

Value: A horse?

King Richard: Slave! I have set my life upon a cast
And I will stand the hazard of the die.
I think there be six Richmonds in the field;
Five have I slain to-day, instead of him. —
A horse! a horse! my kingdom for a horse!

Richard the Third (ca. 1591), Act 5, Scene 4,
by William Shakespeare

© Georgios Kollidas | Shutterstock.com

With this entry, we come to one of the strangest "buried treasures" included in this book. Although burial goods have featured quite prominently thus far, this is the first time that the treasure in question is not a rare, unique, or expensive grave good but the body itself. Considering how many modern *Homo sapiens* have lived and died these past 200,000 years, there is no shortage of skeletons to be found for free, but there are two categories of humans whose remains have an intrinsic value: The bones of Christian saints who were martyred for their faith, which were held to have miraculous powers and were traded for large sums during the Middle Ages as relics; and the bones of God's anointed kings and queens—especially in a country where monarchy is still revered as much as it is in England.

Of course, it helps if the king in question is also historically significant, as one of the main protagonists in the closing act of the War of the Roses (1455–87) between the two great houses of York and Lancaster, and is also something of a cultural icon. Richard III (1452–85), though he only reigned for two years (1483–85), is one of a select band of kings, queens, and emperors whose reigns have been dramatized for the stage by William Shakespeare (ca. 1564–1616). Shakespeare wrote *The Tragedy of King Richard the Third* during the reign of Elizabeth I (1533–1603), the granddaughter of Henry VII (1457–1509), who defeated and killed Richard at the Battle of Bosworth (1485). Unsurprisingly, the play is not kind to Richard, who is portrayed as an evil hunchback with a withered arm—an oath-breaker, usurper, and child murderer.

When Richard's brother King Edward IV (1442–83) died unexpectedly, his 13-year-old son should have succeeded him as Edward V (1470–83). But before he could be crowned, Richard had Parliament declare his brother's marriage invalid and his children illegitimate, thus preventing them from inheriting the throne. He then claimed the crown for himself. Prince Edward and his younger brother, the ten-year-old Richard, Duke of York (1473–83), were taken to the Tower of London and were never seen again, alive or dead. According to Shakespeare, Richard had them smothered as they slept. Although Richard was a good candidate for the murder of his nephews, so was his successor, Henry Tudor, who would have found the two princes just as inconvenient.

What better way to blacken Richard's name than to accuse him of the murder of the young princes in the Tower, whose mother laments them as "those tender babes/Whom envy hath immured within your walls!" (*Richard III*, Act 3, Scene 1). The real coup, of course, was to get the English language's greatest dramatist to do the hatchet job. In the intervening centuries, Shakespeare's monstrous Richard has been played by some of England's leading tragedians, including Laurence Olivier (1907–89), whose chilling screen portrayal of the king in 1955 confirmed him as one of England's most nefarious villains.

There are those, however, who, 530 years after Richard's death and in the face of centuries of Tudor propaganda, continue to work tirelessly for his rehabilitation. Among his most ardent supporters is Philippa Langley (b. 1962), secretary of the Scottish branch of the Richard III Society, who was not only determined to clear Richard's name but also to find his grave and have his remains given a proper royal burial. Although the circumstances of Richard's death were well known—he was hacked to death on the battlefield after being unhorsed—by 1612, the exact whereabouts of his grave had been lost.

"R" MARKS THE SPOT

After Richard had met his gruesome end on Bosworth Field, his corpse was stripped, mutilated, slung over a horse, and taken to the nearby city of Leicester, where it was hurriedly buried in the choir of the Greyfriars Priory church. His was not quite an anonymous pauper's burial but nor was it a king's funeral. In 1534, Henry VII's heir, Henry VIII (1491–1547), had a famous falling out with the Catholic Church over the matter of his many wives, and appointed himself head of the Protestant Church of England. From 1536, he began to dissolve the English monasteries, which refused to accept the break with the papacy or the king's authority. They had also committed the cardinal sins of being extremely rich while paying no taxes to Henry's exchequer. The Leicester Greyfriars was sold to a local landowner, who demolished the church, but kept the monument over Richard's grave, which was now in the open air in his garden.

The house and grounds were later sold and for four centuries roads were built and buildings erected on the site until all traces of the priory, the garden, and Richard's small monument had vanished. The demolition of a building on what was thought to be the site of the priory in 2012 gave local archaeologists a chance to confirm that this was indeed the location of the old monastic buildings, including the priory church, which fortuitously turned out to be under a municipal parking lot. This was the archaeologists'

© Getty Images

MORTAL REMAINS
Richard's skull in situ under
a Leicester parking lot.

first piece of good luck, because had a substantial building been erected over the burial, its foundations would have completely destroyed any evidence.

The subsequent exhumation of the king's remains was filmed for Channel 4's *Richard III: The King in the Car Park*, broadcast on February 4, 2013, with the active participation of Philippa Langley. When she arrived at the lot and stood over a parking bay coincidentally marked with the letter "R," she was certain she was stepping over the dead king's grave. Probably to please the cameras and Ms Langley, the Leicester University archaeological team began digging at the spot where she had "felt" the king's presence and immediately uncovered human remains in a medieval burial. In what turned out to be a second and even greater piece of archaeological and televisual luck, the team had found the skeleton of a man with a deformed spine, whose skull and body showed evidence of having died in battle. Moreover, as they extended the trench, they realized that it was in the middle of the choir of the former church, exactly where Richard was supposed to have been laid to rest.

After comprehensive scientific tests, including the carbon dating of the skeleton, a forensic examination of the body, and the genetic testing of known descendants of Richard's sister, who shared his mitochondrial (maternal) DNA, the University of Leicester was able to confirm with a 99.9 percent degree of certainty that these were indeed the remains of Richard III. Although Richard did have a serious sideways curvature of the spine—known as scoliosis—he was not a classic hunchback like Quasimodo; nor did he have Shakespeare's withered arm or lopsided leer. A facial reconstruction produced by a leading forensic artist revealed a handsome man in his prime with particularly fine, almost feminine features. By the standard of our age, Richard was not a *nice* man, but he was no worse than most of his contemporaries, including Henry VII, and he was certainly not the tragic monster that Shakespeare created and that history now remembers.

BANK OF SPAIN: *NUESTRA SEÑORA DE ATOCHA* TREASURE

1622

TREASURE

Burial goods

Hoards

Shipwrecks

Religious objects or places

Artworks

Gemstones

Circumstance of loss: Sunk during a hurricane off the Florida Keys

Rediscovery: Found by salvage expert Mel Fisher

Historical significance: The wealth of the New World that ruined the Old World

Value: $450 million

Within a week [of the sinking], salvage efforts were made. The Atocha *was found near the last Key of Matecumbe. Her mizzenmast was protruding above the water in 55 feet of water—too deep for divers. Salvors failed to find the* Margarita, *but did salvage the* Rosario.

***Shipwrecks of Florida* (1998) by Steven D. Singer**

BANK OF SPAIN
Part of the vast treasure recovered from the *Atocha*.

© National Geographic | Getty Images

In the three previous entries, I featured treasures that represented a tiny fraction of the wealth of pre-Columbian Native America looted by Spanish conquistadors and treasure hunters, who beyond all other commodities sought gold—the metallic element *Aurum*, which owes its value to its rarity. Even with modern mining methods, the supply of gold on the earth's surface is remarkably small and finite, because early on in our planet's history, the heavier elements sank to the earth's iron core, which is literally "gold-plated." Gold is unevenly distributed across the globe, and in many regions, it has to be acquired by trade, theft, or war.

The Byzantine Empire (395–1453) minted the gold *solidus* as its principal unit of currency, but the Western Roman Empire (30–476 CE) and its successor states in Europe, where gold was in short supply, had to make do with silver. Thus, Spain and Portugal, whose navigators first reached the New World, were particularly "gold hungry." Gold has the added attraction of being one of the few metals that does not tarnish, along with copper, the only other metal that is not a dull, functional gray, making it the material of choice for jewelry and other luxury artifacts. In terms of its practical applications, however, is has all the usefulness of a chocolate hammer: It is far too soft to be made into tools, and anyone depending on gold armor for protection will quickly discover that it is not only cripplingly heavy but also very poor at deflecting steel blades and arrows.

In 1492, when Christopher Columbus (1451–1506) sailed the ocean blue, the Catholic Spanish kingdoms of Castile and Aragon had only just completed the *Reconquista*, the reconquest of the Iberian Peninsula from Islamic rule. Their most Catholic majesties celebrated their victory by expelling the Jews from the kingdom, crippling its economy and banking system. Although they did not know it at the time, in reaching the Americas first, they had won the equivalent of history's biggest lottery jackpot: A continent-sized empire, full of untapped natural resources, whose inhabitants were technologically vulnerable, as the most advanced cultures were still living in the Stone Age in terms of their military hardware, and health-wise, because they had no immunity to Old World diseases.

I have earlier sketched the sad history of the conquests of the Aztecs of Mexico, the Inca of Peru, the Maya of Yucatán, and the Musica of Colombia—defeated by Spanish steel, gunpowder, and smallpox. From an impoverished, fragmented, and partly foreign-dominated land, Spain suddenly became the richest country on earth, and like a modern-day lottery winner, went on a spending spree, investing in palatial new cities, the best luxury goods money could buy, and vast armies and fleets, acquiring a huge amount of Old World real estate to add to her vast American empire, with holdings in the Low Countries (present-day Belgium and Holland), Italy, Portugal, and North Africa, and also splashing out enough cash to buy the crown of the Holy Roman Empire (see "Sroda treasure" pp. 159–162).

Blinded by the luster of the huge amounts of bullion they pillaged from the ruins of Tenochtitlan and Cuzco, the Spanish did not immediately realize that gold and silver were as rare in the Americas as they are anywhere else. In the eighteenth century, they would discover the true price they had to pay for the theft of Aztec and Inca treasure. The British, French, and Dutch, who had been denied the easy pickings of Central and South America, had to make do with the much less promising wilderness of North America. But instead of basing their economies on the exploitation of finite resources—gold, silver, and gems—they developed mercantile and industrial networks, importing raw materials and exporting manufactured goods worldwide.

What is striking about the pillaged wealth of the New World is how bad the Spanish were at getting it back to Spain. In 1566, they instituted a yearly convoy of treasure, or "plate," fleets (from the Spanish word for silver, *plata*) between Seville and Havana, Cuba, carrying colonists, books, and textiles to the Americas, and returning laden with tropical woods, silver, gold, gems, pearls, spices, sugar, and tobacco. A single treasure galleon might carry an average of two million *pesos*, or "pieces of eight" (0.88 ounces/25 g of silver). Naturally, the treasure fleets were a tempting prize for enemy navies, as well as pirates and privateers,

© M.M. | Creative Commons

WORLD STANDARD
Colombia's Muzo emeralds are said to be the finest.

"ATOCHA MOTHERLODE"

and others were lost to the hurricanes that regularly ravage the Gulf of Mexico and the Caribbean.

In 1622, the galleon *Nuestra Señora de Atocha* was due to sail with the 27 other vessels of that year's plate fleet, after collecting cargo from ports in Colombia and Panama. The quantity of treasure from Peru and Bolivia delivered by mule train from the Pacific coast of Panama to Portobelo on the Atlantic coast was so great that it took eight weeks to load it onto the *Atocha*. After further delays in Havana, the fleet set sail six weeks behind schedule, at the peak of the North Atlantic hurricane season. On September 4, the fleet was caught in a storm near the Florida Keys and suffered the loss of seven ships. The *Atocha* sank in 55 feet (16.7 m) of water on a sandbank later christened the "Bank of Spain" because of the vast amount of treasure discovered there.

The loss of the treasure galleons was quickly reported, and five survivors from the 265-strong complement of the *Atocha* were rescued clinging to the ship's mizzenmast, which was still above water. Salvage efforts to recover her cargo began at once, but the wreck was too deep for free divers. However, before more sophisticated equipment could be brought from Havana, another hurricane tore off the mast and stern castle, making it impossible for the Spanish to relocate the wreck.

Salvage expert Mel Fisher (1922–98) discovered the sunken galleon in 1985, from which he recovered the $450 million "*Atocha* Motherlode," consisting of 114,000 silver pieces of eight, gold coins, 40 tons (36 metric tons) of silver and gold bars, and Colombian emeralds from the Muzo Mine, whose production is of such high quality that it sets the international standard for emeralds. According to the ship's manifest, still preserved in the Archives of the Indies in Seville, this only represents half the treasure the *Atocha* was carrying. Still missing are 300 silver bars, and more gold and Muzo emeralds that were probably stored in the captain's cabin in the stern castle. In 2011, divers 35 miles (56 km) from the Keys discovered artifacts thought to be from the *Atocha*, including an emerald ring valued at $500,000, raising hopes that the *Atocha* account at the "Bank of Spain" has not yet "dried up."

CRY "GOLD!" FOR SCOTLAND: TREASURE OF LOCK ARKAIG

1746

TREASURE

Burial goods

Hoards

Shipwrecks

Religious objects or places

Artworks

Gemstones

Circumstance of loss: Hidden from the English in a cave near Loch Arkaig

Rediscovery: Not yet found

Historical significance: The loss of the money prevented the Stuarts from attempting another rising to recover the English throne

Value: 40,000 gold *louis*

The two [French] privateers Le Mars *and* La Bellone *sailed from Nantes in April with 40,000 louis d'or for the prince, unaware of his defeat at Culloden. Anchoring in Loch-nan-Uamh, the French began to unload the money (later to become notorious as the 'Loch Arkaig treasure').*

Charles Edward Stuart (1988) by Frank McLynn

Fans of the film *Braveheart* (1995), featuring the stirring deeds of Scots freedom fighter William Wallace (d. 1305), a.k.a. Mel Gibson (b. 1956), would be well advised to skip this entry because the story of Prince Charles Edward Stuart (1720–88), The Young Pretender, does not reflect well on the prince, his advisers, and his supporters in Scotland, who tried to restore him to the English and Scottish thrones in 1745.

The Stuart dynasty had had an uneasy relationship with the English ever since the reign of Mary, Queen of Scots (1542–87), who was beheaded by her cousin, Elizabeth I (1533–1603). Nevertheless, because Elizabeth died childless, it was Mary's son, James VI of Scotland and I of England (1566–1625), who inherited the Crown, forming the first union of the two kingdoms. The Stuarts were Catholics or Catholic sympathizers, allied to England's traditional enemies, Spain and France, which made them deeply suspect to the Protestant English nobility and loathed by the Protestant English populace. Charles I (1600–49) single-handedly managed to trigger the only republican episode in English history (1640–60), and was executed for his pains. His restored son Charles II (1630–85) had a more successful reign, but his successor, the unpopular, autocratic James II (1633–1701), was deposed and exiled.

© Public domain

PRINCE CHARMING
Charles Stuart was no
William Wallace.

Rather than try another republican experiment, the British chose to crown James II's Protestant daughter, Mary II (1662–94), who died without issue and was succeeded by her younger sister, the childless Queen Anne (1665–1714). On her death, the acceptable Protestant Stuart line of succession ended, leaving Parliament with a difficult decision: Recall James II's son, James Edward Stuart, the Old Pretender (1688–1766), who had been living in exile in France, or find a distant royal relation who was not only Protestant but also willing to take on the English and Scots, whose kingdoms had been officially joined by the Act of Union of 1707.

In 1714, the English persuaded the elderly, stolid George, Elector of Hanover (1660–1727), who spoke only German and never bothered to learn English, and who never really took to his new realm and rebellious subjects, to become Britain's first true constitutional monarch as George I.

Not only was he a Protestant but he also had a male heir, who succeeded him as George II (1683–1760), whose line leads, with a few kinks, to the present queen, Elizabeth II (b. 1926).

The Stuarts, however, were not going to give up their birthright without a fight. James Edward Stuart attempted a first invasion of England with French support in 1715, and therefore known as the "Fifteen." The Stuarts' main power base was among the surviving Catholic nobility in the west of England, and among the Scots, both Protestant and Catholic. The first Jacobite rising (from the Latin for James, Jacobus), which was badly planned and even more poorly executed, ended in a fiasco, and rather than challenging the Hanoverian dynasty, helped it to consolidate its hold on power. Rather than submit to a Catholic king in the pay of the hated French, Spanish, and the pope, the English preferred to rally around their fat, cantankerous old German king. In 1745, it was the turn of James Edward's son, Charles Edward, to attempt to restore his family to the throne, in the second Jacobite rising, known as the "Forty-five."

THE BONNIE PRINCE

Charles was 25, handsome (at least in his portraits), and cut a dashing figure in Highland military dress, even though he had no military training or experience. He had grown up at the decadent French court of Versailles, the palatial home of the absolute Catholic Bourbon Ancien Régime, whose own days were numbered. His model, Louis XV (1710–74), commanded the love and respect (and, if not, the fear) of his loyal Catholic subjects—the Protestant French having been persecuted, imprisoned, forced to convert, or exiled. Charles Edward would be immortalized by a later age as a heroic but tragic romantic figure, "Bonnie Prince Charlie," the subject of ballads, poems, and adventure novels, which, as is often the case, glossed over a rather sordid series of miscalculations, mistakes, and betrayals that led to the Forty-five's failure. You will not find many latter-day Scots Nationalists, now campaigning for their independence from the United Kingdom, who will call for a restoration of the Stuart line as the kings of a newly independent Kingdom of Scotland.

In July 1745, Charles landed in Scotland with no army and little money, to raise the Jacobite standard of revolt against the Hanoverians who, by then, had been 31 years on the throne. George II, though not at all dashing, and not much more popular or anglicized than his father, had nevertheless reached an accommodation with the English Parliament and peerage, the

English population, and many among the Lowland Scots. Charles came with nothing more than promises: of French troops and Spanish gold. The French fleet was caught in a storm, and the army never materialized, but the gold did start arriving. The first installment was delivered in 1745 but fell into the hands of clansmen loyal to King George. In 1746, a second much larger sum of around 40,000 *louis d'or*, or 960,000 *livres*, arrived on board two French ships (see quote, p. 183), which was given into the custody of Scots clansmen loyal to the prince.

By then, however, the Jacobite cause had been lost. The rising had started well: Charles raised an army of Highlanders, captured the Scottish capital, Edinburgh, crossed into England, and took the border garrison town of Carlisle.

DEATH OF FREEDOM
The Forty-five ended in disaster at the Battle of Culloden.

With the bulk of the English army fighting on the Continent, Charles met little resistance and reached Swarkestone Bridge, Derbyshire, 125 miles (200 km) north of London. Panicked by false rumors that the English had mustered a large army to protect the capital, Charles retreated, giving the English time to assemble a real army and go on the offensive. The English and Scots met for the climatic battle of the rising (and the last pitched battle to be fought on British soil) at Culloden, on April 16, 1746. Trying to imitate William Wallace's successes against the English 450 years earlier, the Highlanders charged the English line, only to be mown down by musket fire and grapeshot.

With Charles on the run, which included an episode when he had to disguise himself as a maid to avoid capture, Jacobite clan chiefs, including Cluny Macpherson (d. ca. 1765), who were also wanted men, hid the French and Spanish gold near Loch Arkaig about 15 miles (24 km) north of Fort William in the Highlands. In 1753, Charles sent Archibald Cameron (1707–53) to recover the treasure, but he was arrested and executed as a rebel. Charles, always short of funds, continued to search for the Loch Arkaig treasure, finally accusing Cluny Macpherson of embezzling all or part of it. In 1850, a few gold *louis* were unearthed near the loch, possibly all that was left of Bonnie Prince Charlie's fabled French and Spanish gold.

HOT OFF THE PRESS: DUNLAP BROADSIDE OF THE DECLARATION OF INDEPENDENCE

1776

TREASURE

Burial goods

Hoards

Shipwrecks

Religious objects or places

Artworks

Gemstones

Circumstance of loss: Hidden from the British or used to frame a painting

Rediscovery: Found in a painting bought in a flea market for $4

Historical significance: One of 26 surviving broadsides of the 200 printed by John Dunlap on the evening of July 4, 1776

Value: $8.14 million

We hold these truths to be self-evident, that all men are created equal, that they are endowed by their Creator with certain unalienable Rights, that among these are Life, Liberty, and the pursuit of Happiness.

Declaration of Independence, in Congress, July 4, 1776

"WE HOLD THESE TRUTHS…"
Jefferson drafted the Declaration of Independence.

Before embarking on this entry, I should explain why I have decided to include the Dunlap broadside of the American Declaration of Independence in the category "Religious objects or places." Primarily, it was a matter of expediency, as the object in question did not fit into any other available category, but secondarily, because the Declaration of Independence, like the Stars and Stripes and the Constitution, is held in such high honor in the United States, that it also seemed somehow appropriate to place it alongside sacred artifacts and religious relics. As evidence of its sanctity, I present the one sentence quoted overleaf, which established the entire concept of human rights, giving it legal validity for the first time in human history.

In the previous entry, I examined the early successes of England's Hanoverian dynasty against the Jacobite risings by the Stuart pretenders to the English throne. In the current entry, we look at what might be considered to be the dynasty's greatest failure: the loss of the Thirteen Colonies in the American War of Independence (1775–83). The shock of the British defeat was so great that it was thought to have caused the third Hanoverian king of England, George III (1738–1820), to go insane. His illness, however, was a physical ailment that caused the symptoms of mental instability.

The course of the American war is so well known that it does not need to be repeated here in any detail. Starting with a demand for greater self-government under the slogan, "No taxation without representation," the colonists were driven by inept British policies to fight for full independence from the Crown. In June of 1776, the Second Continental Congress appointed "The Committee of Five," which included John Adams (1735–1826), Thomas Jefferson (1743–1826), and Benjamin Franklin (1706–90), to produce the draft Declaration of Independence — the document that more than any other symbolizes the birth of the United States of America and sets out its guiding principles.

Jefferson wrote most of the initial draft, which the committee presented to Congress on June 28. The document was debated for a further two days after Congress had voted for secession from the British Crown on July 2. The delegates cut about one-quarter of the initial text and made further changes in wording and style, which together produced one of the modern world's most important political documents. Congress ratified the Declaration on July 4—henceforth celebrated as Independence Day. All that now remained was the small matter of defeating Great Britain, the eighteenth-century global superpower, whose empire already encompassed far-flung territories on which the sun never set, and whose armies and navies surrounded the new United States. The Americans, as my readers hardly need to be reminded, led by George Washington (1732–99), prevailed, with a little help from the Marquis de Lafayette (1757–1834) and the French, who were finally able to avenge centuries of humiliations at the hands of the English.

Ratifying the Declaration of Independence was one thing, but letting the 13 colonies know that they were now the United States of America was quite another in an age before film, television, smart phones, and the Internet. There was no handy @GeorgeWashington Twitter feed to let the new Americans know what had been decided in their name in Philadelphia. Apart from word of mouth, town criers, and the mail, the only way to circulate information was through the printed word. On the evening of July 4, Irish-born John Dunlap (1747–1812), a Philadelphia printer and bookseller, who had obtained the printing contract for the Continental Congress, was sent the final draft of the Declaration. Overnight, he printed 200 broadsides of the document for immediate distribution throughout the newly independent states.

AN AMERICAN BROADSIDE AGAINST THE BRITISH

A broadside was a large-format printed sheet that was used to display official proclamations, news of important events, commercial advertisements, and also popular songs and ballads. Like modern posters, they were printed on one side, and were meant to be disposable, although there were also fine-art broadsides of poetry for more permanent display in the home. Apart from Jefferson's and several other handwritten drafts and the final copy of the Declaration and its facsimile made in 1823 to replace the damaged original, a Dunlap broadside is as close as anyone can get to acquiring an original version—a small but very important piece of American history.

There are 26 surviving Dunlap broadsides of the Declaration, most owned and displayed by important national and overseas institutions, including

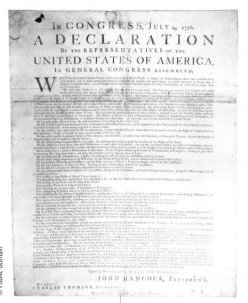

SHORT RUN
One of the 26 surviving
Dunlap broadsides.

the Library of Congress and the New York Public Library, which makes the circumstances of the finding of the twenty-fifth broadside even more noteworthy. In 1989, financial analyst Donald Scheer was on the lookout for an old frame at a flea market in Adamstown, PA. He spotted a frame that he liked, framing a picture he didn't particularly care for, but for which he paid the princely sum of $4—at which the seller probably rejoiced at getting so good a price for a dud picture, and as it turns out, a dud frame, as well. When Scheer removed the painting, the frame fell apart, revealing an old printed sheet, which turned out to be a copy of the Declaration of Independence. Most people might not have thought much of it—old printed sheets were often used as backing for framing pictures. And how the Declaration got there is a matter of conjecture. Was it just a handy piece of paper used to frame the painting, or was it hidden on purpose so that the British would not find it?

Scheer, however, took the print to be valued and discovered that it was one of the original Dunlap print-run of 200, only three of which have ever been in private hands. When he put the print up for sale at auction in 1991, it fetched $2.42 million, a considerable return on his original $4 investment. Nine years later the print was sold at auction a second time, fetching $8.14 million. In addition to the Dunlap broadsides held by American institutions and government agencies, three broadsides are in the possession of the National Archives of Great Britain: Two were sent to London by Vice Admiral Richard Howe (1726–99) in 1776, and, the third, of unknown provenance, turned up in 2008 in a box of documents.

ECCLESIASTICAL PLUNDER: TREASURE OF LIMA

1820

TREASURE

Burial goods

Hoards

Shipwrecks

Religious objects or places

Artworks

Gemstones

Circumstance of loss: Said to have been hidden on Cocos Island

Rediscovery: Not yet found

Historical significance: Hastened the demise of Spain's American empire

Value: $247 million

It eluded Franklin Roosevelt, Sir Malcolm Campbell and Errol Flynn, but now an explorer from Melton Mowbray could be on the trail of a multi-million-pound hoard of gold, silver and jewelry stolen by pirates and buried on a treasure island.

"British Expedition to Pacific 'treasure island,'" *The Daily Telegraph*, **August 5, 2012**

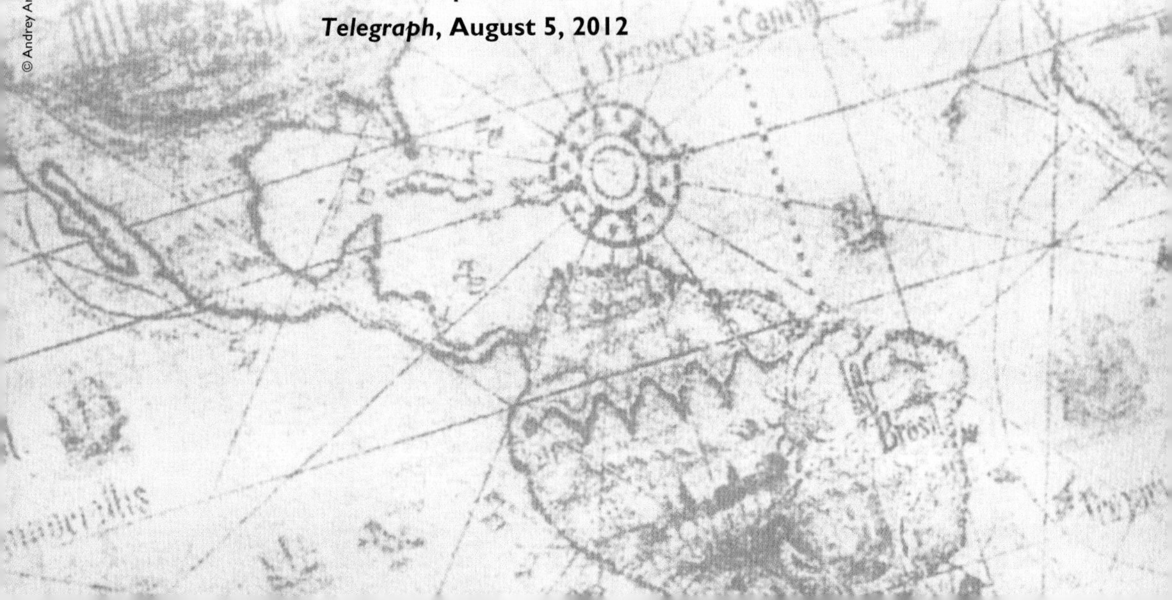

© Andrey Armyagov | Shutterstock.com

MISCALCULATION
Jose de la Serna entrusted the treasure to a British merchantman.

The American War of Independence (1775–83), which I covered in the previous entry, heralded the "Age of Revolutions" that was founded on the ideals of the eighteenth-century philosophical movement known as the European Enlightenment. The French monarchy would succumb in its turn to a revolution in 1789, and the Revolutionary and Napoleonic Wars (1792–1815) would complete the process, radically transforming the political map of the world by putting an end to many absolute monarchies in Europe, as well as several colonial empires, either directly or indirectly.

Although there was no foreign military intervention in Spain's American possessions, the conquest of the Iberian Peninsula by Napoleon Bonaparte (1769–1821), who placed his brother Joseph (1768–1844) on the Spanish throne in 1807, hastened the disintegration of Spain's overseas empire. South America became divided between competing "juntas," some staying loyal to the Bourbon claimant to the Spanish throne, while others, inspired by the American and French revolutions, aspired to emancipation and independence.

There were many among those who fought for independence who hoped to unite the continent into a single national entity on the U.S. model, but the movement to create the Estados Unidos de Sudamerica (United States of South America) was thwarted by rivalries between the different juntas, who fought one another and had to put down revolts of their Native American subjects, who sensed that the time had come to recover their independence from their hated colonial masters. After the restoration of the Bourbon monarchy in Spain in 1813, the Spanish Crown attempted to re-establish its rule in the Americas, but the empire had had its day. Argentina and Chile declared their independence in 1816 and 1818, and in 1819, the two countries signed a pact to liberate Peru, which remained the continent's loyalist stronghold.

The triumvirate of the second supreme director (president) of Chile, Bernardo O'Higgins (1778–1842), General José de San Martin (1778–1850), and British Admiral Thomas Alexander Cochrane (1775–1860), proclaimed the Independence of Peru in 1821. However, it would take another five years, and the intervention of South America's liberator,

Simon Bolivar (1783–1830), in 1824, to bring hostilities to a successful conclusion. By 1826, all the former colonial possessions of the Spanish Crown in South America had won their independence.

Together with New Spain (Mexico), Peru was among the oldest Spanish conquests on the continent, and, as the former territory of the Inca Empire, also one of the richest. In addition to the treasures stolen from Native American peoples of Peru and Colombia (see "Treasure of Lake Guatavita," pp. 167–170), the Spanish had discovered considerable silver deposits in Bolivia, which were exploited with slave labor, and the proceeds sent back to Spain in the yearly treasure fleet (see "*Nuestra Señora de Atocha*, pp. 179–182), to fund Spain's extravagant lifestyle and European wars. Ultimately, even the vast wealth expropriated from a whole continent was not enough to balance Spain's books, and by the end of the eighteenth century, it was bankrupt, and itself ripe for revolution.

TREASURE ISLAND

The French Bonapartist interlude probably did not hasten by very much the inevitable loss of empire, but it made the process more complex, because royalist elements were able to appeal to nationalist sentiment to maintain control of the South American colonies. A year before San Martín proclaimed Peruvian independence, the capital Lima was already on the verge of insurrection. In a panic, the civil and ecclesiastical authorities in the city thought it would be best to ship the treasury of both state and church to Mexico rather than risk it falling into rebel hands.

© Public domain

ISLAND TALES
The treasure is one of several buried on Cocos Island.

According to the inventory, there were 113 solid gold religious statues, including a life-size Madonna holding the Christ child, 200 chests of jewels, 273 swords with jeweled hilts, 1,000 diamonds, several solid gold crowns, and 150 gold and silver chalices, the whole valued at around $247 million.

José de la Serna (1770–1832), the viceroy of Peru, entrusted the vast haul of treasure to the British merchantman *Mary Dear*, captained by William Thomson, and lightly guarded by an escort of six soldiers and several clerics. Instead of sailing to Mexico as chartered, Thomson and his crew turned pirate, slaughtered the Spanish escort, and diverted to Cocos Island, 350 miles (560 km) off the Pacific Coast of Costa Rica, where, according to Thomson, in classic pirate style, they buried the loot somewhere. Before the pirates could make their getaway, to lie low before they returned at a later date to reclaim the treasure, the *Mary Dear* was captured by a Spanish warship, and the crew, except for the captain and the first mate, who had promised to lead the Spaniards to the treasure, were executed, forever silencing the majority of the men who knew its real location. The Spaniards took the two survivors back to the island, but the Englishmen escaped into the jungle, never to be seen or heard of again.

The isolated and usually uninhabited Cocos Island, said to be the inspiration for Michael Crichton's (1942–2008) *Jurassic Park* (1990), and for Robert Louis Stevenson's (1850–94) *Treasure Island* (1883), seems to have been popular with pirates, as another two pirates are supposed to have hidden their ill-gotten hoards there: the English pirate Bennett Graham, who supposedly stashed 350 tons (317 metric tons) of gold on the island; and the Portuguese buccaneer Benito "Bloody Sword" Bonito (d. 1821). The lure of so much potential loot has attracted around 300 treasure-hunting expeditions since 1820, including one led by President Franklin D. Roosevelt (1882–1945) and another by movie star and screen pirate Errol Flynn (1909–59). The most determined treasure hunter was the German August Gissler (1857–1935), who came equipped with two separate treasure maps, and who spent 19 years on the island between 1889 and 1908 excavating a complex network of tunnels, some of which can still be visited today. His total haul, for almost two decades of hardship and hard work was a grand total of six gold coins.

Cocos Island has now been designated a UNESCO World Heritage Site for its unspoiled natural environment and rich wildlife. Although the Costa Rican government actively discourages treasure hunters from coming to the island, it reluctantly gave permission for a British team to search for the treasures using the latest in remote-sensing technology, including a ground-radar robot "snake," airborne 3-D imaging cameras, and a keyhole drill that can reach 100 feet (30 m) into caves with minimal disturbance.

THE LAST PIRATE: JEAN LAFITTE'S TREASURE

1821

Circumstance of loss: Treasure reportedly hidden in several locations in Louisiana

Rediscovery: None reportedly found

Historical significance: Jean Lafitte was one of the last buccaneers, with a fleet of pirate ships under his command operating from a series of pirate strongholds

Value: The end of the Pirates of the Caribbean

Hand in hand with the romances went the stories of lost and buried treasure. The prosaic reality is that pirates and privateers lived hand to mouth, were improvident when they had money, and kept plying their trade because they saved none.

The Pirates Lafitte (2006) by William C. Davis

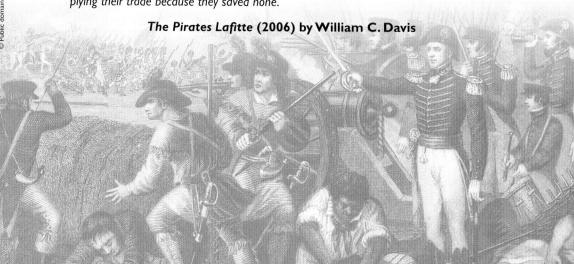

Pirates, with a Yo-ho-ho, a parrot, a wooden leg, and a bottle of rum — not to forget the main ingredient: a treasure chest full of stolen gold doubloons and gemstones — have been a B-movie staple since Douglas Fairbanks (1883–1939) swashed and buckled his way through the role of the Black Pirate, in the 1926 film of the same name, to today's frankly absurd but highly entertaining Disney franchise *Pirates of the Caribbean* (2003–present), starring Johnny Depp (b. 1963), as the very difficult to kill Captain Jack Sparrow.

HIGH-SEAS ENTERPRISE
Lafitte was more businessman than buccaneer.

As is often the case with Hollywood cowboys, knights in shining armor, and gladiators, pirate movies romanticize the very harsh and often sordid lives and deaths of the protagonists, turning them into maritime Robin Hoods who robbed the rich (and usually fat and corrupt) Spanish officials and redistributed the gold to the deserving poor. In reality, pirates were cutthroats, who dealt out death and destruction to anyone they encountered and blew their money on the eighteenth-century version of "sex, drugs, and rock 'n' roll." It was not by accident that the Jolly Roger — the flag bearing a variant of the skull-and-crossbones motif — was chosen as the pirate emblem. A black Jolly Roger signified that quarter would be given if the merchantman surrendered quickly, but a red one meant that no quarter would be given under any circumstances. Pirates did not expect mercy from their captors, nor did they give it to their victims.

The adventures of fictional pirates are nevertheless based on the lives and exploits of real buccaneers and privateers active during the "Golden Age" of Caribbean piracy, in the run-up to and immediately after the War of the Spanish Succession (1701–14) that was being fought in Europe. Famous first-generation pirates included Sir Henry Morgan (ca. 1635–88), John Rackham (a.k.a. Calico Jack; 1682–1720), Edward Thatch (a.k.a. Blackbeard; ca. 1680–1718), and, most successful of all in terms of ships captured, Bartholomew Roberts (1682–1722). A quick reckoning of their ages at time of death, however, demonstrates that their lives and careers were short, often ending on the end of a hangman's rope.

Morgan, a semi-official pirate, or "privateer," who was issued with letters of marque by the English Crown that allowed him to prey on the ships and colonies of Spain with impunity—from the English Royal Navy, if not the Spanish Royal Navy—lived longer than most and was knighted for his piratical services to the Crown. Thatch, Rackham, and Roberts, whose names inspired terror among the settlers of Spanish America and the West Indies, died at the comparatively young ages of 38 and 40. Piracy, while its financial rewards could be considerable, was not a long-term career option.

The pirates of today's East African waters who prey on giant, lightly crewed supertankers and container ships—to ransom the crews, ships, and cargoes for millions of dollars—have a lot in common with the pirates that operated in Spanish Main in the seventeenth and eighteenth centuries. The regions where the pirates operated in the seventeenth century, as is the case with where pirates operate now, were in a state of semi-permanent warfare, with corrupt, failed, and rogue states incapable or unwilling to police their own territory and waters. The waters of the Caribbean were the frequent battlegrounds for the fleets of Spain, France, and England, whose governments issued letters of marque to privateers to attack each other's settlements and commercial shipping during hostilities.

The myriad islands and archipelagos of the Caribbean Sea—Jamaica, Tortuga, and the Lesser Antilles—provided ideal bases from which the pirates could operate unhindered by the overstretched naval forces of the colonial administrations. However, after the Peace of Utrecht (1714) ended the War of the Spanish Succession, the European powers realized that the pirates, whom they had found useful as irritants during wartime, were now seriously threatening the economy of the Caribbean, which produced most of the sugar consumed on Europe's tables. By the early 1720s, England's Royal Navy and a strengthened Spanish coastguard had all but eliminated the pirate menace from the Caribbean.

PIRATE INC.

The second phase of piracy in the region coincided with another period of wide-ranging social, economic, and political changes triggered by the American War of Independence (1775–83) and ensuing Anglo-American conflict (1812–15) and the French Revolutionary and Napoleonic Wars (1792–1815), which themselves triggered independence movements in Central and Latin America (1810s–1820s), which resulted in the foundation of new nation-states (see previous entry), while at the same time creating many opportunities for a new generation of pirates and privateers.

In 1803, Napoleon Bonaparte (1769–1821), soon to declare himself emperor of France, sold the French colony of Louisiane, named for King Louis XIV (1638–1715), and henceforth known as Louisiana, and its main port of New Orleans, to the United States for $230 million at the 2012 exchange rate—a bargain at any price, as it gave the U.S. a prime beachfront property on the Gulf of Mexico and the Caribbean, which had previously been a European preserve. The year 1807 saw two legal measures with far-reaching long-term impacts on the economy of the region, which also provided lucrative opportunities for those with business acumen, loose morals, and fast ships: The British Crown abolished the slave trade, making it a crime for a British ship to carry slaves; and the United States government passed the Embargo Act that barred all American ships from docking at foreign ports to prevent the seizure of U.S. merchant shipping during the wars between Britain and France.

The Embargo Act, which was designed with the best of intentions to protect neutral American shipping, had the effect of instantly crippling America's maritime trade, especially that of the thriving port of New Orleans, which relied heavily on trade with the Caribbean colonies of Spain, France, and England. The field was wide open for two freelance entrepreneurs, Jean Lafitte (ca. 1776–ca. 1823) and his older brother, Pierre (1770–1821), to supply goods to the merchants of New Orleans, except that in this case, the U.S. government defined the goods as "contraband," and the entrepreneurs as "smugglers" and "pirates."

There are two theories about the origins of the Lafittes: that they were the sons of colonists from French Saint-Domingue (now part of Haiti) who migrated to Louisiana in the 1780s, or that they were born in metropolitan France. In 1805, the brothers were already operating a lucrative smuggling operation into New Orleans, whose scope and profits only increased after the Embargo Act. They set themselves up on the Island of Barataria in the bay of the same name, which was sufficiently out of the way to avoid notice by U.S. customs and coastguard. However, they were not satisfied with the modest returns from smuggling, and outfitted a schooner to engage in much more lucrative acts of piracy, seizing ships and their cargoes. By 1814 they had a small fleet of ships operating out of Barataria.

When Britain and the U.S. went to war in 1812, the Lafittes were caught between the two camps. The British feared that the brothers would throw in their lot with the U.S., while the Americans feared the opposite. In September 1814, an American squadron attacked Barataria and seized Jean Lafitte's crews, ships, arsenal, and $500,000 worth of contraband, though he himself managed to escape. When General and future U.S. President Andrew Jackson (1767–1845) arrived in New Orleans to defend the city from a threatened British invasion, he found the "Big Easy" almost undefended, with a few thousand raw recruits and just two ships to resist the approaching British fleet. Lafitte offered his and his crew's services for a full pardon. Jackson agreed and together the two men won the Battle of New Orleans fought on January 8, 1815.

Rather than rest on their laurels and continue to serve their new adopted homeland, the Lafittes became involved in the Mexican War of Independence (1810–21), notionally acting as spies for the Spanish Crown. Jean went to Galveston Island, then part of Spanish Texas, to spy on Mexican revolutionaries. True to his past, however, Lafitte set up a privateering and piracy operation on the island that took advantage of poorly drafted U.S. anti-slavery statutes that allowed the resale of slaves captured from enemy ships. He remained in Galveston until 1821, until the U.S. government ordered his eviction after his crews had attacked American shipping. After burning down his home and HQ, the Maison Rouge, he supposedly escaped with his treasure aboard the *Pride*. Beaten but never defeated, Lafitte continued to live from piracy and smuggling, until he met his match and was killed during a battle with two heavily armed Spanish privateers in the Gulf of Honduras in 1823.

As for Lafitte's rumored caches of treasure, none has ever been found. This has not stopped treasure hunters from going to extraordinary lengths to try to find them. In the 1920s, a private consortium dammed and drained Indian Bayou, Louisiana, in a quest for stashed gold; all that was recovered was a Native American dugout canoe. Other locations that have been extensively explored for Lafitte's treasure include Galveston, Texas, Grand Isle in Barataria Bay, and Contraband Bayou, which runs through the City of Lake Charles, Louisiana. Thus far, the only people to profit from Lafitte's piracy are the citizens of Lake Charles, who celebrate his life and legend in Contraband Days, an annual festival held in May.

TREASURE

Burial goods

Hoards

Shipwrecks

Religious objects or places

Artworks

Gemstones

SHOGUN'S BOUNTY: TOKUGAWA GOLD

1868

Circumstance of loss: Hidden just before the fall of the last shogun

Rediscovery: Not yet found

Historical significance: The legend is resurrected during economic crises in Japan

Value: 4 million gold ryo

During the 1870–80s, the 1930s, and the 1990s, times of economic instability, the countryside surrounding Tokyo witnessed a corresponding influx of treasure hunters looking for Tokugawa gold.

Asian Popular Culture (2013) edited by John Lent and Lorna Fitzsimmons

We last visited Japan in the eleventh century (pp. 140–143) when a climatic naval battle between two samurai clans established the pattern of government that would endure until the nineteenth century. Although the emperor sat on the imperial throne in the ceremonial capital of Kyoto in Western Japan, his days occupied in complex court ceremonial and religious ritual, he was more the high priest of the Shinto religion than a temporal ruler. The real power was held by feudal lords, who, after defeating their rivals, were granted the title of shogun by a grateful sovereign. The longest and last of this succession of military dictatorships was the Tokugawa Shogunate, or *Bakufu* in Japanese (1600–1868), founded by Tokugawa Ieyasu (1543–1616).

Fearing that Japan would slowly turn into a European dependency and become corrupted by Christianity, in 1633 Ieyasu decreed that the country would be closed to all foreigners, save for a very limited number of Dutch and Chinese merchants, who were given access to the artificial island of Dejima in the port city of Nagasaki. All outside influences, including the Christian religion, were outlawed, and Japanese converts persecuted, forced to convert, or executed. While China, Southeast Asia, and India gradually succumbed to Western imperialism and colonialism, Japan, almost uniquely in Asia, managed to remain isolated and closed to practically all foreign intercourse until 1853, when a naval squadron commanded by Commodore Matthew Perry (1794–1858) of the United States Navy achieved the greatest diplomatic coup of the age by forcing the shogun to open Japan's ports to foreign trade.

© Public domain

PACIFIC OVERTURES
Perry opened Japan to foreign trade.

Japan, whose military technology had progressed little since the seventeenth century, was outgunned by the Western powers, which imposed unequal trade treaties, just as they had done all over Asia. The Bakufu, once a powerful leading force in the Japanese empire, was now powerless in the face of the rapacious foreign powers and Japan's rebellious feudal lords, who were all scheming to topple the Tokugawa and take their place. Had the country still been isolated, there might have been a change of shogun from one samurai clan to another and not much else. However, the arrival of foreign powers complicated the situation. The more conservative elements, which were also the main opponents of the Bakufu, endorsed

LAST SHOGUN
Yoshinobu retired, making way for the restoration of direct imperial rule.

the backward-looking policy of *Sonno Joi* ("Revere the Emperor and expel the barbarians").

"Revering the Emperor" did not mean making him de facto ruler of the country; it was merely a way for the feudal lords to use the imperial institution to overthrow the Tokugawa and establish their own legitimacy. Through the 1850s, the Bakufu, ably led by Tairo (equivalent of prime minister) Ii Naosuke (1815–60), attempted to reach some kind of accommodation with the Western powers, while modernizing Japan, and trying to control the rebellious feudal lords. Ii arranged for the succession of the fifteenth and last shogun, Tokugawa Yoshinobu (1837–1913), and began a radical program of reform, playing the Western powers against one another to prevent foreign intervention in what would soon become a civil war between the Bakufu and imperial loyalists.

One of the most progressive officials in Ii's administration was Oguri Kozukenosuke Tadamasa (1827–68), who visited the U.S. in 1860 as a member of the goodwill mission sent to sign a Treaty of Amity and Commerce between the two countries. Upon his return to Japan, he took on several important posts, including *kanjo bugyo* (commissioner of finance), who was responsible for the Bakufu's finances and its reserves of gold, held in the treasury of Edo Castle.

Unfortunately, conservative samurai opposed to Ii's policies assassinated the tairo in 1860. Within seven years the shogun had been deposed, and in 1868 Japan celebrated the official restoration of the Emperor Meiji (1852–1912) and the permanent abolition of the post of shogun. Although the emperor moved from the western capital of Kyoto to a new palace in Edo, renamed Tokyo (the "Eastern Capital"), he was no more powerful than his forebears—his role was carefully circumscribed by the Meiji Constitution, with all the real power going to the feudal lords who had won the civil war for the control of Japan after the shogun's abdication.

TOKUGAWA INSURANCE POLICY

Japan was not a rich country, certainly not in terms of its gold bullion, having few sources of gold itself, but the Bakufu had been in power for over two and a half centuries—time enough for even the most improvident of regimes to put by a little for a "rainy day." The highest denomination in Japan, the gold *ryo*, was an oblong-shaped coin with rounded ends that weighed approximately 0.6 ounces (16.5 g). One ryo was worth 60 silver coins or 4,000 copper coins. The thousand-dollar bill of its day, the ryo had a greater purchasing power in pre-Meiji Japan than in more gold-rich economies that were still on the Gold Standard. In the novels of Edo Japan, 100 ryo represented a considerable fortune.

When the rebels took over Edo Castle after the shogun's resignation, they found the strong rooms of the treasury empty. The most logical explanation was that the gold had already all been spent on modernizing the country's armed forces, and on heavy industrial projects such as a shipyard and Japan's first modern steelworks. However, there was another, more intriguing theory about the fate of the Tokugawa gold: Before his death, Ii Naosuke had planned to hide between 3.6 million and 4 million ryo, amounting to anything up to 72 tons (66 metric tons) of gold, as a war chest to ensure the survival of the Bakufu. As commissioner of finance, Oguri would have followed through with Ii's plan and buried the gold on Mount Akagi in modern-day Gunma Prefecture, north of Tokyo.

Exhaustive exploration of several locations on Mount Akagi have failed to unearth a single ryo. The hopeful treasure hunters include several of Japan's leading commercial TV channels, which have funded televised excavations. Repeated failures have not dampened the enthusiasm for the treasure, especially in Japan's current straitened economic times. One theory holds that Oguri, who was an accomplished scholar, knew his Chinese classics, including Sun-tzu's *Art of War* (ca. 600 BCE), which recommended that a war chest be divided to avoid the whole being discovered by the enemy, and that a trail of disinformation be created to hide the whereabouts of different treasure caches.

The simplest thing would have been to ask Oguri what had happened to the Bakufu's bullion reserves. In 1868, however, Oguri was no longer in office. He had fallen out of favor for his opposition to the regime's military campaign against imperial loyalists, and had retired to a village in Gunma. In the chaotic period immediately after the imperial restoration, government troops arrested and executed Oguri as a leading official of the former regime, silencing for good the one man who knew the real fate of the shogun's treasure.

SEEDS OF REVOLUTION: MISSING FABERGÉ EGGS

1917

Circumstance of loss: During the fall of the House of Romanov in 1917

Rediscovery: Not yet found

Historical significance: If not a direct cause of the Bolshevik Revolution, a very visible symbol of the inequalities of wealth and power that triggered it

Value: $125 million

The Czarevitch Egg [....] Carved from a single block of deep blue lapis lazuli, it was covered by an elaborate golden cage-work containing several motifs, of which the most prominent was the Romanov double-headed eagle. Within the egg was the surprise—a portrait of Alexis, naturally, framed by another Romanov eagle made of platinum and set with more than two thousand diamonds.

***The Extraordinary Story of the Masterpieces That Outlived an Empire* (2008) by Toby Faber**

I have never been, nor am I ever likely to be, a supporter of Communism, or of any other ideology of the extreme left or right. As a student of history, I am only too aware that the totalitarian regimes that they inevitably spawn have been responsible for the greatest crimes against humanity—be it Hitler's (1889–1945) Holocaust (1933–44) of the Jewish people, or Stalin's (1878–1953) Holodomor (1932–33), perpetrated against his own Ukrainian and Russian countrymen. However, the extravagance of the treasures featured in this entry—the missing imperial Fabergé eggs—may shed some light on why Communism triumphed in Russia in 1917, and also help to explain why the last representatives of the Romanov Dynasty (1613–1917), Nicholas II (1868–1918), his wife Alexandra (1872–1918), their son, Alexei (1904–18), and their four daughters, Olga (1895–1918), Tatiana (1897–1918), Maria (1899–1918), and Anastasia (1901–18), died in a hail of bullets in Yekaterinburg.

© Public domain

GILDED COUPLE
The czar and czarina were out of touch with their subjects.

Pre-revolutionary Russia sat in a somewhat anomalous geopolitical position astride Europe and Asia. European Russia looked to the south and west, to Constantinople (now Istanbul), capital of the former Byzantine Empire, which had given her the Cyrillic alphabet, Orthodox Christianity, and the imperial institution, modeled on the "Caesars," which is the origin of the Russian word "czar," and toward the glittering capitals of Western Europe, especially the "City of Lights," Paris. In religion, language, and culture, however, vast tracts of the empire were more properly part of the Islamic Near East, Central Asia, or East Asia, as the empire spanned the whole continent from the shores of the Black Sea to the Pacific coast.

Czar Peter the Great (1672–1725), though an autocrat like his forebears, liked to think of himself as an "enlightened" eighteenth-century European monarch. He abandoned the cramped medieval Moscow, with its wooden houses, onion-domed churches, and the forbidding Kremlin Palace, to build himself a new capital, Saint Petersburg, further west, on the shores of the Baltic Sea, which he and his successors embellished with neo-Classical Italianate churches and palazzos, built along canals and around great piazzas. Despite many attempts at reforms and modernization, Russia remained a backward agricultural economy on a continent that was rapidly modernizing and industrializing. It was not until the reign of Alexander II (1818–81) that serfdom—a form of slavery that kept Russia's peasantry tied to the estates of the landed aristocracy—was abolished. Although hailed as "the Liberator," Alexander was murdered by an ungrateful anarchist and was succeeded by the more conservative Alexander III (1845–94), who reversed some of his father's liberal reforms.

UNDERDEVELOPED
Marx thought Russia too backward for Socialism.

Alexander's successor, Nicholas II, was also a natural small-c conservative, but not a particularly harsh or bad ruler. The worst that can be said about him was that he was indecisive, badly advised, and so out of touch with what was happening in his own country that he sleepwalked into revolution. At the beginning of the twentieth century, Russia had a population of some 135 million, the vast majority of whom were farmers. In 1904, the earnings of the poorest class of landless farming families averaged 220 rubles a year, while the great aristocratic magnates earned 527 times more, or around 116,500 rubles. Although this might have been acceptable in 1717, when this was the state of affairs Europe-wide, by 1917, the rest of the developed world had moved on. After 141 years of intellectual, social, political, and industrial revolution, the citizens of the most advanced countries of North America and Europe had won their human and civil rights, with universal suffrage, equality before the law, and freedom of speech and conscience—all things conspicuously absent in Czarist Russia.

In the monumental *Das Kapital* (1867–94), Karl Marx (1818–83) predicted the historical inevitability of the passing of Capitalism, whose cycles of boom and bust would finally destroy it, and the emergence of a Communist utopia run by the proletariat, who would seize the "means of production," and do away with the bourgeoisie. If he thought of the Russian imperial family at all, Marx probably considered them to be an outdated relic of a former age. But Marx did not foresee the proletarian revolution as breaking out in a country as economically and socially backward as Russia. England or Germany, which had the most developed economies, and the largest working classes, were the states that he saw as being ready for

Communism. Capitalism and liberal-democracy, as it turned out, were far more resilient and adaptable than Marx foresaw, and it was the West that triumphed at the end of the Cold War (1948–91), when the Communist Soviet Union collapsed into social, political, and economic chaos.

Now we can finally return to my comment in the opening paragraph, claiming that the subject of this entry, the imperial Fabergé eggs, will help the reader understand why the Romanov dynasty did not survive as constitutional monarchs, such as those of Britain, Spain, and the Netherlands. Cocooned in their palaces and mansions in westernized, elegant Saint Petersburg, the imperial family and the rest of the Russian aristocratic elite lived in a dream world of court balls, elegant dinner parties, concerts, and theatrical and country outings, complete with all the pomp and ceremony a 300-year-old dynasty could muster. Their world, however, had all the solidity and staying power of a soap bubble.

From March 2013, my American readers can join the rest of the world in "enjoying" a "Kinder Surprise," a chocolate egg made by the Italian confectioner Ferrero that contains a small self-assembly plastic toy. In 1938 the FDA banned the sale of any candy with a concealed toy or trinket with the laudable aim of saving America's tiny tots from choking as they greedily devoured their treats. However, at the time of writing, a U.S. confectionery manufacturer has succeeded in producing a Kinder-type egg that has passed the FDA's stringent safety rules. We are fortunate that the FDA was not around in 1885, when Alexander III commissioned the first surprise egg as an Easter gift for his wife, Maria (1847–1928).

FABERGÉ SURPRISE

Crafted by the court jewelers Fabergé, the "Hen Egg" was definitely not a chocolate confectionery. Outwardly it is the plainest looking of the extravagant collection of imperial eggs made for Alexander III and then for his son Nicholas II, who continued the tradition until the end of his reign. The outside of the gold egg is enameled to look like a real hen's egg, but like a Russian doll, it opens to reveal several "surprises." The first is a beautifully fashioned gold yolk, inside which is a tiny golden hen; the fowl is also hollow and once contained a tiny replica of the Imperial crown made of diamonds, on which hung a ruby pendant (both now lost).

We do not know how surprised the czarina was, but she liked it so much that the imperial family commissioned a total of 52 eggs, eight of which

MINIATURE GEMS
One egg cost many times
the annual income of
most Russians.

went missing during or after the Russian Revolution of 1917. The missing eggs are: "Hen with Sapphire Pendant" (1885), "Cherub with Chariot Egg" (1888), "The Nécessaire Egg" (1889), "Alexander III Portraits Egg" (1896), "Mauve Egg" (1897), "Empire Nephrite Egg" (1902), "Royal Danish Egg" (1903), and the "Alexander III Commemorative Egg" (1909). The surviving imperial eggs are displayed in important public collections in Russia and overseas, several having been taken out of the country by members of the royal family and others sold by Stalin to obtain foreign currency to pay for the modernization of the Russian economy. The themes of the eggs include members of the imperial family, nature (the seasons, plants, and animals), imperial palaces, and notable Russian achievements and anniversaries.

If readers (and the FDA) can set aside their concern that the empresses broke their teeth on their jeweled surprises, thinking they were chocolate, they will realize how the fabulously expensive gems symbolized the huge gulf that separated the czar from the vast majority of his subjects in the years leading up to the Russian Revolution. While millions of his countrymen starved or were exploited in factories and tenant farms, and their demands for fair wages and political reform were brutally repressed by the czar's secret police, Nicholas was giving his wife and mother casual Easter gifts that were worth many times a peasant or worker family's yearly income.

Although Fabergé eggs very rarely come on the market, the "Rothschild Egg," a novelty timepiece from which a diamond cockerel emerges flapping its wings, nodding its head, and crowing each time the clock strikes the hour, was sold at auction in London in 2007. This luxurious piece of egg-shaped kitsch broke all records, fetching $13.3 million, even though it had not been made for the Russian imperial family. In my valuation for the eight missing imperial eggs, I've valued them fairly conservatively at $15.6 million each, giving their potential finder a grand total of $125 million.

GOLD MIRAGE: LASSETER'S REEF

1931

TREASURE

Burial goods

Hoards

Shipwrecks

Religious objects or places

Artworks

Gemstones

Circumstance of loss: The location of the gold reef died with Lasseter

Rediscovery: Not found

Historical significance: A damn good yarn

Value: Entirely imaginary

In some ways a uniquely Australian legend, the story of Lasseter's Reef neatly fits the template common to "lost treasure" folklore across the world: an intrepid male explorer stumbles on a fabulous trove but loses its location in his struggle to return to civilization alive.

Great Australian Stories (2010) by Graham Seal

There is no better stimulus to the human imagination than naked, unbridled greed. Combine greed with large amounts of treasure and the Great Depression (1929–39), and, if you're raising funds for an expedition to find a lost gold mine, you're onto a winner. The most famous lost mine story is the fictional *King Solomon's Mines* (1855), by Sir Henry Rider Haggard (1856–1925), whose plot features a vast hoard of hidden treasure in the remotest and, of course, "darkest," heart of Africa. By the nineteenth century, the treasures of the ancient kingdoms of Africa, the Americas, and Asia had all been found, plundered, and spent. The precious metals that were left would have to be prospected for and mined out of the ground the hard way, increasingly in the unexplored regions of North America, Africa, and Australia.

The nineteenth century was famous for many "gold rushes," notably the California Gold Rush of the 1840s, and the Kalgoorlie Gold Rush in Western Australia in the 1890s, when farmers, shopkeepers, laborers, and professional men gave up their homes, families, and careers to rush headlong into the wilds on the rumor that gold nuggets could be picked off the ground. A few returned very rich men; most came back poorer than they had arrived, bereft even of their dreams of striking it rich; and not an inconsiderable number found a small fortune in gold only to lose it — to thieves and conmen, if they were lucky; or to murderers, if they were not.

There was yet another class of hopeful prospector: One who returned to civilization with tales of a major find, which he needed help — in funds — to mine, making him and his backers rich men. No doubt quite a few of them were conmen sniffing a good opportunity to swindle some ready cash; a few might have actually found something; and yet others might have deluded themselves into believing they had made a big find, to make up for the disappointment of repeated failure. Embellished and passed down the generations, these tales of huge gold deposits just waiting for someone to pick them up have spawned a plethora of books, TV shows, and movies — whose authors are, as usual, the only people to profit from the supposed "unsolved mystery."

LASSETER'S RIDES

I shall let the readers themselves decide into which of the above categories — unlucky but genuine prospector, clever conman, or deluded fantasist — Australian gold prospector Lewis Lasseter (1880–1931) best fits, though my money is on number three. In 1929, the 49-year-old Lasseter claimed to have made a huge gold find in the arid desert center of Australia. From the very beginning, however, his story was not entirely straight, and he told at least two versions, the first in 1929 and the second in 1930, each with different timeframes and locations for the find. In the first version, he'd made the discovery on the edge of the MacDonnell mountain range in the Northern Territory in 1911. When state officials checked out his claim, they discovered that between 1908 and 1913, Lasseter had leased a farm near the small town of Tabulam, New South Wales, many thousands of miles away in eastern Australia, and therefore was unlikely to have been where he claimed in 1911.

In the second version, which he produced to recruit backers to fund an expedition to locate and mine the reef, he changed the date from 1911 to 1897 — probably to cover his Tabulam tracks. He claimed that at the age of 17, when he was riding from Queensland in northeastern Australia to the West Australian gold fields of Kalgoorlie — a distance of 2,300 miles (3,700 km) — he stumbled across the fabulous gold reef, around 620 miles (1,000 km) west of Alice Springs in the Northern Territory. He described the reef to Australian officials, geologists, and potential investors as a quartz formation measuring seven miles (11.2 km) long, 12 feet (3.6 m) across, and four to seven feet (1.2 to 2.1 m) high, bulging with gold seams.

Just after making the discovery, the young Lasseter got into trouble but was rescued by a passing Afghan camel drover. Although the camel is a native of Arabia, it is well suited to the desert conditions of central Australia, and many animals brought as beasts of burden in the nineteenth century had, by the twentieth, gone feral and roamed free; so this part of the story, at least, rings true. The helpful Afghan took Lasseter to the camp of a surveyor working in the area, but for reasons that are not entirely clear, though they went back to the reef together, they failed to fix its exact location. For the next three decades, Lasseter said that he had been looking for the reef, a task made more difficult because the formation was often hidden from view by sand after the floods of the region.

By 1930 he had managed to persuade a group of private investors to back his scheme, raising the considerable sum of $80,000. The seven-man expedition led by bushman Fred Blakeley was unusual in that it had motorized vehicles at a time when pack animals would have been the norm, and it also had an aircraft for reconnaissance. The expedition left

GOLDEN DREAMS
Lasseter lived and
died a pauper.

Alice Springs in July but soon ran into difficulties, which included the loss of the airplane. Lasseter, who was supposed to guide the expedition to its goal, was vague and uncooperative. When Lasseter announced that they had gone 150 miles (240 km) too far north of the reef's general location, Blakeley accused him of being a fraud and called the expedition off.

Lasseter, however, decided to continue with one companion and a few camels. During their wanderings, Lasseter set off on his own toward the rock formation known as Kata Tjuta (The Olgas). He returned to camp with samples, which he kept hidden, and the news that he had rediscovered the reef. He refused to tell his companion its exact location—understandably, if he really had found the reef at last. At this, the two fell out and the other man departed, leaving Lasseter in the desert with a few supplies and two camels.

In March 1931 a tracker sent out to find Lasseter discovered a badly decomposed body, which he could not positively identify, and Lasseter's personal effects and diary in a cave. According to the diary, Lasseter had lost his camels and had been stranded in the desert. He was rescued by a band of nomadic Australian Aborigines, but after falling out with them, he had died of exhaustion and hunger, apparently trying to reach Uluru (Ayers Rock), which is 208 miles (335 km) southwest of Alice Springs.

There is a final twist to the story of Lasseter's Reef. In addition to the many fruitless expeditions to try to locate the reef, there were reports of sightings of Lasseter on the West Coast of the U.S. after his supposed demise in 1931. According to one source, he absconded with a large sum of money raised from investors, and lived out the rest of his days in San Francisco where he died sometime in the 1950s.

SPOILS OF WAR: NAZI GOLD

1945

TREASURE

Burial goods

Hoards

Shipwrecks

Religious objects or places

Artworks

Gemstones

Circumstance of loss: Disappeared into the banking system in 1945

Rediscovery: A private lawsuit by the World Jewish Congress against the Swiss banks and the Swiss government has recovered $1.25 billion

Historical significance: Shedding light on the murky world of international finance that was corrupt long before the current financial crisis

Value: $1.96 billion

The report documents the greatest thefts by a government in history: the confiscation by Nazi Germany of an estimated $580 million of central bank gold—around $5.6 billion in today's values—along with indeterminate amounts of other assets during World War II.

U.S. Department of Commerce and International Trade report on the recovery of gold stolen by Germany (1997)

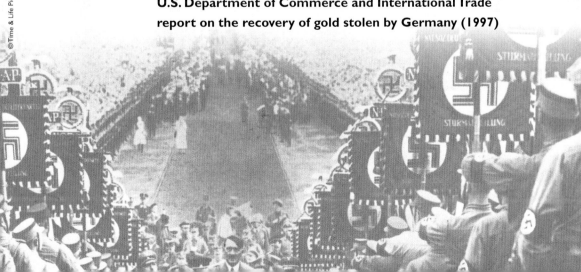

© Time & Life Pictures | Getty Images

The Second World War (1939–45) is usually portrayed as the modern era's first ideological war, ranging the forces of totalitarianism, racism, fascism, militarism, and ultra-nationalism against those of the free market, liberalism, and democracy (not forgetting the American Way, and mom's apple pie). Although this portrayal is by no means wrong, as the former description fits the Axis powers (Nazi Germany, Fascist Italy, and Imperial Japan) and the latter characterization, the Allies (the U.S., the UK and its dominions, the Free French, Poles, and Dutch, but not the Soviet Union, which was a totalitarian dictatorship of the Left), it does not tell the whole

story of what made Germany start the world's costliest conflict in terms of people killed and material damage caused. The Second World War, like any other human conflict, also had economic causes.

In one sense, the war was between the haves and the have-nots; Britain, France, and, to a lesser degree, the U.S, had extensive overseas possessions that increased their political, cultural, and economic clout in the world. Germany, Italy, and Japan, who had come to statehood in the second half of the nineteenth century, had been denied the benefits of empire. But as we saw in the entries on Spain's ill-gotten American gains, the possession of a large imperial domain could be either a boon or a curse. The vast amounts of bullion that the Spanish plundered from the Americas actually set them back economically, especially when compared to the countries of northern Europe that had to earn their wealth through manufacture and trade.

WARMONGER
Hitler financed his wars with looted gold.

The second thing we have to remember is that the 20-year period from the Treaty of Versailles (1919), which brought the First World War to a close, to the beginning of the Second World War, was a time of profound economic instability and dislocation. First, there was the reconstruction necessitated by the Great War, which had transformed the map of Europe, with the dissolution of the Austro-Hungarian, German, and Ottoman empires, and which led to the emergence of a plethora of new nation states. The Allies, led by the French, imposed particularly harsh conditions on Germany, including heavy reparations in both money and goods, and the loss of territory. Germany was effectively bankrupt, but Britain and France were faring little better economically. Added to the destruction and huge loss of life from the war, a disastrous flu pandemic, christened the "Spanish Flu" (1918–20), killed a further 3 to 5 percent of the world's population, unfortunately mostly fit, young adults of working age who had managed to survive the war.

There was a brief period of respite and recovery during the "Roaring Twenties," a period of affluence and excess based on real estate bubbles and stock market speculation, which came to a disastrous end in the Wall Street Crash of 1929. With the U.S. economy in serious trouble, the world entered a ten-year period of recession that was made worse by protectionist legislation enacted by the major countries. Weak economies like Germany suffered the most from the financial crisis. Worse, it was still saddled with paying war reparations for the First World War, an added humiliation that Adolf Hitler (1889–1945) exploited to the full in his bid for power.

For all their vaunted efficiency, the Nazis were not particularly good economists. Under Hitler's rule, Germany was still bankrupt and defaulted on its foreign loans. As Germany could not borrow on the international financial market, Hitler was able to claim in his uniquely vehement style that Germany was a "victim" of an international conspiracy of Jewish financiers and bankers. Hitler's plan to re-arm Germany and make it one of the world's superpowers did not come cheap. Faced with huge debts and no ready sources of cash, he did exactly what many former European leaders had done since the medieval period: He targeted the country's wealthiest minority, the Jews, who for historical reasons were Germany's leading bankers and businessmen, envied by both the landed aristocracy and the Christian middle classes.

The expropriation of Jewish property in Germany began as soon as Hitler got to power in 1933. It reached its climax on Kristallnacht (Night of Broken Glass), on November 9–10, 1938. But even the considerable wealth of Germany's Jewish community was not sufficient to finance Hitler's plans. In 1938, Hitler imposed the Anschluss, forcefully uniting Austria with the German Reich, and seized half of Czechoslovakia, conquering the second half in 1939, moves that gave him access to more Jewish wealth, as well as assets and gold reserves belonging to the former national governments and central banks of the two countries. The inability and unwillingness of Britain and France to oppose German aggression encouraged Hitler to try to make another financial and real-estate acquisition by invading Poland, after signing a non-aggression pact with the leader of the Soviet Union Joseph Stalin (1879–1953). Poland was a step too far, even for the pacifist administrations of Britain and France, which declared war on Germany on September 1, 1939.

HITLER'S RESISTIBLE RISE

In 1941, German dramatist Bertold Brecht (1898–1956) wrote *The Resistible Rise of Arturo Ui*, while he was living in exile in Finland. The play satirized the rise of Hitler and the Nazi Party in Germany by portraying the führer as the 1930s Chicago mobster, Arturo Ui, who attempts to corner the Windy City's cauliflower racket, murdering his mob rivals in the process. Brecht's caricature of the upper echelons of the Nazi Party as gangsters is not far off the mark. Although Hitler and his cronies may have believed in their absurd pseudo-scientific theories about racial purity and their rants about the "destiny" of the Aryan race — the German people who were not of Jewish, Slavic, or Roma origin — many of their actions were dictated by pure greed.

In May 1940, Hitler invaded Belgium, the Netherlands, and Luxembourg, placing the gold reserves of their central banks within his grasp, adding to those of Austria, Czechoslovakia, and Poland. It is estimated that Germany's gold reserves increased by $71 million between 1938 and 1939, and by a further $550 million during the war, including $223 million from Belgium and $193 million from the Netherlands, amounting to around $5.6 billion at current values. Add to this the wealth that his troops and the German secret police, the Gestapo, were taking from the Jews of occupied countries, and Germany was suddenly in the money. Nazi expropriation was not limited to gold and hard currency reserves; it included property, businesses, and valuables such as jewelry, antiques, and artworks from private and public collections.

Had Britain sued for peace in 1941, the Third Reich would have vastly expanded its territory to the east, and would have dominated Western Europe, while Russia dominated the eastern half of the Continent. Fortunately for the world, Britain refused to submit to Hitler's threats and repulsed his planned invasion. Hitler broke his non-aggression pact with Stalin, and attacked the Soviet Union — the biggest blunder of his military career, as it had been of Napoleon I's (1769–1821) in 1812. A few months later, the U.S. entered the war on the Allied side after Japan's attack on Pearl Harbor, and the rest, as they say, is history. Hitler committed suicide in his bunker in Berlin on April 30, 1945, to escape capture by the advancing Red Army. Those too cowardly to take even the coward's way out and take their own lives were tried and executed for war crimes and crimes against humanity. Hitler's "Thousand Year Reich" had lasted a mere twelve years.

In 1946, the U.S., Britain, and France established the Tripartite Gold Commission to recover the gold stolen by Germany and return it to its rightful owners, which included Albania, Austria, Belgium, Czechoslovakia, Greece, Italy, Luxembourg, the Netherlands, Poland, and Yugoslavia. After recovering all the gold they could find in German vaults, and receiving claims from national governments, the commission realized that it could only reimburse 65 percent of the claims. The commission was wound up in 1998, which means that a cool $1.96 billion remains unaccounted for. According to a top-secret report carried out by the U.S. State Department in 1946, and declassified in 1996, the Vatican Bank confiscated a large haul of Nazi gold held in Switzerland, which it placed in its own Swiss bank accounts for "safekeeping." The Vatican, needless to say, has strenuously denied the American claims.

WHERE'S THE MONEY?

However, the Swiss connection with missing Nazi assets was proven in 2000 when the Swiss banks and government settled a private lawsuit filed by the World Jewish Congress, agreeing to pay $1.25 billion in restitution to Jewish victims of Nazi wartime confiscations. This does not address the outstanding national claims made to the Tripartite Gold Commission. However, it is likely that a great deal of the missing $1.96 billion in gold was laundered through Swiss institutions immediately after the war. Other neutral countries, such as Portugal, received payments in gold for raw materials for the armaments industry during the war, and other recipients of the stolen gold might include countries sympathetic to the Nazis, such as Argentina.

TREASURE

Burial goods

Hoards

Shipwrecks

Religious objects or places

Artworks

Gemstones

THE MARCOS BILLIONS: YAMASHITA'S GOLD

1945

Circumstance of loss: Looted valuables from Japanese-occupied Southeast Asia

Rediscovery: Thought to have been found in the Philippines, and seized by President Ferdinand Marcos

Historical significance: A smokescreen for far more serious financial crimes on behalf of the Philippines government under Marcos

Value: $13,275,848.37

Once on American turf, the Marcoses were hit by lawsuits accusing them of theft and conversion of recovered treasure, human rights abuse and racketeering related to that treasure.

Gold Warriors (2003) by Sterling and Peggy Seagrave

The second great theater of conflict during the Second World War was the Pacific, where the Japanese confronted the British Empire and the United States. In 1941, Japan attempted to cripple the U.S. Pacific Fleet in its infamous attack on Pearl Harbor, while it also mounted an invasion of the British colonies of Malaya (now Malaysia) and Singapore. Where the Imperial Japanese Navy (IJN) failed to sink the all-important U.S. aircraft carriers that were out to sea at the time of the raid, the Imperial Japanese Army (IJA), led by General Tomoyuki Yamashita (1885–1946), henceforth known as "the Tiger of Malaya," succeeded in taking the British completely by surprise and capturing 130,000 British, Indian, and ANZAC troops—the single greatest surrender in British military history.

Imperial Japan's aggression was not as ideologically motivated as Nazi Germany, although there were strong racist, militarist, and ultra-nationalist components to imperial ideology. Japan had fought on the winning side in the First World War (1914–18), but it felt that it had been cheated in the postwar settlements. For Japan, which had few natural resources of its own, access to the markets and cheap natural resources of Asia to feed its growing industrial sector was an extremely pressing problem, especially after the beginning of the Great Depression, when its main Western export markets shrank or were closed by protectionist legislation.

Though Japan had coal reserves, it was critically short of iron ore and petroleum, which it had to purchase from Indonesia, then the Dutch East Indies, and from Britain and the U.S. In 1941, in response to Japanese aggression in China and French Indo-China, the Free Dutch, British, and American governments imposed an embargo on further sales of iron ore, steel, and petroleum to Japan. Faced with the imminent collapse of her economy and the paralysis of her armed forces, which were dependent on imported fuel, the Japanese went on the offensive.

PYRRHIC VICTORIES

After the raid on Pearl Harbor and the fall of Singapore, the Japanese were temporarily the undisputed masters of China, Southeast Asia, and the Pacific, as far south as Australia and east as the island of Midway. They had finally obtained the natural resources with which to conduct the war, but their greatest strategist, Admiral Isoroku Yamamoto (1884–1943), who had planned and executed the raid on Pearl Harbor, knew that, even as Japan celebrated its victory over the U.S. Navy, the war had already been lost. Japan's armed forces, already overstretched in China, on the

© Public domain

FALL GUY
Yamashita had no interest in acquiring a personal fortune.

borders of India, in the Philippines, and across the islands of the Pacific, would never be able to defeat the combined forces of the United States and Great Britain. The U.S., in particular, had vast supplies of manpower, stocks of natural resources, deep pockets, and a military-industrial complex that was immune from foreign attack.

As Yamamoto had predicted, the Japanese war machine had a finite supply of men and equipment, which the Americans, moving across the Pacific, succeeded in destroying. With the bulk of the IJN and aircraft carriers gone, the Japanese lost control of the seas and skies, and their cities, industry, commercial shipping, and troops became vulnerable to relentless Allied bombing raids. After the Battle of Midway (1942), it was only a matter of time before the Americans pushed the Japanese back to the home islands. Unfortunately for humanity, Japan's inevitable defeat took another three years and the dropping of the first two A-bombs, on Hiroshima and Nagasaki in August 1945, to force the unconditional surrender of Japan and of its overseas forces. Yamashita, now in command of the Philippines, surrendered on September 2. Held responsible for the atrocities committed by his subordinates, he was convicted of war crimes and executed in 1946.

SHOE MONEY

Like all invading armies, the Japanese armed forces helped themselves to the property and wealth of conquered territories. However, unlike the Germans, who actively sought gold, which they needed to purchase vital war materiel from neutral countries such as Portugal, Japan had gone on the offensive to seize the natural resources—petroleum, iron ore, rubber, and food supplies—that it needed for the war effort. As the Japanese had acquired what they needed, there was little real reason for them to go after gold bullion. I am not saying that the Japanese, like any other people, do not value wealth, but what they consider to be "treasure" is sometimes very different from the European and American conceptions.

Westerners, as has been well documented in many earlier entries, value gold for its own sake—to be used for lavish, visible displays of personal wealth. With the exception of the short-lived Azuchi-Momoyama period

(1568–1600), when all things glittery and golden were in fashion in the empire, Japanese aesthetics have shied away from conspicuous displays of wealth. In a country where the epitome of good taste is a single flower in a bamboo container, a misshapen earthenware tea bowl, or a stark ink-wash painting, a piece of gemstone-studded gold treasure has very little appeal.

There were probably many incidences of looting by Japanese troops; however, I do not agree with Sterling and Peggy Seagrave, who argued in *Gold Warriors* (2003) that the IJA and imperial family, aided by Japan's *yakuza* gangs, engaged in the systematic looting of gold bullion and precious artifacts from China and Southeast Asia, which were destined to be shipped by the IJN to Japan. It is far-fetched to suggest that Hirohito, the Emperor Showa (1901–89), whose main interest in life was the study of the *Hydrozoa*, an obscure family of microscopic marine animals, was the criminal mastermind who organized the operation.

According to the Seagraves, the looted treasure is supposed to have been taken to the Philippines in 1945, where the IJA was under the command of General Tomoyuki Yamashita, the conqueror of Malaya and Singapore. Although he was executed for war crimes, many historians argue that his conviction was unfair. Yamashita, by all accounts, was an honorable man, who punished his subordinates for looting and atrocities. Unlike some of the more rapacious Nazi leaders, who were little better than gangsters and who stole artworks, property, and money, Yamashita was a distinguished career soldier dedicated to serving his country and emperor, and with little interest in amassing a personal fortune. If he had been a crook like Hitler and his gang, instead of surrendering to the Americans, he would have tried to escape with his ill-gotten gains to a neutral country.

Nevertheless, the Seagraves assert that, acting on behalf of the imperial family, Yamashita ordered the looted treasure of Asia to be hidden in various locations in the Philippines, including Baguio City in northern Luzon, the site of the general's later formal surrender to the Americans. In 1988, Filipino-soldier-and-locksmith-turned-treasure-hunter Rogelio Roxas (ca. 1943–93) filed a lawsuit in Hawaii against former president of the Philippines, Ferdinand Marcos (1917–89) and his wife Imelda (b. 1929). He claimed that, in 1971, he had acquired a three-foot-high (0.9 m) solid-gold Buddha weighing 2,200 pounds (1,000 kg), and 24 gold bars, part of a much larger hoard of treasure, hidden in a cave in Baguio

MARCOS' BILLIONS
The treasure was a
smokescreen for
money laundering.

City. Roxas sold seven of the bars and put the Buddha on the market. Hearing of the find, Marcos had Roxas arrested and tortured until he revealed the location of the cave, whose contents he then recovered himself.

Both Marcos and Roxas died before the lawsuit was settled, but the case continued with new principles: Roxas' estate vs the president's widow, Imelda Marcos. In 1996 a Honolulu jury awarded the Roxas estate a record $40 billion in compensatory damages, but the Hawaii Supreme Court overturned the award in 1998 on the grounds that there was insufficient evidence as to the exact value of the treasure that Roxas had found in the cave. However, the court did confirm that Roxas had found Yamashita's gold, which had later been stolen on the order of Ferdinand Marcos. In 2000, the court valued the Buddha and 17 gold bars at $13,275,848.37, a judgment confirmed by the Hawaii Supreme Court in 2005 and the United States Ninth Circuit Court of Appeal in 2006.

A series of court decisions in the U.S., however, do not confirm the existence of Yamashita's gold or of Roxas's solid gold Buddha. The Marcoses were in power in the Philippines from 1965 to 1986, during which time they embezzled billions of dollars from the Filipino people. The couple hid their loot in foreign accounts, and they managed to preserve a great deal of the cash after Marcos was deposed, despite the best efforts of the new Philippines government to recover it. It is possible that Marcos used the story of Yamashita's gold as a convenient cover to launder the billions that he had stolen while in office. But if the gold Buddha did really exist, it was probably sold long ago to buy Imelda a few more pairs of shoes.

CULTURAL ATROCITY: AMBER ROOM

1945

TREASURE

Burial goods

Hoards

Shipwrecks

Religious objects or places

Artworks

Gemstones

Circumstance of loss: Looted by the Germans in 1941; probably destroyed

Rediscovery: A few pieces of the room not made of amber were recovered

Historical significance: One of the many artworks looted by the Nazis and lost, believed destroyed at the end of the war

Value: $142 million

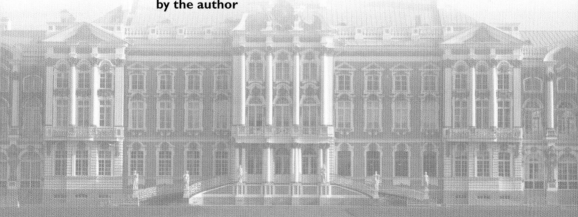

The Amber Chamber at the Catherine Palace on the outskirts of Saint Petersburg, Russia, was once called the "eighth wonder of the world." Originally built for an eighteenth-century Prussian king, the room, consisting of panels and decoration made of six tons of Baltic amber with gold detailing, was presented as a gift to Tsar Peter I.

"Amber," *Fifty Minerals that Changed the Course of History* **(2012) by the author**

The previous two entries featured gold bullion looted by the Germans and Japanese during the Second World War. Gold represented but a small fraction of the private and public property that the Germans seized from occupied countries between 1938 and 1945. One inventory drawn up by the Nazis themselves listed 21,903 artworks and antiques, including 5,281 paintings, pastels, watercolors, and drawings; 684 miniatures, glass and enamel paintings, illuminated books, and manuscripts; 583 sculptures, terracottas, medallions, and plaques; 2,477 pieces of antique furniture; 583 tapestries, rugs, and embroideries; 5,825 objects of decorative art; 1,286 artworks of East Asian origin; and 259 artworks from Classical antiquity. When the Allies started bombing Germany's cities, these priceless treasures were hidden in bunkers and mineshafts for safekeeping.

While many artworks were reunited with their owners after the war, many pieces that had been stolen from Jewish owners were never reclaimed, because entire families had been wiped out during the Nazi Holocaust that claimed six million victims among Europe's Jewish community. An estimated 20 percent of the artworks currently on the European art market were taken during the war and were never returned to their rightful owners. While the Nazis were the main perpetrators, the Soviets, too, did their fair share of looting in occupied German territories, removing anything of value as reparations for the huge losses they had suffered during the invasion of the Soviet Union in 1941.

The Second World War, while it had ideological and financial causes (see "Nazi Gold," pp. 213–217), was also a "cultural war," with its own "cultural atrocities." Along with iconic buildings, artworks form part of a country's "soul." For example, we could not imagine Paris without the *Venus de Milo* (pp. 93–99) and the *Mona Lisa* any more than without the Eiffel Tower or the Louvre. Looting artworks and destroying buildings, therefore, are in a very real sense, "crimes against culture." Because the Nazis planned to annihilate the Soviet Union not just politically and militarily but also socially and culturally, they were particularly destructive in their attacks on the artistic and cultural heritage of occupied Russia.

When the Germans reached the outskirts of Leningrad (now Saint Petersburg) in 1941, they captured the Catherine Palace, the czars' summer residence at Tsarskoye Selo. Anything of value that could be moved had been taken away for safekeeping, but there was one treasure, the palace's "Amber Room," which was too large and fragile to move without causing it considerable damage. The palace curators had attempted to hide the room beneath wallpaper. The Germans, however, were not deceived, and within 36 hours they had dismantled and crated the priceless treasure that was known as the "Eighth Wonder of the World." Ironically, the room was an eighteenth-century collaboration between German and Russian craftsmen, when the two countries had been allies in a war against a common enemy, Sweden.

Amber, the fossilized sap of ancient trees, is found in the Baltic region of northern Europe. Known to the Arabs as *anbar*, amber has been traded along the "Amber Road" that links the Baltic to the Mediterranean since the Neolithic period (10,000–7000 years BP). Baltic amber found its way to ancient Egypt, where it formed part of the sumptuous grave goods of Tutankhamun (ca. 1341–1323 BCE; see pp. 30–35). During the Middle Ages, it was the main source of wealth of the crusading order of Teutonic Knights, who were known as the "Lords of Amber"—yet another Germanic connection with the Amber Room, as much of its material must have at one time passed through the hands of the Germanic order.

In certain cultures, when a guest to your home heaps praise on one of your possessions, it is good manners for you to offer them the item. When the host is King Frederick William I of Prussia (1688–1740) and the guest, the Czar of all the Russias, Peter the Great (1672–1725), it is unlikely that the host is going to get away with the gift of a silver gilt saltshaker or teapot. What the czar particularly admired when he visited Frederick William's Berlin City Palace was a room entirely decorated in amber sculpted in the exuberant, florid Rococo style by Andreas Schlüter (1664–1714). The room, which featured gold-leaf mirrors and mosaic decorative panels, was lit by hundreds of candles in ornate sconces, whose light reflecting off the amber panels must have given visitors the impression that they were swimming through liquid gold. Once installed in the Catherine Palace, the Amber Room was enlarged and renovated several times, until it contained of 6 tons (5.4 metric tons) of amber and covered =592 square feet (55 m²).

The dismantled panels, mosaics, and mirrors of the Amber Room were shipped to Königsberg Castle, where sections of it were put on public

© Public domain

GO WEST
Peter the Great built a new capital on the Russian Baltic.

EIGHTH WONDER

© RIA Novosti | Alamy

REPLICA
Both Amber Rooms were
collaborations between
Russia and Germany.

display. In 1997 one of the stone mosaics reappeared in the possession of the relatives of one of the soldiers who had been tasked with packing the room for transportation to Germany. As for the amber panels, there are various theories as to their fate. The first, and least likely, is that the Amber Room is intact somewhere in a subterranean bunker or mineshaft. Amber, being of organic origin, degrades over time, and it is very unlikely that if it did survive the war intact, it would have survived decades of peace.

The most likely explanation of the room's fate is that it was destroyed, either in 1944, in a British bombing raid that caused a fire in the castle, or in April 1945, during the battle for the town between the Soviet Red Army and the German garrison, when fire again seriously damaged the castle. The Soviet investigator charged with finding out what had happened to the Amber Room made conflicting reports about when and how it had been destroyed, but this has been interpreted as the Soviets making sure that they were not blamed for the room's destruction, and that the responsibility for this cultural atrocity rested with the Germans or British.

In 1979, confirming the room had been lost forever, the Soviet government commissioned a replica of the Amber Room to be made using prewar photographs. The work, which took 24 years and cost $142 million, reunited the original creators of the room. The reconstruction, executed by Russian craftsmen with 6 tons (5.4 metric tons) of Baltic amber, was paid for by a German corporate donor. In 2003 President Vladimir Putin (b. 1952) and German Chancellor Gerhard Schröder (b. 1944) jointly opened the new Amber Room. I am sure that Schröder lavished praise on the reconstructed Eighth Wonder of the World, and that Putin thanked him and sent him home with a silver gilt saltshaker.

MAHARAJA'S BEST FRIEND: PATIALA NECKLACE

1948

TREASURE

Burial goods

Hoards

Shipwrecks

Religious objects or places

Artworks

Gemstones

Circumstance of loss: Disappeared from the royal treasury in 1948

Rediscovery: The necklace, minus its major stones, was found in London in a second-hand jewelry store

Historical significance: A sample of the extraordinary wealth of India's princely states before Indian independence

Value: $30 million

In 1925 […] Sir Bhupindra Singh, Maharajadhiraja, Great King of Kings, the ruler of Patiala, opened his treasury and handed over his most valuable pieces to Cartier. The fabulous collection of stones included the "Victoria" or "De Beers" diamond of 234.69 carats, which became the centerpiece of the great ceremonial necklace.

Cartier (2007) by Hans Nadelhoffer

PLAYBOY PRINCE
The rajahs were the celebrities of the early twentieth century.

After gold, nothing better says, "I am stinking rich," than a brace of diamonds. Strange, when you think of it, however, because diamond is composed of one of the commonest elements on earth, carbon—common coal—or, as Henry Kissinger (b. 1932) put it more pithily: "A diamond is a chunk of coal that is made good under pressure." When subjected to the huge pressures and temperatures in the liquid mantle under the earth's crust, carbon changes its molecular structure, turning into a proverbially hard, translucent lattice of perfect octahedral crystals. Although white diamonds are traditionally the most prized for jewelry, especially for Western engagement rings, chemical impurities give diamonds a wide range of hues, the most common being yellow and brown. Diamonds are sized in carats—a metric unit of mass equivalent to 0.007055 ounces (0.2 g).

Natural diamonds of any kind are rare, and large, high-grade diamonds are rarer still. The world's finest stones come from the Kimberley region in South Africa, home of the famous De Beers Company. In 1888, not long after the foundation of De Beers Consolidated Mines, miners unearthed the largest diamond then found, the 234.65-carat "De Beers Diamond." A giant crystal measuring 1.87 inches (4.76 cm) along its longest axis, the De Beers is light yellow in color, though the adjective does not do justice to the prismatic qualities of the gemstone once faceted. It was surpassed by the massive Cullinan Diamond, discovered in 1905, weighing a spectacular 1.36 pounds (621.35 g), with a mass of 3,106.75 carats, which, when cleaved, faceted, and polished, literally became the "jewel in the crown" of British kings and queens. Yet the De Beers remains the seventh largest diamond in the world.

Before the discovery of the Kimberley mines, the world's largest diamonds came from India, the most famous being the 105-carat Koh-i-Noor ("Mountain of Light"), mined in northern India for Hindu kings between the eleventh and thirteenth centuries, who had mounted it as the eye of a goddess (it was later appropriated by the British royal family). While the elites of some cultures eschew visible displays of wealth, preferring flawlessly tailored clothes in the finest materials, matched with one or two priceless accessories, those of others like to demonstrate their wealth and power by weighing themselves down with as much jewelry as they can.

Foremost among those who would make America's most bling-loving "gangsta" rap artists look positively underdressed were India's native princes, be they Hindu, Sikh, or Muslim, who appeared in public looking like bejeweled Christmas trees. Unsurprisingly, when the De Beers went on display at the Exposition Universelle in Paris in 1889, it attracted the attention of Rajinder Singh (1872–1900), the Maharaja of Patiala in northeastern India. Although the raja never had the stone mounted in a piece of jewelry, it is thought that he wore it to set off the turban that all Sikhs must wear.

Patiala was part of the Sikh Empire (1749–1849), one of the successor states that replaced the disintegrating Mughal Empire (1526–1857), which itself succumbed to the British Raj (1857–1948). The Raj was a historical oddity; it had begun as a purely commercial enterprise—built on territorial gains made by the British East India Company (1600–1874), which acquired a vast land empire in Bengal in the late eighteenth century that it administered with mounting difficulties. In 1857, Indian troops rebelled, staging the largest uprising against British rule in the nineteenth century.

After the rebellion, formerly known as the "Indian Mutiny," was suppressed, the British Crown took over the government of India, and the reigning British monarch, Queen Victoria (1819–1901), took the grandiloquent title of "Queen Empress of India." From the start, the Raj was a political patchwork of provinces directly administered by a British governor and "princely states"—Indian kingdoms that had sided with the British in exchange for a measure of self-government. Patiala, though part of the Sikh confederacy that had fought against the British, had switched sides at just the right moment, ensuring the survival of its royal house.

During the 91 years of British rule, the princely states were denied the main pastime that had kept them occupied for the preceding two millennia: wars with their neighbors. Fabulously wealthy but with no real power, the rajas of India became the world's billionaire playboys of the first half of the twentieth century, looking for new and ever more extravagant, self-

JEWEL IN THE NECKLACE

indulgent ways to spend their money, while many of their impoverished subjects continued to live in the most appalling poverty, the regular victims of pandemics, natural disasters, and famines. Rajinder's successor Bhupinder (1891–1938) was a typical representative of his class, though neither Hindu or Muslim, but Sikh. Legend has it that he drove around his kingdom in a fleet of 20 Rolls Royce limousines. He was the first man in India to own an aircraft, for which he built the country's first civilian airstrip. He erected numerous palaces, lodges, and temples in the exuberant Raj style, which married Western amenities with Indian architecture. A keen sportsman, he represented his country in cricket in 1911, and laid out India's highest cricket pitch at his mountain retreat in 1893.

Among his greatest extravagances, we must count the fabulous Patiala necklace, commissioned in 1925. On one of his regular visits to Paris, the raja brought with him a case containing the family's most treasured gems, including the still unmounted De Beers diamond, which he entrusted to the French jeweler Cartier to create a necklace that he would wear on state occasions. Cartier's gaudy Art Deco confection consisted of five platinum chains encrusted with diamonds, with a central cascade of seven large diamonds ranging from 18 to 73 carats, including an 18-carat brown diamond, and flanked by two Burmese rubies with a combined mass of 29.58 carats. The De Beers hung from the bottom chain, roughly over the raja's solar plexus. The necklace, which took three years to make, contained 2,930 diamonds with a total mass of 962.25 carats (6.78 ounces/192.45 g), and has been valued at $30 million at 2013 prices.

In 1948, the British, sometimes cajoled, persuaded, prodded, or embarrassed by Indian independence campaigner Mohandas "Mahatma" Gandhi (1869–1948), granted India its independence. An important element of the negotiations was the fate of the princely states and their constitutional relationship with the new governments of India and Pakistan. Although the rajas survived independence, they lost many of their privileges, and were hit by major tax hikes. In order to pay the IRS, many royal families resorted to selling land and possessions acquired over the centuries. The necklace disappeared from view shortly after independence, and the most likely explanation is that the raja's heirs broke it up and sold the larger stones piecemeal to raise money. At the last sighting of the De Beers, the stone fetched $3.16 million at auction in 1982.

In 1998, an eagle-eyed collector spotted the remnants of the necklace, shorn of its larger diamonds and two rubies, in a second-hand jewelry store in London. Cartier purchased the necklace, intending to restore the piece to its former glory. Of course, the major stones were long sold off, and a stone as large as the De Beers was not available. Cartier first attempted to replace the missing stones with natural gems such as white sapphires and white topazes, but the results were disappointing. In the end, Cartier decided to replace the seven large diamonds with synthetic diamond, cubic zirconium, and the Burmese rubies with synthetic rubies. An exact replica of the De Beers was created with either synthetic yellow sapphire or yellow cubic zirconium. Manmade cubic zirconium is the closest substance to natural diamond, refracting light in the same way.

© Getty Images

SUBSTITUTIONS
Cartier restored the necklace with artificial gems.

This much more "democratic" Patiala necklace, combining the original design and craftsmanship of Cartier—"the jeweler of kings and the king of jewelers"—with modern synthetic stones that cost a fraction of the price of the originals, took four years to recreate. It has since been displayed worldwide, latterly at the Field Museum in Chicago, where it formed part of the 2013 exhibit, "Maharaja: The Splendor of India's Royal Courts." The colorful history of the Patiala necklace chronicles the rise and fall of two world empires: the splendor and decay of the courts of India's maharajas, and of the British Empire, which once ruled both South Africa, where the De Beers diamond was dug up, and the Indian subcontinent, where it found a temporary home on the inflated chest of a maharaja.

THE TRUTH IS DOWN THERE: VICTORIO PEAK TREASURE

1949

Circumstance of loss: Various theories as to the origin of the treasure

Rediscovery: "Doc" Noss claimed to have found the treasure, but there is no official record of any discovery of gold at the peak

Historical significance: A damned good story—someone should turn it into a movie

Value: $1.7 billion

What Doc Noss discovered deep in the heart of Victorio Peak that afternoon has become one of the most controversial topics in American history, one that involves the discovery of wealth beyond imagination, one that led to murder, lawsuit, and the ultimate involvement of the United States government.

New Mexico Treasure Tales (2003) by W. C. Jameson

I'm very surprised that Hollywood has not yet snapped up the story of the Victorio Peak treasure, because, potentially, it's a red-hot big-screen property. It has all the makings of a Lucas or Spielberg blockbuster: the treasure, of course, a sadistic Spanish conquistador, a renegade French Catholic priest, a deposed Mexican emperor, an Apache war chief, and a murdered treasure hunter—all mixed up with the U.S. Department of Defense and a top-secret missile range in New Mexico; the only thing that is lacking is a crashed flying saucer and a couple of injured aliens. But before the reader imagines that Victorio Peak has the eerie symmetry of Devil's Tower, Wyoming, which won the Oscar for best supporting topographical feature in Spielberg's *Close Encounters of the Third Kind* (1977), I'm afraid it is a rather uninspiring rocky outcrop, with sloping sides, like many others in the Hembrillo Basin of New Mexico.

What Victorio Peak lacks in physical impact, it makes up for in mystery and controversy, as the rumored hiding place for a treasure that included an estimated 16,000 gold bars, as well as gold artifacts, jewels, and silver bullion, said to be worth $1.7 billion, which American former showman turned gold prospector Milton "Doc" Noss found by accident while on a deer-hunting trip with his wife, "Babe" (d. 1979) and a group of friends in 1937. According to Doc's later account, he had wandered off on his own to look for water when he came across a concealed entrance to the peak. Investigating further, he found a notched wooden pole that could be used as a crude ladder attached to the side of a manmade shaft. Although he told Babe about the discovery, Doc kept it secret from the others.

The couple returned a few days later with ropes and flashlights, and in good Indiana Jones style, Doc climbed down the 60-foot (18 m) shaft. At the bottom he found several small rooms decorated with Native American murals; these led to another 125-foot (38 m) shaft extending deep into the heart of the mountain. He descended into a large natural cavern, where he made a sensational but gruesome find: human skeletons bound to stakes, looking as if they had been left to die a slow painful death from thirst and hunger. He discovered a total of 27 skeletons, some restrained and others piled together in small side chambers. As he continued to explore, he found a hoard of treasure that included coins, jewels, ornate swords, and a gold statue of the Madonna—an eerie echo of the treasure that had gone missing from Lima over a century before (see pp. 191–194).

In a deeper cavern, Doc found what looked like thousands of metal bars stacked against the wall, which were so heavy he had trouble lifting one. Stuffing his pockets with some of the more portable coins and gems, Doc climbed back to the surface and told his wife of his discoveries. She insisted that he go back for one of the heavy metal bars. Her instincts turned out to be good because when he handed her a small bar, she scratched off the grime to reveal that it was made of solid gold. Over the next few months, Doc continued to explore the tunnels and caves inside the peak. Each time, he brought out more priceless artifacts, including a gem-studded crown, and around 200 gold bars.

At this point the reader might justifiably ask why the Nosses did not cash in their huge gold strike, and retire as the 1930s version of Bill and Melinda Gates? The government, of course—if in doubt, always blame the government. In Executive Order 6102 of 1933 and the Gold Reserve Act of 1934, the U.S. government, trying to stabilize the dollar during the Great Depression (1929–39), outlawed the ownership, trading, and sale of gold by American citizens anywhere in the world. All gold, except for some items of jewelry and collectors' coins, had to be sold to the Treasury, which deposited it at bullion depositories like Fort Knox. So the Nosses were not just vandals, disturbing what might have been an important archaeological site, but also criminals in the eyes of the Federal law.

HOUSE OF THE GOLDEN CAVE

If Doc's claims are accurate, how had close on $2 billion in gold and treasure made its way deep underground in an isolated location in New Mexico that was until the late nineteenth century the stronghold of Native American tribes that vigorously resisted the settlement of their ancestral lands? The sheer amount described by Doc would suggest that many people must have been involved in moving the treasure to the peak, excavating the shafts and caves over a long period of time, and one would imagine that there would have been first-hand accounts by participants and their relatives. According to Babe Noss, Doc found ancient documents in the cave, whose originals have all vanished, but she did produce a copy of a document dated 1797 that seems to be a cryptic set of instructions for finding the exact location of La Casa del Cueva de Oro ("The House of the Golden Cave"), by using the sun's position at high noon.

The first theory about the treasure's provenance was that it was the fruit of the Spanish conquest of the southwestern U.S. by Juan de Oñate

(1550–1626), also known as "the last conquistador." Although Oñate did indeed found New Mexico and subdue many Native American peoples of the region, it is unlikely that he would have amassed so vast a store of gold and gems, because, unlike the Aztec and Inca, they did not have large quantities of accumulated wealth. Another legend about the peak is that the gold was mined and smelted into ingots by members of a small community led by a French missionary called Philippe La Rue in the late 1790s. When the colonial government in Mexico heard about his mining operation, they dispatched soldiers to investigate, and claim the king of Spain's "Royal Fifth." La Rue had the mine sealed and the entrance hidden, leaving the ingots inside. He died under torture without revealing the whereabouts of the gold.

© Advanced Source Productions | Creative Commons

LAST CONQUISTADOR
Oñate might have assembled the treasure.

As Doc also described artifacts and documents dating to the nineteenth century, two other theories have emerged about the origins of the treasure. The first is that it belonged to Maximilian I (1832–67), who had a three-year tenure as Emperor of Mexico before being deposed and executed by firing squad by Republican revolutionaries. Before his death, he is rumored to have sent gold and valuables to the United States for safekeeping, though it is unclear how these would have ended up buried under Victorio Peak. The second is that the treasure is the loot accumulated by the Chiricahua Apache war chief Victorio (ca. 1825–80), who fought successful campaigns against both the U.S. and Mexican armies, until he was cornered and killed by the Mexicans in the state of Chihuahua. The 5,499-foot (1,676 m) peak, formerly known as Soledad (Solitude), was renamed for Victorio, who used the area as a hideout. Some have speculated that the skeletons tied to stakes were the remains of prisoners tortured to death by Victorio's band, and that the treasure was stolen from his American and Mexican victims.

Doc leased land and filed mining and treasure trove claims on and around the peak to establish his claim to the treasure. The treasure itself, however, remained extremely elusive. Whatever he removed from the peak, Doc hid in the desert in locations that he kept secret even from his wife. In 1939,

FIGHTING UNCLE SAM

Doc hired a mining engineer to enlarge the shaft leading into the mountain. The pair used too much dynamite and succeeded in burying the only access route under tons of rock and rubble. In 1945, Doc divorced Babe, and in 1947 married for a second time. In 1948, Doc reached an agreement with Charles Ryan, a Texan with experience of drilling for the oil industry, to reopen the shaft in exchange for $25,000 in gold. In the meantime, Babe had filed a counter-claim, and was trying to prevent her ex-husband from mining at the peak. The delay caused an argument between Doc and Ryan, which ended in the Texan shooting Doc, who died on the spot with the lordly sum of $2.16 in his pocket.

Babe retained her claim on the peak, but her efforts to clear the shaft were unsuccessful. In 1955, the White Sands Missile Range took over the Hembrillo Basin, canceling all other claims and leases in the area. This led to protracted legal action involving various parties, including Babe, Doc's second wife, the State of New Mexico, the Department of Defense, and the landowner who had leased the land to the military. The court ruled that Babe could mine the land but only with the army's consent, and thus she was denied access to the peak. In 1961, it appeared that the military themselves had been mining at the peak. Babe asked the State of New Mexico to intervene and all mining operations were halted. In 1963 and 1977, the army allowed two limited treasure-hunting expeditions, but neither uncovered any trace of the treasure.

Babe died in 1979, without ever finding the treasure, but her heirs continued to lobby the army for permission to reopen the mine. The story appeared in the national media across the U.S., with claims and counter-claims that the army had removed the gold, which was now in the vaults of Fort Knox. Finally, in 1989, a special act of Congress allowed the Noss heirs access to the peak, but so far nothing has been found. The truth is definitely out there, but in this case, it might be that the treasure of Victorio Peak is as imaginary as the gold of El Dorado (see "Treasure of Lake Guatavita," pp. 167–70), and some kind of scam dreamed up by former snake-oil salesman and showman Doc Noss and his sometime wife, Babe.

HILL OF GOLD: BACTRIAN TREASURE

1989

Circumstance of loss: Lost after the Taliban takeover of Afghanistan

Rediscovery: Rediscovered in a vault under the Central Bank of Afghanistan in 2003

Historical significance: A rare survival of the looted heritage of Afghanistan

Value: The national heritage of a nation

Gold is often described as treasure. Jewelry from the Bactrian region of Central Asia surely fits that description. Two thousand years ago, gold jewelry and the other ornaments were buried as grave goods in the tombs of wealthy nomads at Tillya Tepe in Afghanistan.

Afghanistan: Forging Civilizations Along the Silk Road (2012) by Joan Aruz and Elisabetta Valtz Fino

© Danita Delimont | Alamy

© Danita Delimont | Alamy

EAST MEETS WEST
Bactria was an
Indo-Greek kingdom.

There is an age-old conflict that runs through the history of human civilization. It is not a conflict between religious faiths or political systems, but between two different lifestyles: the nomad and the settler. For most of the past 200,000 years since *Homo sapiens* emerged from Africa to colonize the planet, humans lived in small bands of nomadic hunter-gatherers, which followed herds of game animals, and migrated with the seasons, driven by the need for food, and perhaps also by curiosity—to see what lay beyond the next valley or mountain ridge. Although our ancestors had language, used tools, wore clothing, and knew how to control fire to cook their food, they were not so different from the herds of herbivores on which they depended for food, or the packs of wolves that competed with them.

And so our species could have gone on forever, crisscrossing the planet like other migratory species. But between 75,000 and 50,000 years BP, something began to happen to the way humans thought and behaved: They achieved what anthropologists call "behavioral modernity"—they began to create art, wear personal ornaments, and bury their dead with ritual care. Tools became ever more sophisticated and varied, and animals were domesticated. It is almost as if a switch had been thrown in the human brain, turning prehistoric humans into people not very different from ourselves. From being hunter-gatherers, many populations became nomadic pastoralists, traveling with their herds to find the best pastures. Then, 10,000 years BP, humans began to settle in one place where they could plant and grow the food crops they had once gathered from the wild.

The first cities grew up along great rivers that could be used to fertilize and irrigate crops: the Nile, the Yellow River, the Tigris and Euphrates, and the Indus. Of course, not all humans settled; there were still bands of hunter-gatherers and nomadic pastoralists in regions not well suited to agriculture, such as the vast expanses of the Central Asian steppe and its mountain and desert fringes. Humanity divided into two, the settled humans becoming ever more urbanized, developing socially and politically, as well as culturally and technologically. The nomads, however, continued very much as they had done for millennia, trading meat, hides, wool, and milk with the towns for the things they could not make themselves.

Central Asian nomads were the first to domesticate the horse, giving them much greater mobility. At some point, the nomads realized that instead of bartering for what they wanted, they could take it by force from settled peoples. Thus began a series of confrontations that has shaped the history of our planet for the last 5,000 years. We saw the consequences of this great division in earlier entries, when empires were destroyed, their treasures quickly buried or lost in the destruction of once mighty cities. Invasions and migrations of nomads brought on the collapse of several great empires in the East and West. The largest and most influential of such events was the conquest of much of Eurasia by the Mongols in the thirteenth century.

We have already visited several points along the Silk Road that linked East Asia to the Near East. In this entry we travel to the part of northern Afghanistan known as Bactria in ancient times. This area is the melting pot of human culture, as it was the meeting point for three great world civilizations: China to the east, India to the south, and the Hellenistic world to the west. The nomadic inhabitants of the region did not build cities or temples, or leave inscriptions and monuments that have allowed archaeologists to identify them and reconstruct their lives and histories. By the very nature of their lifestyles, they left little evidence of their passage on this planet, even though their influence on history was sometimes considerable. In one respect, however, they were not very different from settled humans: in the care they took in the burial of their dead.

The 20,600 gold ornaments that were discovered in six graves at Tillya Tepe ("Golden Hill") in northern Afghanistan just before the Soviet invasion of Afghanistan (1979–89) included jewelry made of gold, turquoise, and lapis lazuli, coins, belts, medallions, and crowns. There is no agreement as to exactly which of the area's many nomadic inhabitants—Scythian, Parthian, or Yuezhi—created the burials, but coins found in the graves date them to the first century CE. The jewels, which are Scythian in style, display marked Hellenistic influences, and the mound burials also included artifacts from faraway India and China. Thought to have been lost during the Soviet invasion or destroyed by the Taliban after the Soviet retreat, the treasure was rediscovered intact hidden in a secret vault in Kabul, a rare survival of Afghanistan's archaeological heritage that will help rebuild this much maligned nation.

CENTRAL ASIAN MELTING POT

TREASURE

Burial goods

Hoards

Shipwrecks

Religious objects or places

Artworks

Gemstones

INTOLERANCE: BAMIYAN BUDDHAS

2001

Circumstance of loss: Blown up by the Taliban in 2001

Rediscovery: The Buddhas may be rebuilt or recreated in some form in the future

Historical significance: The destruction led to the discovery of hidden caves decorated with the world's oldest known oil paintings

Value: The costs of religious fundamentalism

As it turns out, a genuine treasure was hidden behind the two Buddhas destroyed by the Taliban in 2001: caves decorated with 1,000 year-old paintings depicting various scenes from Buddhist mythology. They are believed to be the oldest oil paintings ever found.

"Secrets of the Bamiyan Buddhas" (2009) by Géraldine Véron of the CNRS, Paris

We stay in Afghanistan for this entry on the Bamiyan Buddhas, but for a story with a much more mixed ending than the previous article on the treasure of Tillya Tepe that was rediscovered after the defeat of the Afghan Taliban. I count myself extremely privileged to have visited Afghanistan, not like so many of my countrymen in a military capacity during the NATO invasion of 2001 and subsequent occupation and insurgency, but as a peaceful traveler along the "Hippy Trail" between Europe and India. I visited just before Soviet tanks rolled over the border in 1979 for the USSR's ill-fated ten-year occupation of Afghanistan, which has cost the world so dear in terms of the radicalization of Islamic elements in Central Asia and the Near East.

As a fortunate prewar and pre-Taliban visitor, I can testify to Afghanistan's isolation and underdevelopment in the late 1970s—the country was then ranked among the poorest on earth in terms of per capita income by the UN—but also to the awesome beauty of its natural scenery, its fascinating history revealed by monuments scattered across its arid, mountainous landscapes, and the incredible hospitality and generosity of its people, several of whom told me in broken English, but with visible pride, that Afghanistan was "the best country on earth." I politely concurred because it never does to contradict your host, especially when he is a proud, armed warrior, who was to see off the Soviets in 1989, and who will no doubt see off other forces in the future.

Like many other backpackers, I decided to make the arduous 140-mile (230 km) trip from the capital, Kabul, to see the two giant Buddhas carved into the cliffs of Bamiyan in central Afghanistan. A few hours out of Kabul, we left the paved highway that leads to the western city of Herat and the Iranian border, and turned onto unpaved roads through the mountains toward Bamiyan. I and my half a dozen Western companions traveled not in a comfortable tourist bus but in the back of a pickup truck, trying to protect our rumps from bruising on the metal floor by wedging ourselves between the sides of the truck and our backpacks, and trying to avoid choking on the dust thrown up by the truck by covering our mouths and noses with scarves, while also trying not to pass out from the heat, dehydration, and hunger, as it was Ramadan—the yearly Islamic month of fasting—which in Afghanistan meant that everyone, Muslim or not, had to wait until sunset to eat or drink.

© Tsui | Creative Commons

GONE FOREVER
The large Buddha before and
after the Taliban's vandalism.

**HIDDEN
TREASURES**

Having set off from Kabul in the early morning, the pickup dropped me off in the Bamiyan Valley around lunchtime, where I was greeted by a sight that I shall remember for as long as I live. Set in deep niches carved in the sandstone cliffs stood two giant Buddhas—seeming sentinels of eternity who had withstood everything that man and nature had managed to throw at them for the past 1,500 years. Until, that is, they met their match in the fanatical intolerance of the Afghan Taliban in March 2001.

In the entry on the Mogao Library Cave in Dunhuang (pp. 129–135), I featured rock-hewn Buddhist cave temples at the easternmost end of the Silk Road, where it entered the Chinese sphere of influence. The Bamiyan Buddhas represent the westernmost spread of Buddhism, which did not prosper in the lands west of modern-day Afghanistan and Pakistan. Buddhism was the religion of several rulers of the Kushan Empire (30–375 CE), whose ancestors are strong candidates as the occupants of the golden graves of Tillya Tepe, and who founded the first monasteries in Bamiyan during the second century. The first occupants of the caves in the Bamiyan cliffs were Buddhist hermits from local monasteries, who decorated them with statuary and colored frescoes. The Buddhas themselves, however, were built during the reign of one of the nomadic successors of the Kushans, the Hephthalites, also known as the "White Huns," who ruled a vast empire stretching from Afghanistan to India to the south and China to the east between 408 and 670.

The two statues represent the Buddha Vairocana and the historical Buddha, Shakyamuni, Siddhartha Gautama (ca. 563–ca. 483 BCE). The smaller statue, which measured 115 feet (35 m) tall, was carved between 544 and 595, and the larger statue, measuring 174 feet (53 m), between 591 and 644. Both would have been brightly painted, the larger Buddha in bright red, and the smaller one in several colors, though at the time of my visit, there were no traces of paint left on the statues. While the main bodies of the statues were carved out of the cliff face itself, the detailing of the clothing, face, and hands was added later in layers of mud mixed with straw finished in stucco. A first-hand Chinese account written in the early seventh century described Bamiyan as a flourishing Buddhist center with a dozen monasteries and a community of more than 1,000 monks. The valley remained a Buddhist pilgrimage center until the Islamic invasions of the late seventh century. In the ninth century, the whole of Afghanistan became part of the Saffarid Muslim Empire (861–1003), which effectively eliminated Buddhism in the region.

The trials of the Buddhas were just beginning. Considered to be idols by the Muslim rulers of Afghanistan, they came under repeated attack. In 1221, the non-Muslim Mongols under Genghis Khan (ca. 1160–1227) destroyed Bamiyan, slaughtering its population, but the statues were left intact. There were several artillery attacks on the Buddhas in the seventeenth to nineteenth centuries, with the final attempt managing to destroy the face of the larger Buddha. The stone parts of the statues, however, withstood the weapons and explosives of the early-modern period.

The destruction of the Buddhas by the Taliban using modern explosives and mines, however, has not been an unmitigated disaster, because subsequent investigation of the cliff behind the statues revealed a hidden treasure: around 50 caves decorated with frescoes of the Buddha and Buddhist stories, dating from the fifth to the ninth centuries, which were probably sealed before the arrival of iconoclastic Muslim invaders, and which also contained fragments of rare Buddhist manuscripts. Additionally, when archaeologists analyzed tiny fragments of paint, they were amazed to discover that several are oil paintings—the first in the world—predating the earliest known Italian and Flemish oils by six centuries.

HIDDEN SECRETS
Caves behind the Buddhas hold the world's first oil paintings.

© JERRYE & ROY KLOTZ MD | Creative Commons

TREASURE

Burial goods

Hoards

Shipwrecks

Religious objects or places

Artworks

Gemstones

LATE BLOOMER: VAN GOGH MUSEUM THEFT

2002

Circumstance of loss: Two paintings stolen from the Van Gogh Museum

Rediscovery: Not yet found

Historical significance: Masterworks by the world's greatest and most highly respected Post-Impressionist painter

Value: $30 million

In December 2002, two thieves used a ladder to climb to the roof and break in to the Vincent Van Gogh Museum, Amsterdam, The Netherlands. In just a few minutes the thieves stole two paintings.

**Number five on the "FBI Top Ten Art Crimes" list
(www.fbi.gov; retrieved May 21, 2013)**

The great irony about the treasures featured in this entry—two works by the Dutch Post-Impressionist Vincent van Gogh (1853–90), *View of the Sea at Scheveningen* (1882) and *Congregation Leaving the Reformed Church in Nuenen* (1884), stolen from the Van Gogh Museum, Amsterdam, in 2002—is that during his lifetime, he could not have given away the paintings to passing strangers, let alone raised the slightest interest among professional art thieves. Although many recognized van Gogh as a talented artist during his lifetime, including his younger brother Theo (1857–91), Post-Impressionist painter Paul Gauguin (1848–1903), and printmaker and illustrator Henri de Toulouse-Lautrec (1864–1901), he was a famously troubled individual, whose mental instability led to his early death aged 37.

© Public domain

Van Gogh's reputation, however, was to be transformed. Retrospective exhibitions disseminated his work among a new generation of artists and collectors. By the middle of the twentieth century, van Gogh was recognized as one of the world's greatest Post-Impressionist painters. Along with Pablo Picasso (1881–1973), he attracted the highest prices at auction and in private sales, while earning the ultimate accolade: His work was forged. In the 1980s and '90s, van Gogh paintings regularly broke records for the most expensive oil paintings. In 1987, *Irises* (1890) made $59.6 million at auction, a price so high that the successful bidder could not raise the full amount, and the painting was sold on to the Jean Paul Getty Museum in Los Angeles. In 1990, his *Portrait of Doctor Gachet* (1890) smashed all records by fetching $82.5 million. In 1993, one of the three versions of *A Wheatfield with Cypresses* (1889) sold for $57 million, and in the 1990s, his *Self Portrait with Bandaged Ear* (1889) sold privately for an estimated $80–90 million.

TROUBLED GENIUS
Van Gogh is seen as the world's greatest Post-Impressionist.

The staggering prices paid for works by van Gogh were bound to attract the less than desirable attention of criminals. In 1988, thieves broke into the Kröller-Müller Museum in the Netherlands and stole three paintings by the artist: one of several versions of his earliest noted work, *The Potato Eaters*, as well as *The Weaver's Interior*, and *Dried Sunflowers*. The thieves returned *The Weaver's Interior* with a ransom note for the other two asking for $2.5 million. The police recovered the two missing paintings in 1989

**THINGS THAT
GO BUMP IN
THE NIGHT**

without a ransom being paid. In 1991, there was a much more ambitious theft of 20 paintings from the Van Gogh Museum itself, which included another version of *The Potato Eaters*. Although the thieves managed to take the paintings out of the building, they were found in an abandoned car 35 minutes after the theft. Unfortunately, three van Gogh masterpieces were seriously damaged. Four men, including two museum guards, were convicted of the crime and sent to prison.

The two heists above represent the more conventional types of art theft: The first is holding a famous artwork for ransom (far easier than kidnapping a person, as a painting is easy to hide, does not need feeding or watching, and won't try and run away); the second is the theft of famous artworks to order. Even the dimmest thief will realize that he could never sell a painting as distinctive and well known as *The Potato Eaters* on spec on the black market. However, there have been thefts of extremely prominent paintings that have been done on the order of unscrupulous private collectors, who one imagines in a darkened subterranean vault, admiring the filched masterpiece that they could just as easily have viewed during the opening hours of the museum they were stolen from.

© Public domain

MISSING I
The stolen landscape that has never been recovered.

The world's largest art theft occurred in the early hours of March 18, 1990, when thieves broke into the Isabella Stewart Gardner Museum in Boston, MA, making off with a haul of artworks estimated at $300 million, which included several paintings by Rembrandt, oils by Vermeer and Manet, and five drawings by Degas. None of the artworks has ever been recovered despite the offer of a $5 million reward. There are a further two more recent types of art crime: thefts by terrorist organizations; for example, the looting of Iraqi antiquities to fund the insurgency in Iraq and terrorist operations overseas; and thefts by drug cartels, who use artworks as substitutes for large amounts of cash, bullion, or gems, which are less easy to hide and smuggle across borders.

Despite improved security after the 1991 robbery, the Van Gogh Museum was hit again in 2002. Van Gogh painted the two stolen works early on in his career when he was living in the Hague (1881–82) and later in the village of Nuenen, where his father had been appointed pastor in 1882, and where van Gogh stayed between 1883 and 1885. The paintings do not have the vibrancy and vivid color palette of later works executed in the south of France between 1888 and his death two years later.

Van Gogh painted the *View of the Sea at Scheveningen* not from memory or from sketches, but while standing on the beach in a strong wind that plastered his painting with sand, grains of which are still visible in the thick layers of paint. He painted *Congregation Leaving the Reformed Church in Nuenen* for his mother while she was convalescing from a broken thighbone in 1884. It originally depicted his father's church on its own, but van Gogh later added members of the congregation, and leaves to the trees to give the painting more life and color.

© Public domain

MISSING II
The two stolen works are worth $30 million.

Although two men were arrested and convicted of the robbery, the paintings have not yet been recovered, despite the museum's offer of €100,000 ($129,000) for information leading to their recovery. Although a tempting sum, the reward is dwarfed by the estimated value of the paintings themselves, which was set by the FBI Art Crime Team at $30 million.

TREASURE

Burial goods

Hoards

Shipwrecks

Religious objects or places

Artworks

Gemstones

A QUESTION OF OWNERSHIP: LA PEREGRINA PEARL

2011

Circumstance of loss: Not lost, but sold to a private buyer, so out of the public eye

Rediscovery: Now in private hands

Historical significance: A significant artifact in the history of the past five centuries

Value: $11,840,000

According to Garcilaso de la Vega, who says he saw [La Peregrina] at Seville in 1597, this was found in Panama in 1560 by a [black slave] who was rewarded with his liberty, and his owner with the office of alcalde of Panama.

The Book of the Pearl (1908) by George Kunz and Charles Stevenson

This last entry deals with La Peregrina, the "pilgrim" or "wanderer"—a pearl that, though it has had an extraordinary history, passing through the hands of crowned heads, aristocrats, and celebrities, has never been "lost" in the sense of having completely disappeared. After 2011, however, it did go missing in a sense, because it was sold at auction to a private collector and has since been out of sight in a way that it has not been for most of its 553-year history. Although it has always been privately owned, when it formed part of the crown jewels of several royal houses, it was also a public possession, on show during state occasions and in many royal portraits.

La Peregrina is a large teardrop-shaped natural pearl of great beauty and symmetry that originally weighed 223.8 grains (55.95 carats, or 0.39 ounces/11.2 g). After cleaning and drilling to secure it to its mounting in 1913, its mass was reduced to 203.84 grains. Sources disagree as to the date of the find, but they agree that it was discovered in the Gulf of Panama, near the Islands of Cubagua and Santa Margarita, whose oyster beds were the source of some of the best pearls in the New World. Like the gold and silver of the Americas, the pearls of the Gulf of Panama represented a vast source of wealth for the Spanish Crown. Until the nineteenth century, when British marine biologist William Saville-Kent (1845–1908) discovered how to artificially induce oysters to produce cultured pearls, pearls remained extremely rare and expensive, and natural pearls of the size and quality of La Peregrina were literally worth a king's ransom.

The pearl was most likely fished in the early years of the sixteenth century; the 1560 date given by Kunz and Stevenson (see quote, p. 248) is much too late. King Philip II of Spain (1527–98), who had been gifted with La Peregrina, presented it to his betrothed, Queen Mary I of England (1516–58) in 1553. The Catholic daughter of Henry VIII (1491–1547), who had broken with Rome to divorce Mary's Spanish mother, the queen tried to undo her father's work and reunite the Church of England to the Church of Rome. In order to achieve her ends, she allied herself with England's main European rival and traditional enemy, Catholic Spain, and married her king, Philip II, who was briefly both king of Spain by birth and king consort of England by marriage.

Mary was too old to have children, and upon her death in 1558, the throne of England passed to Mary's younger half-sister, the fiercely Protestant Elizabeth I (1533–1603), bringing an instantaneous and permanent end to

England's alliance with Spain and to any moves to return England to the Catholic fold. La Peregrina returned to Spain, where it formed part of the Spanish crown jewels for the next two and a half centuries. The pearl was a favorite of Spain's queens consort, and the wives of Philip III (1578–1621) and Philip IV (1605–65) were painted wearing the fabulous gem.

THE FRENCH CONNECTION

As we have seen in earlier entries, Spain benefited very little from the vast amounts of gold and silver bullion and the pearls and emeralds that it appropriated from the New World (see "Treasure of Lima," pp. 191–194). While the countries of northern Europe developed trading networks and manufacturing bases, Spain lagged behind, socially, economically, and technologically. By the late eighteenth century, the empire, too, was becoming a huge drain on the public purse, with independence movements inspired by the American and French revolutions. The crisis came in 1808 when Emperor Napoleon I (1769–1821) invaded Spain, placing his elder brother Joseph (1768–1844) on the throne. Joseph's reign did not outlast his brother's emperorship, and the French were expelled from Spain in 1814 by an alliance of the British and Spanish.

HOLLYWOOD ROYALTY
Richard Burton gave the pearl to Elizabeth Taylor.

Joseph escaped to France with some of the Spanish crown jewels, including La Peregrina, which unlike other Napoleonic loot (see "Venus de Milo," pp. 93–99), was never returned to its rightful owners. Joseph bequeathed the pearl to his nephew, who would one day ascend the throne of France as Emperor Napoleon III (1808–73). Napoleon was deposed during the Franco–Prussian War (1870–71) and went into exile in Britain, taking with him the fabulous Peregrina. The ex-emperor sold it to James Hamilton, Duke of Abercorn (1811–85), and the pearl, after having been briefly misplaced twice during social occasions in Windsor Castle and in Buckingham Palace, remained a family heirloom until it was sold at auction at Sotheby's, London, in 1969.

The buyer, while not Old World royalty, was definitely "Hollywood royalty": Actor Richard Burton (1925–84) bought it as a Valentine's Day gift for his then wife Elizabeth Taylor (1932–2011) for a mere $37,000. Burton worked with royal jewelers Cartier (see "Patiala necklace," pp. 227–231) to have it set as the centerpiece of a diamond and ruby necklace. The actress admitted in an interview that the heavy pearl had once fallen off the necklace, and that she had had to rescue it from the mouth of one of her pet dogs—almost the most expensive doggy chew in history! After the actress's death in 2011, the pearl, along with her many jewels and her large collection of designer dresses, went on sale at Christie's, New York. La Peregrina, which was expected to fetch $3–3.5 million, actually sold for a record $11.84 million, the highest price ever paid for a pearl.

With a few exceptions, including La Peregrina, all of the other surviving "lost treasures" featured in this book are rightly in public ownership and on public display. Although it is part of a piece of jewelry that can be worn by one person, La Peregrina is also an important cultural and historical artifact that belongs to humanity as a whole. Maybe La Peregrina now adorns the neck of the wife of a Russian oligarch, a Chinese billionaire, or a Near Eastern oil magnate, or maybe, it languishes in a private display case, or, worse, it sleeps unseen in a bank vault. Where it should be, I would argue, would be as the glittering centerpiece of a museum exhibition—in the Caribbean, where it was found; in Spain, its longest owner; or in France, England, or the U.S., which have all been its temporary home.

© AFP | Getty Images

RECORD BREAKER
The pearl fetched more than three times its estimated price at auction.

FURTHER READING

There are many excellent general reference works available in printed form or online covering many of the entries featured in this book. Still one of the most authoritative is the *Encyclopaedia Britannica*, available for free at most large public, college, and school libraries, and online at britannica.com as a subscription service. Another reference source that is used by authors and journalists is the ubiquitous Wikipedia (en.wikipedia.org). The content of Wikipedia, however, is user-generated, and is not independently verified. As a result there are inaccurate, incomplete, or biased articles included in the wiki databases (articles identified as having problems or a particular bias are often flagged by the site, but the site itself will not edit or delete articles unless they are proved to be bogus or libelous). Nevertheless, Wikipedia and its associated sites provide a good starting point to find basic information and references on a wide range of topics.

In addition to books and articles, I have included the web addresses of general and specialist sites whenever appropriate. All URLs were correct at the time of writing, but it is the nature of the Internet that these change as sites migrate to new service providers or are taken down. If a website is no longer active or has moved, please conduct a search on the topic with an Internet search engine.

The reference materials listed below fall into two categories: In certain instances, they provide detailed accounts of the topics covered in the entries; in others, they give the reader a general background on the period, person, or topic. I have tried to include both whenever these were available. When a source listed is strongly biased either for or against the topic under discussion, I have also included a balancing work supporting the opposite point of view. I have also included materials about entries in other media, including videos (most of these are available at Internet sites such as youtube.com) and also film and TV documentaries or dramatizations of the events described in the entries, though often these do not necessarily stick faithfully to the facts, and take Hollywood liberties with storylines and characters.

Ram in a Thicket

Lieck, Gwendolyn. *Mesopotamia: The Invention of the City*. London, UK: Penguin, 2002.

Woolley, Leonard. *Abraham: Recent Discoveries and Hebrew Origins*. London, UK: Faber and Faber, 1936.

www.britishmuseum.org (for the British Museum's Ram)
www.penn.museum (for Penn State's Ram)

Solar Boat of Khufu

Jenkins, Nancy. *The Boat Beneath the Pyramid: King Cheops' Royal Ship*. New York, NY: Holt, Rinehart and Winston, 1980.

Vinson, Steve. *Egyptian Boats and Ships*. Oxford, UK: Osprey Publishing, 2008.

Egypt's Ten Greatest Discoveries (2008) TV documentary by Zahi Hawass, Discovery Channel.

Phaistos Disk

Haugton, Brian. "The Unsolved Puzzle of the Phaistos Disc" in *Hidden History: Lost Civilizations, Secret Knowledge, and Ancient Mysteries*. Pompton Plains, NJ: Career Press, 2007.

www.interkriti.org (see section on "Phaistos")

Mask of Agamemnon

Homer, trans. by Samuel Butler. *Odyssey*. Digireads.com, 1900/2009.

Martin, Thomas. *Ancient Greece: From Prehistoric to Hellenistic Times*. New Haven, CT: Yale University Press, 2000.

Tutankhamun's Death Mask

Carter, Howard, and A. C. Mace. *The Discovery of the Tomb of Tutankhamen*. London, UK: Dover Publications, 1977.

Reeves, Nicholas. *The Complete Tutankhamun: The King, the Tomb, the Royal Treasure*. London, UK: Thames & Hudson, 1995.

Sarcophagus of Seti I

Mayes, Stanley. *The Great Belzoni: The Circus Strongman Who Discovered Egypt's Ancient Treasures.* New York, NY: St Martin's Press, 2006.

www.soane.org (see section on "Egyptian and classical antiquities")

Treasure of Villena

Soler García, José María. *El tesoro de Villena.* Alicante, Spain: Biblioteca Virtual www.cervantesvirtual.com ("Miguel de Cervantes"), 2005.

www.museovillena.com

Ark of the Covenant

Carroll, Robert, and Stephen Prickett (eds). *The Bible: Authorized King James Version.* New York, NY: Oxford University Press, USA, 2008.

Matthews, Victor. *A Brief History of Ancient Israel.* Louisville, KY: Westminster John Knox Press, 2002.

Raiders of the Lost Ark (1981) dir. by George Lucas, starring Harrison Ford.

Riace Bronzes

Foxhall, Lynn, and John Salmon (eds). *Thinking Men: Masculinity and its Self-Representation in the Classical Tradition.* New York, NY: Routledge, 1998.

Mattusch, Carol. *Greek Statuary: From the Beginning to the Fifth Century B.C.* Ithaca, NY: Cornell University Press, 1994.

Panagyurishte Treasure

Bonfante, Larissa. *The Barbarians of Ancient Europe: Realities and Interactions.* Cambridge, UK: Cambridge University Press, 2011.

www.archaeologicalmuseumplovdiv.org (see "Thracian art")

Qin Shi Huang's Terracotta Army

Capek, Michael. *Emperor Qin's Terra Cotta Army.* Minneapolis, MN: Lerner Publishing, 2008.

Man, John. *The Terracotta Army: China's First Emperor and the Birth of a Nation.* London, UK: Random House, 2010.

Alexander the Great's Sarcophagus

Green, Peter. *Alexander the Great and the Hellenistic Age.* London, UK: Phoenix, 2007.

Heckel, Waldemar, and Lawrence Tritle (eds). *Alexander the Great: A New History.* Hoboken, NJ: Wiley-Blackwell, 2009.

Antikythera Mechanism

Marchant, Jo. *Decoding the Heavens: Solving the Mystery of the World's First Computer.* Cambridge, MA: Da Capo Press, 2009.

www.antikythera-mechanism.gr

Holy Grail

Baigent, Michael, Richard Leigh, and Henry Lincoln. *Holy Blood, Holy Grail.* New York, NY: Random House, 2009.

Malory, Thomas. *Le Morte Darthur: The Winchester Manuscript.* Oxford, UK: Oxford University Press, 1485/1998.

Indiana Jones and the Last Crusade (1989) dir. by George Lucas, starring Harrison Ford.

Dead Sea Scrolls

Vanderkam, James C., and Peter Flint. *Introduction to the Dead Sea Scrolls, The Meaning of the Dead Sea Scrolls.* New York, NY: HarperCollins, 2002.

dss.collections.imj.org.il (digital Dead Sea scrolls)
www.english.imjnet.org.il (Shrine of the Book, Jerusalem)
www.loc.gov ("Scrolls," Library of Congress online exhibit)

Venus de Milo

Curtis, Gregory. *Disarmed: The Story of the Venus de Milo*. New York, NY: Random House, 2003.

www.louvre.fr ("Chefs d'oeuvre du Louvre," Official website of the Louvre Museum, section on the *Venus de Milo*)

Chausa Treasure

Cort, John. *Framing the Jina: Narratives of Icons and Idols in Jain History*. Oxford, UK: Oxford University Press, 2009.

bstdc.bih.nic.in (see section on Patna)

Neptune Dish

Bédoyère, Guy de la. *Roman Britain: A New History*. London, UK: Thames & Hudson, 2010.

Hobbs, Richard. *The Mildenhall Treasure (Objects in Focus)*. London, UK: British Museum Press, 2012.

Sutton Hoo Ship Burial

Carver, Martin (ed). *The Age of Sutton Hoo: The Seventh Century in North-western Europe*. Woodbridge, Suffolk: Boydell Press, 1992.

www.britishmuseum.org (current owner of the Sutton Hoo treasure)

Pereshchepina Treasure

Curta, Florin, and Roman Kovalev (eds). *The Other Europe in the Middle Ages: Bulgars, Khazars and Cumans*. Leiden, The Netherlands: Brill, 2008.

hermitagemuseum.org (current owner of the Pereshchepina treasure)

Pakal's Death Mask

Martin, Simon, and Nikolai Grube. *Chronicle of the Maya Kings and Queens: Deciphering the Dynasties of the Ancient Maya*. London, UK: Thames & Hudson, 2000.

Schele, Linda, and Peter Matthews. *The Code of Kings: The Language of Seven Sacred Maya Temples and Tombs*. New York, NY: Scribner, 1998.

Staffordshire Hoard

Leahy, Kevin, and Roger Bland. *The Staffordshire Hoard*. London, UK: British Museum Press, 2009.

www.staffordshirehoard.org.uk

Mogao Library Cave

Whitfield, Susan, and Neville Agnew. *Cave Temples of Mogao: Art and History of the Silk Road*. Los Angeles, CA: J. Paul Getty Trust, 2000.

idp.bl.uk (International Dunhuang Project)

Bayeux Tapestry

www.bayeuxtapestry.org.uk

www.normandie-heritage.com (in French)

www.tapestry-bayeux.com (museum displaying the tapestry)

Imperial Japanese Regalia

Nobutaka, Inoue et al. *Shinto: A Short History*. London, UK: Routledge, 2003.

Yamamura, Kozo. *The Cambridge History of Japan*, vol. 3. Cambridge, UK: Cambridge University Press, 1990.

Genghis Khan's Tomb

Dittrich, Luke. "Conjuring Genghis Khan: Albert Yu-Min Lin, Explorer," *National Geographic Magazine*, 2009, and website, December 2009/January 2010.

Weatherford, Jack. *Genghis Khan and the Making of the Modern World*. New York, NY: Random House, 2004.

Nanhai One

Qingxin, Li, trans. William Wang. *The Maritime Silk Road*. Beijing, China: China Intercontinental Press, 2006.

www.unesco.org (section on "Underwater Cultural Heritage")

Treasure of the Knights Templar

Barber, Malcolm. *The New Knighthood: A History of the Order of the Temple.* Cambridge, UK: Cambridge University Press, 1994.

Haag, Michael. *The Tragedy of the Templars.* London, UK: Profile Books, 2012.

Sroda Treasure

Heer, Frederich. *The Holy Roman Empire.* London, UK: Phoenix Giant, 2002.

Tyler, Elizabeth (ed). *Treasure in the Medieval West.* Woodbridge, Suffolk: Boydell Press, 2000.

Moctezuma's Treasure

Prescott, William. *The History of the Conquest of Mexico and Peru.* Lanham, MD: Cooper Square Press, 2000.

Thomas, Hugh. *The Conquest of Mexico.* London, UK: Random House, 2004.

Treasure of Lake Guatavita

Labbé, Armand. *Colombia Before Columbus.* New York, NY: Rizzoli, 1986.

Salomon, Frank, and Stuart Schwartz (eds). *The Cambridge History of the Native Peoples of the Americas: South America.* Cambridge, UK: Cambridge University Press, 1999.

Sacred Cenote

Adams, Richard. *Prehistoric Mesoamerica.* Norman, OK: University of Oklahoma Press, 1991.

Coggins, Clemency Chase. *Artifacts from the Cenote of Sacrifice, Chichén Itzá, Yucatán.* Cambridge, MA: Harvard University Press, 1992.

Remains of Richard III

Baldwin, David. *Richard III.* Stroud, UK: Amberley Publishing, 2012.

www.le.ac.uk/richardiii (University of Leicester website)

www.richardiii.net (Richard III Society website)

Nuestra Señora de Atocha Treasure

Singer, Steven D. *Shipwrecks of Florida.* Sarasota, FL: Pineapple Press, 1998.

Stradling, R. A. *Philip IV and the Government of Spain.* Cambridge, UK: Cambridge University Press, 1988.

Thomas, Hugh. *Rivers of Gold: The Rise of the Spanish Empire 1490–1522.* London, UK: Weidenfeld & Nicolson, 2004.

Treasure of Loch Arkaig

McLynn, Frank. *Charles Edward Stuart: A Tragedy in Many Acts.* New York, NY: Routledge, 1988.

Preston, Diana. *The Road to Culloden Moor—Bonnie Prince Charlie and the '45 Rebellion.* London, UK: Constable and Robinson, 1998.

Dunlap Broadside of the Declaration of Independence

Goff, Frederick Richmond. *The John Dunlap Broadside: The First Printing of the Declaration of Independence.* Washington, DC: Library of Congress, 1976.

McCullough, David. *John Adams.* New York, NY: Simon & Schuster, 2001.

Treasure of Lima

Coping, Jasper. "British expedition to Pacific 'treasure island' where pirates buried their plunder," *The Daily Telegraph.* London, UK, August 5, 2012.

Lynch, John. *The Spanish American Revolutions, 1808–1826.* London, UK: W. W. Norton & Company, 1986.

Jean Lafitte's Treasure

Davis, William C. *The Pirates Laffite: The Treacherous World of the Corsairs of the Gulf.* New York, NY: Harcourt Books, 2005.

www.contrabanddays.com (Annual pirate festival held at Lake Charles, Louisiana, in honor of Jean Lafitte)

Tokugawa Gold

Lent, John and Lorna Fitzsimmons (eds). *Asian Popular Culture: New, Hybrid, and Alternate Media.* Lanham, MD: Lexington Books, 2013.

Wert, Michael. *Meiji Restoration Losers: Memory and Tokugawa Supporters in Modern Japan.* Cambridge, MA: Harvard University Press, 2013.

Fabergé Eggs

Faber, Toby. *Fabergé's Eggs: The Extraordinary Story of the Masterpieces That Outlived an Empire.* New York, NY: Random House, 2008.

www.mieks.com (Dutch site in Dutch and English, featuring a very thorough history of the Fabergé eggs)

Lasseter's Reef

Idriess, Ion. *Lasseter's Last Ride: New Light on Lasseter's Lost Reef.* Sydney, Australia: Angus & Robertson, 1931.

Seal, Graham. *Great Australian Stories: Legends, Yarns and Tall Tales.* Sydney, Australia: Allen & Unwin, 2010.

Nazi Gold

Bower, Tom. *Nazi Gold: The Full Story of the Fifty-Year Swiss–Nazi Conspiracy to Steal Billions from Europe's Jews and Holocaust Survivors.* Toronto, ON: HarperCollins Canada, 1997.

Sayer, Ian and Douglas Botting. *Nazi Gold: The Story of the World's Greatest Robbery—And Its Aftermath.* Edinburgh, UK: Mainstream Publishing, 1998.

Yamashita's Gold

Costello, John. *The Pacific War: 1941–45.* New York, NY: HarperCollins, 2009.

Seagrave, Sterling and Peggy Seagrave. *Gold Warriors: America's Secret Recovery of Yamashita's Gold.* New York, NY: Verso, 2003.

Amber Room

Bunn, David. *The Amber Room.* Peabody, MA: Hendrickson Publishers, 2013.

Levy, Adrian. *The Amber Room: The Fate of the World's Greatest Lost Treasure.* London, UK: Bloomsbury, 2009.

Patiala Necklace

Allen, Charles and Dwivedi Sharada. *Lives of the Indian Princes.* London, UK: Century Publications, 1984.

Nadelhoffer, Hans. *Cartier.* New York, NY: Chronicle Books, 2007.

Victorio Peak Treasure

Boswell, R. and D. Schweidel. *What Men Call Treasure: The Search for Gold at Victorio Peak.* El Paso, TX: Cinco Puntos, 2008.

Chandler, David. *100 Tons of Gold.* New York, NY: Doubleday, 1975.

Bactrian Treasure

Aruz, Joan and Elisabetta Valtz Fino. *Afghanistan: Forging Civilizations Along the Silk Road.* New York, NY: Metropolitan Museum of Art, 2012.

Baumer, Christoph. *The History of Central Asia: The Age of the Steppe Warriors.* New York, NY: I. B. Tauris, 2012.

Bamiyan Buddhas

Hansen, Valerie. *The Silk Road: A New History.* Oxford, UK: Oxford University Press, 2012.

Morgan, Llewelyn. *The Buddhas of Bamiyan.* London, UK: Profile Books, 2012.

Van Gogh Museum Theft

Heugten, van, Sjraar. *Van Gogh: The Master Draughtsman.* London, UK: Thames & Hudson, 2005.

www.vangoghmuseum.nl (official website of the museum where the theft took place)

La Peregrina Pearl

Finlay, Victoria. *Jewels: A Secret History.* New York, NY: Random House, 2007.

Kunz, George and Charles Stevenson. *The Book of the Pearl: Its History, Art, Science, and Industry.* Mineola, NY: Dover Books, 1908/2001.